Language, Culture, and Education in an Internationalizing University

Critical Perspectives on Language, Mobility and International Education

Series Editors:
Kumari Beck (Simon Fraser University, Canada)
Angel M. Y. Lin (Simon Fraser University, Canada)
Yang Song (Fudan University, China)
Michelle Mingyue Gu (The Education University of Hong Kong, Hong Kong)

This book series aims to provide a trans-disciplinary space for scholars to publish critical studies revolving on the intertwined relations between language, mobility and international education in different geopolitical, cultural and societal contexts. It welcomes submissions from both established scholars and dynamic, emergent scholars.

Also available in the series:

The Value of English in Global Mobility and Higher Education: An Investigation of Higher Education in Cyprus, by Manuela Vida-Mannl

Language, Culture, and Education in an Internationalizing University

Perspectives and Practices of Faculty, Students, and Staff

Edited by Kumari Beck and Roumiana Ilieva

BLOOMSBURY ACADEMIC
LONDON • NEW YORK • OXFORD • NEW DELHI • SYDNEY

BLOOMSBURY ACADEMIC
Bloomsbury Publishing Plc, 50 Bedford Square, London, WC1B 3DP, UK
Bloomsbury Publishing Inc, 1359 Broadway, New York, NY 10018, USA
Bloomsbury Publishing Ireland, 29 Earlsfort Terrace, Dublin 2, D02 AY28, Ireland

BLOOMSBURY, BLOOMSBURY ACADEMIC and the Diana logo are trademarks of
Bloomsbury Publishing Plc

First published in Great Britain 2024
Paperback edition published 2026

Copyright © Kumari Beck, Roumiana Ilieva and Contributors, 2024, 2026

Kumari Beck, Roumiana Ilieva and Contributors have asserted their right under the
Copyright, Designs and Patents Act, 1988, to be identified as Authors of this work.

For legal purposes the Acknowledgments on p. xvii constitute an extension
of this copyright page.

Cover design: Charlotte James
Cover image © filo/ iStock

All rights reserved. No part of this publication may be: i) reproduced or transmitted in
any form, electronic or mechanical, including photocopying, recording or by means of
any information storage or retrieval system without prior permission in writing from the
publishers; or ii) used or reproduced in any way for the training, development or operation
of artificial intelligence (AI) technologies, including generative AI technologies. The rights
holders expressly reserve this publication from the text and data mining exception as per
Article 4(3) of the Digital Single Market Directive (EU) 2019/790.

Bloomsbury Publishing Plc does not have any control over, or responsibility for, any
third-party websites referred to or in this book. All internet addresses given in this
book were correct at the time of going to press. The author and publisher regret any
inconvenience caused if addresses have changed or sites have ceased to exist,
but can accept no responsibility for any such changes.

A catalogue record for this book is available from the British Library.

Library of Congress Cataloging-in-Publication Data

Names: Beck, Kumari, editor. | Ilieva, Roumiana, editor.
Title: Language, culture, and education in an internationalizing university : perspectives and practices
of faculty, students, and staff / edited by Kumari Beck and Roumiana Ilieva.
Description: 1. | New York : Bloomsbury Academic, 2024. | Series: Critical perspectives on language,
mobility and international education | Includes bibliographical references and index.
Identifiers: LCCN 2023058385 (print) | LCCN 2023058386 (ebook) | ISBN 9781350211711 (hbk) |
ISBN 9781350211759 (pbk) | ISBN 9781350211735 (epub) | ISBN 9781350211728 (ebook)
Subjects: LCSH: International education--Canada. | Children of immigrants--Education--Canada. |
Multicultural education--Canada. | Language and education--Canada. | Language and culture--Canada.
| Education, Higher--Moral and ethical aspects--Canada. | Education and globalization--Canada.
Classification: LCC LC1090 .L278 2024 (print) | LCC LC1090 (ebook) |
DDC 378.71--dc23/eng/20240414
LC record available at https://lccn.loc.gov/2023058385
LC ebook record available at https://lccn.loc.gov/2023058386

ISBN: HB: 978-1-3502-1171-1
PB: 978-1-3502-1175-9
ePDF: 978-1-3502-1172-8
eBook: 978-1-3502-1173-5

Series: Critical Perspectives on Language, Mobility and International Education

Typeset by Deanta Global Publishing Services, Chennai, India

For product safety related questions contact productsafety@bloomsbury.com.

To find out more about our authors and books visit www.bloomsbury.com and
sign up for our newsletters.

We dedicate this book to two dear friends and colleagues who are no more.

Aisha Ravindran

Aisha was a doctoral student working with Roumi. When Aisha started her program, I (Roumi) met a truly warm and incredibly smart woman and we became not only academic colleagues but shared friendship, laughter, and a desire to make a difference in the life of students for whom English is not a mother tongue. Aisha was a voracious reader whose scholarship engaged with a whole gamut of complex and nuanced understandings of postqualitative methodologies and posthumanist agency enactments. Talking with Aisha was participating in an intellectual feast, and her academic work contributes to overcoming deficit views of international students in educational contexts and beyond. Aisha's big heart and great mind have left an indelible impression on faculty and students associated with the doctoral program in Languages, Cultures, and Literacies at Simon Fraser University.

Marela Dichupa

Marela was a fellow graduate student who became involved in international programs in our Faculty of Education around the same time that we did. A gifted artist, educator, scholar, and social justice activist, Marela brought critical perspectives to internationalization practices and was fearless in her calling out of racism that international students experienced. She was a passionate advocate for students and committed to taking action against all forms of injustice. We recall the many animated conversations about race, Spivak, the gaze and the counter-gaze, the patriarchy, intercultural "everything," teaching, professors, and quite simply "being" in the world.

We miss you both very much, and hope that this book reflects the critical perspectives you brought to our scholarly work, and the ethical and principled stance you took in your lives and in your praxis.

Contents

List of Figures	ix
Series Editor Foreword	x
Foreword	xii
Preface	xiv
Acknowledgments	xvii

	Introduction: Framing Internationalization, Language, and Cultural Difference *Kumari Beck and Roumiana Ilieva*	1
1	Faculty Experiences of Teaching With/in Cultural Difference in an Internationalizing University *Kumari Beck*	25
2	Content Area Faculty Engagement with Language Matters in an Internationalizing University *Roumiana Ilieva*	49
3	Narratives on IELTS Test Writing, Preparation, and English Learning of Chinese International Students in Canada *Zhihua (Olivia) Zhang*	71
4	Internationalization as Intercultural Capital or "I Feel I Am a Cultural Transformer" *Aisha Ravindran (posthumous manuscript) and Roumiana Ilieva*	91
5	Pre-service Teachers' Experiences of Learning with/in Cultural Difference in Study Abroad *Jas K. Uppal-Hershorn and Kumari Beck*	109
6	Challenges Faced by Japanese English Teachers Applying Knowledge after Study Abroad *Steve Marshall and Brent Amburgey*	129
7	Staff as Third Space Professionals *Chelsey Laird and Kumari Beck*	147
8	The Experiences of Staff Regarding Language in the Internationalizing University *Camila Miranda and Roumiana Ilieva*	169
9	Implementing a Post-entry Language Assessment in a First-Year Engineering Course to Center Academic Language and Literacy in an Internationalizing University *Amanda Wallace and Michael Sjoerdsma*	191
10	Critical Perspectives Toward Assessing Impact and Outcomes in Language Development within Business Education *Valia Spiliotopoulos*	211

11	The Development and Impact of a Linguistically Responsive Classroom Series to Address Linguistic Diversity in Higher Education *Amanda Wallace, Eilidh Singh, and Fiona Shaw*	233
12	Closing Reflections *Kumari Beck and Roumiana Ilieva*	255

List of Contributors	259
Index	263

Figures

10.1	Student profile and diagnostic information	218
10.2	Impact assessment results—student perceptions of improvement before and after writing course	223

Series Editor Foreword

Critical Perspectives on Language, Mobility and International Education

This series publishes state-of-the-art, interdisciplinary scholarship that addresses educational issues in international education with a specific focus on the complex relations among linguistic practices, transnational mobility of students and academics, and material-semiotic resources of meaning-making. The book series aims to provide a transdisciplinary space for scholars to publish critical studies investigating the contemporary manifestations of international education in different geopolitical, cultural, and societal contexts. The books in the series may include research monographs, edited volumes, and theory-based textbooks on the themes of the book series such as critical pedagogies for international education. The editors welcome proposals from experienced and emerging scholars and specifically invite proposals that feature a range of scholarship in edited collections.

We are experiencing an exponential growth of academic mobility across borders in higher education, K-12 schools, and other educational settings. These dynamics of international education are expressed in intensified transnational flows of linguistic, cultural, and epistemic resources; transplantation and adaptation of institutional models for curriculum design and educational management; and mobilities of students and academics. The field of international education, once reflecting educational activities among schools, higher education institutions, and communities across nations, is now known as the internationalization of education, a process bringing an international dimension to education. These processes and the very notion of international, founded in colonial relations and practices, need to be critically examined in the context of inequitable geopolitical power relations, the neoliberal orientation of internationalization of education, and cultural imperialism.

Meanwhile, international policies and initiatives coming from the Global South, as well as stakeholders from regions and communities not traditionally associated with international education, have been transforming the one-directional flow of international students from the Global South to the Global

North. The diversification of the directions of mobility for both students and academic faculty members has in turn challenged the previously seldom questioned legitimacy of the Global North as the center of knowledge production.

In applied linguistics and sociolinguistics, the global spread of English-medium instruction (EMI) courses and programs becomes an increasingly significant research area as EMI simultaneously risks reinforcing the dominance of English while providing opportunities for students' social mobility and worldwide redistribution of cultural and linguistic capital. There is also a huge demand for content-and-language-integrated pedagogy to help resolve tensions in academic English language capacity and the teaching and learning of content knowledge.

Proposals are invited that include but are not limited to scholarship that highlights and features: perspectives and epistemologies from and of the Global South; Indigenous perspectives and epistemologies on the topic of language, mobilities, and international education; critical perspectives on international education worldwide; decoloniality in approaching language, mobility, and international education; a dual focus on language and mobility issues in international education; and interdisciplinary and innovative approaches and methodologies in response to the ever-changing ecology of international education.

Foreword

Despite increasing immigration, mobility, and the emergence of plurilingual identities, official education policies and curriculum in Canada have not expanded to include the explicit development of plurilingual repertoires or societal plurilingualism in classrooms. This is one of the key perspectives presented in the insightful and thought-provoking book, *Language, Culture, and Education in an Internationalizing University: Perspectives and Practices of Faculty, Students, and Staff*. This edited volume, put together by my much-admired colleagues and dedicated researchers Kumari Beck and Roumiana Ilieva, is the first of its kind in the field, presenting a unique microcosm of an Anglo-dominant Canadian university's internationalization process from the vantage points of its key players—the faculty, students, and staff.

As a researcher and educator in plurilingual and intercultural education, and an "international" faculty member myself, I have found this book to be a rich, textured study that candidly captures the many contradictions in the institutional discourses, policies, and practices of an internationalizing university. It provides an intricate tapestry of experiences, highlighting the tensions created by a still rather parochial system attempting to attract international students, which is still not well prepared to support and adapt to the changing needs of an increasingly pluricultural and plurilingual student body.

Critiquing the gap between the rhetoric of lofty ideals of official internationalizing discourses and the actual institutional policies and practices (e.g., an admissions system designed mainly for domestic students, lack of support to faculty faced with the increased linguistic and cultural diversity), the book lays bare the uncomfortable reality that the primary driver of internationalization processes in many Canadian universities is financial gain. However, international students are still often viewed through a deficit lens, framed by standard English ideologies and an entrenched Western-led colonialist mind-set.

While offering a critical analysis of these ideologies and practices, the authors do not stop at mere critique. They also present the possibility of alternative perspectives and practices, and show the agency of those faculty and staff members who go beyond their officially defined roles to support and value the diversity these international students bring.

The authors have conducted their research ethically and critically, shedding light on the many contradictions in the process of internationalization of higher education in Canada and beyond. By illustrating the challenges and tensions experienced by the key participants, they have contributed significantly to our understanding of this complex and contested process. The authors of the book do not claim to provide all the answers. However, it does serve as a significant stepping stone toward addressing these challenges in a manner that values and respects the diversity of our international student body.

Language, Culture, and Education in an Internationalizing University: Perspectives and Practices of Faculty, Students, and Staff thus offers an invaluable contribution to the scholarship of our field. It is a must-read for educators, policy makers, and anyone interested in the internationalization of higher education. I am confident that readers will be, as I have been, challenged, enlightened, and inspired by the diverse and insightful analysis and perspectives shared in this book.

Angel M. Y. Lin
Simon Fraser University
& The Education University of Hong Kong

Preface

This book began many years ago in conversations among four graduate students who found themselves in the middle of planning and preparation for a new Master of Education program in Teaching of English as an Additional Language designed for international students. The four students were Anne Scholefield, Bonnie Waterstone, Roumi, and Kumari. Internationalization of higher education was a new consideration in Canadian higher education, and our university had adopted it with great enthusiasm. Our master's program was one of two designated international programs in the Faculty of Education. In developing the program and teaching in it, we had varied experiences of teaching, administering, and supporting the students. We wrote about them and the program in a paper titled "Locating Gold Mountain: Cultural Capital and the Internationalization of Teacher Education."

> We are four educators working in the post-secondary system: we have been colleagues and friends through graduate study, and beyond. Even as our friendships have been forged through compatible interests and worldviews, more recently we have come together as a team (coordinator, instructors, mentors and sounding boards) for a Master of Education program that falls under the umbrella of International Education in the Faculty of Education at Simon Fraser University (SFU). This paper presents our reflections as we navigate the complex practices of this program and, through a description of some of the dilemmas we have faced, enables links between theory and practice as we seek a way to align internationalization to ethical practice. (Beck et al. 2007, 1)

We, Roumi and Kumari, took up faculty positions at SFU, and with Bonnie were the founding members of the Centre for Research on International Education (CRIE) in our faculty. Anne, a teacher educator with the international education module, left the university when her contract ended but continued her work in the field elsewhere. Bonnie took up the coordinating role of the international graduate program where she maintained her critical practice until she too left the university.

Where is CRIE now? Reflecting on our aspirations for CRIE at the time, our research has had some impact in guiding our faculty's internationalization activities in the strategic plan over the past few years. We are still committed to the direction for our work set by our small collective. In some ways, however, little has changed: we are still navigating the complexity of internationalization, still troubled by, and frustrated with, the money-making machine that internationalization has become, and still trying to remain aligned to ethical principles and praxis in the face of many challenges.

Throughout the early years of CRIE, we engaged vigorously with graduate students interested in the topic of university internationalization and many of them worked as research assistants (RAs) on projects we embarked on. Without the support of these students much of the work that guides our current thinking on the topic shared here would not have been possible. Some of them also completed their graduate research on topics aligned with our studies, and the work of several of these scholars is presented in chapters in this book. However, as there is no dedicated institutional financial support for the center and as fewer students nowadays seem to be able to afford living solely off RA salaries given the significant increase in costs of living, CRIE activities have been negatively impacted, including the completion of this book.

Although we noted that the ideas and issues we write about in this book are not new for us, the thought of putting a book together did not arise for either of us until we invited our colleague, Professor Angel M. Y. Lin, to be part of the CRIE Steering Committee. Angel, a Tier 1 Canada Research Chair in Plurilingual and Intercultural Education, brought new energy to CRIE and suggested that we add a greater focus on publications in the work of the center. How else, she argued, would people know about the work? So when the book series *Critical Perspectives on Language, Mobility and International Education* (Beck, Lin, Song, and Gu 2020) was approved, we submitted a proposal for consideration.

The proposal was approved during the pandemic, and we naively thought we would have all the time we needed to complete the book. The reality was that the book's completion was greatly delayed by the pandemic, which, as we are all aware, impacted a large part of humanity and demonstrated inequitable material effects on various groups. Like most people, our contributors and we had to face the difficulties of isolation in both personal and professional lives, the mental and physical effects of COVID-19-related illness and its aftermath, and caregiving and other family commitments that dominated our days. The nature of university teaching and learning also changed significantly, and for many of us, devoting time to academic writing was overcome by other priorities. Now that we are back on track, we hope that the research shared in the book could offer some points of connection to academics and graduate students working and studying in internationalizing universities. If our experience is anything to go by, it is difficult to keep aligned with and strive for ethical and equitable relations and practices when we are situated in institutions, indeed, a system, that is focused on competitiveness and economic gains. The work discussed here speaks to the possibilities to initiate or be part of pockets of resistance to the neoliberal agenda pervading higher education settings, especially in engaging respectfully with language and cultural differences in the superdiverse universities of our times.

Our experience of collaborating with colleagues in CRIE and beyond has shown how collectives are the way forward—and if there is a legacy of CRIE, it is that.

Acknowledgments

We wish to respectfully acknowledge the xʷməθkʷəy̓əm (Musqueam), Sḵwx̱wú7mesh Úxwumixw (Squamish), səlilwətaʔɬ (Tsleil-Waututh), q̓íc̓əy̓ (Katzie), kʷikʷəƛ̓əm (Kwikwetlem), Qayqayt, Kwantlen, Semiahmoo, and Tsawwassen peoples on whose unceded traditional territories our three campuses reside. We benefit daily and were able to write this book because we occupy these lands as uninvited guests of these Coast Salish Peoples.

We wish to acknowledge the following who helped to make this book a reality:

The authors—for your contributions, for your patience in waiting for the book project to be completed, and for your persistence and hard work in completing your chapters against many odds;

Professor Angel M. Y. Lin who nudged us into submitting a proposal for this book;

The Editorial Staff at Bloomsbury Press, in particular, Laura Gallon, Sarah MacDonald, and Maria Giovanna Brauzzi, without whose guidance and support this book would not have been published. You had patience, and had faith in our capacity to complete, especially when we were facing challenges along the way;

Our reviewers who helped us strengthen the chapters presented here;

Our Research Assistants Juliana Ferreira, Carol Suhr, and Neha Aurora from the Centre for Research on International Education;

Professor Özlem Sensoy, Director, Cassidy Centre for Educational Justice for making the CCEJ Research Assistant team available to us for the final tasks in the production process;

A very special thank you to Research Assistant Mehtab Purewal from the Cassidy Centre for Educational Justice who stepped in at the eleventh hour to help us with reference style, formatting, indexing and finalizing the manuscripts;

Our families who supported us in this endeavor, believed we can bring it to fruition, and took on additional daily tasks to allow us to focus on the work.

Introduction

Framing Internationalization, Language, and Cultural Difference

Kumari Beck and Roumiana Ilieva

This book, an edited collection, explores and highlights the experiences of students, faculty, and staff who are embedded in the processes of internationalization in one representative Anglo-dominant Canadian university as they learn, teach, and work in the intersections and interplay of culture, language, and international activity. It is a book in the series *Critical Perspectives on Language, Mobility and International Education*, and the authors, at the time of conducting their research, were all faculty, staff, or graduate students at Simon Fraser University in Canada. The purpose of our book is to present a multidimensional micro-level account of the experiences of university stakeholders (faculty, students, and staff) engaged in internationalization activities and practices, in order to understand how they are addressing and dealing with these conditions and influences. We hope these perspectives will enrich researcher knowledge, support higher education instructors with new ideas, and provide administrators with insights into the role that nonacademic staff might play in an internationalizing university. Overall, we hope to provide insights into the complex mix of language, culture, and internationalization in internationalizing higher education institutions.

What insights, you may ask, can be gained from a close look at one university site in Western Canada and what relevance might this book have for researchers and practitioners in other contexts? From our experience of connecting with researchers and practitioners across Canada and internationally over the years, we have been able to see parallels and common themes in the work of others in different contexts. Those cases have proven valuable to us in trying new approaches in the classroom, taking a different methodological pathway in our research, or being inspired by a new idea. Our hope is that readers will find the same—resonate with the work of the researchers and with the participants in the research, to find commonality with their own experiences. We are not trying to generalize, nor make claims about the global applicability of the findings in the studies featured here. We are also not attempting to present a comprehensive representation of the full range of issues and perspectives prevalent in an internationalizing university. The authors in this book are colleagues and graduate students with whom we have researched critical issues and share concerns regarding internationalization that have arisen in the course of our work at the university. The issues may not be wide ranging but the close attention to a few of them allows us to offer a more complex and multidimensional view and understanding of what we believe are common topics in contemporary higher education settings.

Much of internationalization research has been applied (de Wit 2014, 98), or concerned with policy matters at the institutional level, with few opportunities to connect with everyday experiences at the individual level. This book is our attempt to provide a fresh understanding of internationalization efforts on the ground. Following Dorothy Smith (1996, 2005), it is, in some ways, a sociology, a close look at some of the relations and practices of internationalization, and the ways in which institutional and policy discourses influence and order them. From her seminal work on institutional ethnography (IE) where she discusses the relations of ruling as a feminist inquiry, we draw on Smith's (1996) notion of "standpoint": "to be understood as a way of directing attention to the starting place of the inquiry" (76–7). Our starting place is curiosity about people's experiences of the everyday world of internationalization. In some chapters, the experiences that are brought to light are those of the participants in the research, and in some other contributions, in particular, those inquiring about practice, the experiences are those of the researchers themselves. Thus, aligned with IE, we are "work[ing] from the interests and concerns of actual people" (Smith and Griffin 2022, 77).

In the rest of this introductory chapter, we provide a summary overview of the internationalization of higher education, including a focus on Canada and the university where the authors conducted their research. This is followed by a brief discussion of theoretical perspectives informing our understandings of culture, language, and internationalization and their interconnections. We conclude with an overview of the chapters in the book.

Internationalization of Higher Education

Globalization and internationalization have changed the terrain of higher education in the twenty-first century (Knight 2014). Internationalization of higher education, however, has been claimed to be separate and distinct from economic globalization (Knight 2008). It has been a scant three decades since the internationalization of higher education has grown from a novel idea into a central feature of higher education (de Wit 2014) and a billion-dollar industry in the Global North (Luke 2010; Naidoo and Jamieson 2005).

Often conflated or confused with globalization of education, internationalization of higher education has been generally described as an integration of an international, intercultural, and global dimension in all aspects of higher education (Knight 1994). Recognizing the exponential growth of academic mobility across borders and the importance of this for higher education, Hudzic (2011) introduced the notion of comprehensive internationalization: "a commitment, confirmed through action, to infuse international and comparative perspectives throughout the teaching, research, and service missions of higher education. It shapes institutional ethos and values and touches the entire higher education enterprise" (1). Contrary to the ideals of internationalization expressed through these definitions and scholarly discussions, internationalization is dominated by an economic orientation and "academic capitalism" (Jones, Leask, and de Wit 2021; Marginson 2006; Stein 2019).

The intensification in the global mobilities of people is being reflected in the dramatic increase of international student mobility, often from countries from the Global South to higher education institutions in the Global North. Over five million students a year, globally, leave their home country to take up the identity of "international student" in higher education institutions elsewhere (OECD 2020). This cross-border academic mobility is the most visible element of the internationalization of higher education, and most commonly associated with it. In the past two decades alone, there has been increasing competition among postsecondary institutions (PSIs) in the Global North to recruit international students, valued for the essential revenue they bring in the face of declining public funding for the higher education sector (Marginson 2006; Trilokekar and Kizilbash 2013). "[U]niversities strive for competition, revenue, and reputation/branding" (de Wit and Altbach 2021, 35). The commodification and marketization of international higher education is far from the aspirations of the early proponents of internationalization who saw in internationalization possibilities to realize global citizenship, intercultural learning and international mindedness among students, and in integrating a more global ethos across the services and operations of higher education institutions (Knight 2008; de Wit 2014).

Amidst growing critiques of the "edubusiness" (Luke 2010) of internationalization, scholars have declared that it has lost its way (Knight 2014), even announced the death of internationalization (Brandenberg and de Wit 2011) and challenged the notion that internationalization is inherently beneficial (Stein et al. 2016). In response to the increasing gap between rhetoric and reality, de Wit and Hunter (2015) attempted to provide direction by enhancing the influential Knight definition to include intentionality and clarity of purpose: "[t]he *intentional* process of integrating an international intercultural or global dimension into the purpose, functions and delivery of post-secondary education *in order to enhance the quality of education and research for all students and staff, and to make a meaningful contribution to society*" (3, emphasis in original). Neither critique nor revisions of definitions and conceptualizations, however, have influenced the direction of internationalization, which remains market-driven.

These developments brought attention to the need for an ethical and principled internationalization in all its dimensions. In our own work, we have advocated for internationalization that is grounded in practices of social justice and educational sustainability (e.g., Beck and Ilieva 2019; Ilieva, Beck, and Waterstone 2014). Another revisioning of internationalization has also emerged with a concept known as "intelligent internationalization" (Rumbley 2015), aspiring to align with the common good rather than economic goals, and to foster and develop a more sustainably just, globally connected, and interculturally competent society. Along the same lines, Jones, Leask, and de Wit (2021) have put forward a compelling argument for socially responsible internationalization. Beck (2021) has even considered the possibility of a "post-internationalization" borrowing from the post-development scholars and grounded in the degrowth movement. All of these developments point to the desire for a different kind of internationalization reflected in the growth of what is known as critical internationalization studies (Stein 2019). Sharon Stein, one of the leading scholars in this movement, also founded the Critical Internationalization Studies Network which "brings together scholars, practitioners, educators, students, and community organizations interested in reimagining dominant patterns of relationship, representation, and resource distribution in the internationalization of education" (CISN n.d.). With this growing network, critiques of internationalization are becoming mainstream (Stein and McCartney 2021). What has proven to be challenging, however, is going beyond critique to "imagine internationalization otherwise" (Andreotti et al. 2016).

Systemic change appears to be near impossible, but is it possible to create spaces for a different kind of engagement? Stein and McCartney (2021) ask: "What kind of internationalization would be adequate to the task of preparing people to respond to these [global, planetary] challenges in more sober, mature, discerning, and accountable ways?" (9). And in response, we agree with the authors that

> in the end there is no fixed answer, just many partial, imperfect propositions in the short term (each of which may reproduce some colonial patterns, or create new ones) and the long-term work of examining the limits of the existing system and asking how we got here, why it is so difficult to imagine otherwise and how we might experiment responsibly and self-reflexively not just with alternative approaches to internationalization, but alternative thinking about alternatives. (9)

We align ourselves with perspectives that call for the reimagination of patterns of engagement in contexts of internationalization that respect difference, reciprocity, and equitable relationships and seek to dismantle coloniality. These values are foundational for our work and the work shared by the contributors to this book. What we also acknowledge is that reimagining may be short term, and that the responses to the current systemic problems may be partial and imperfect.

The Canadian Context

Historical context: As with developments in other countries, Canada's international engagement began post–World War II with development assistance to countries in the Global South, which was supported by federal policy on international development assistance, known as humane internationalism (Trilokekar 2010). These activities resulted in the growth of academic mobilities of Canadian faculty to universities in the Global South and international students enrolling in universities in the Global North. These acts of "benevolence" (Jefferess 2008) produced colonial patterns of education and mobility, including the imposition and universalization of Western values and knowledge, and the reification of students from the Global South as objects of development (Schendel and McCowan 2015). In a classic trope of colonialism, international students are sought as cultural assets and simultaneously cast as culturally and intellectually deficient.

These colonial legacies implicate internationalization itself as an imperial project and in the hierarchical ordering of geopolitical relations (Beck and

Pidgeon 2020; Dolby and Rahman 2008; Johnstone and Lee 2017). Further analysis shows how the modern university is structured and maintained by Whiteness (Shahjahan and Edwards 2022) and advances the "modern colonial global imaginary" (Andreotti et al. 2016). The next phase of internationalization in Canada can also be connected to coloniality as economic expansion as international engagement shifted from "aid to trade" (Trilokekar 2010), shifting from a service model to a market model which is evident in internationalization activities in the present.

Internationalization policies: Trade is a notable theme in Canadian policy documents on international education. As there is no federal portfolio for education, which is under the jurisdiction of provinces, the first international education strategy was developed fairly recently by the Ministry of Trade under its Global Markets Action Plan (FATDC 2014). Unsurprisingly, the strategy is focused on marketing education internationally by "branding Canada to maximize success" (10). The benefits listed are for Canadians, including economic prosperity created by incoming international students, job creation, and finding solutions for the skilled labor shortages. Students from developing and emerging economies are targeted in this marketing campaign and are promised "a consistently high-quality education at an attractive price in a tolerant, diverse, safe and welcoming environment" (10). Students are cast as an economic asset, and education is traded as a commodity.

The second strategy continues with recruiting international students in "key global markets" (Government of Canada 2019, 7) and a move into a greater diversification of student source countries. Another focus is encouraging Canadian students to go abroad, but even here, the global learning outcomes are tied to prosperity in a competitive global market. A significant item in this strategy is the access offered to international students for "pathways to permanent residency" (2) and "timely immigration services" (10). This has created mixed messaging regarding the value of a quality education in Canada which has little value in itself other than as a means to greater cultural capital.

In the same year as the first federal policy, the Association of Canadian Deans of Education (ACDE) (2014) launched their *Accord on the Internationalization of Education*, which was both a critique of economic internationalization and a call for principled practices. An important statement by the educational community, the Accord names five principles on which it is founded: equity, economic and social justice; reciprocity; global sustainability; intercultural awareness and respect; and equitable access. These principles explicitly address concerns about internationalization, including its economic orientation; the sharp increases in student mobility affecting institutional capacity to respond to service demands; and the challenges arising from increasing uncertainty, complexity, and inequity in social conditions. The Accord also names risks associated with these concerns, including the uncritical adoption of exploitative practices, personal and social disruption, neocolonial practices, and risk to participants engaged in international activities. Among the benefits named are the potential for "enriching and enhancing educational experiences for all students" (2) and possibilities for systemic change.

There was much hope following the signing of this Accord by over fifty Faculties of Education across Canada that the Accord would have a greater influence over the practices of internationalization. There has been little institutional reporting or follow-up, and as Stein (2019) argues, "while the institutionalization of critique can have strategic benefits for those seeking change, it does not necessarily represent an unreservedly positive development, especially when institutions or other organizations mobilize critique in tokenistic and selective ways" (4–5). In this kind of environment, where systemic change is hard to achieve, it is even more important that we are able to highlight the ways in which faculty and staff are engaging with the challenges of internationalization in whatever way they are able to.

International students: Numbers and economics constitute much of the news about international students. To convey an idea of the intensification of internationalization in Canada, where our research is located, here are some recent statistics. Canada ranks as the world's fourth most popular destination for international students and hosted 621,565 students in 2021, a 16 percent increase over the previous year, and a 135 percent increase since 2010 (CBIE 2022). In 2022, 807,750 international students were enrolled in educational institutions in Canada at all levels of study. These numbers constitute an increase of 31 percent over the previous year, a 40 percent growth over the previous five years, and almost 170 percent growth over the past decade (CBIE n.d.). The majority of these students were enrolled in PSIs.

Statistics Canada (2021) observed some interesting patterns about international student enrollment in Canada: over the past few years, it is international students who have increased the overall enrollment in PSIs. From the academic year 2018/19 to 2019–20, international student enrollment increased by 13.7 percent while Canadian student enrollment declined by 0.9 percent overall. In this context, universities and colleges in Canada have come to rely on international student tuition to the extent that many institutions are forced to apply budget cuts when international student enrollment declines.

While Canadian PSIs actively recruit international students promising a quality education and a welcoming and safe environment, there are increasing media and research report accounts of challenges faced by international students. Beyond the common challenges of culture shock, loneliness, and financial stresses, there has been a sharp increase in more troubling issues such as racism, multiple forms of discrimination, bullying, sexual assault, and mental health issues (Appia 2021; Canada Bound Immigrant n.d.; Dey and Williams 2021; Houshmand, Spanierman, and Tafarodi 2014). Incidents of racism increased during the pandemic, affecting those of Asian heritage in particular, who were the target of racism and hatred.

Beyond the students whose daily lives are impacted, such issues affect the conditions faced by faculty in their classrooms and impact their role as mentors, and by staff who serve international students in their day-to-day work. The research featured in this book was completed prior to the pandemic, and so the escalation of racism, discrimination, and financial stress, for example, do not appear in the data. This does not mean that racism was not an issue or that it does not exist. On the contrary, racism in higher education has been an invisible issue and an under-researched area of higher education (e.g., Henry and Tator 2009).

The University

The University, located on the west coast of Canada, has eight faculties and offers programs on three campuses as well as through distance and online education. It has been actively involved in international activities for over thirty years including: an international student presence on campus, study abroad programs such as field schools, student and faculty exchanges, credit and noncredit instructional program delivery, and development assistance, delivered either in Canada or overseas. The University has established 290 partnership agreements in over 55 countries, 42 of them with partners ranked in the world's top 200 universities. Exchanges, field schools, work, and study abroad options are available in over fifty countries. Three hundred global co-op placements are offered annually in more than twenty-five countries. Research and international development activities are being conducted in over fifty-five countries. In 2022, over 6,100 international students were enrolled at the University, including 4,872 undergraduates comprising 20.7 percent of 23,536 undergraduates, and 1,294 graduates who were 34 percent of the graduate population of 3,805.

There are a number of administrative offices and services that were designed to support international students, such as a specialized student services office, the Student Learning Commons in the library, welcome guides, health and counseling, a study lounge dedicated to international students, a mentoring program, workshops and special events, a Global Connections program. Some of the chapters in the book highlight how some services may be either a mismatch or are inadequate in meeting the multiple complex needs of the diverse range of international students, prime among them, language support.

We are noticing a recent trend regarding terminology related to internationalization and international activities among Canadian universities. The term "internationalization" has been quietly dropped in favor of "global engagement." At our university, support for international students is administered under Student Services, and the rest of the international portfolio is under the Vice President Research and International. SFU International is described as "the university's hub for international relationships, knowledge and resources to enhance and mobilize the global reach of SFU's teaching, research and community engagement" (SFU International n.d.). The most recent strategic plan cites global impact, global partnerships, and global networks as the focus, highlighting research and programs. Using the UN Sustainable Development Goals as a framework, global engagement activities and programs are aligned with goals of sustainability.

The goals of sustainable development and social justice are a move in the right direction in recognizing that internationalization is more than the recruitment of international students. The term "global engagement" also centers attention on research and teaching as the educational sites for such engagement rather than the cultural diversity of students. However, the separation of international student recruitment from the university's stated commitments to international or global engagement is paradoxical while the university is reliant on international student tuition, in itself, an inequitable and largely unsustainable practice. This serves as a move to innocence and allows the institution to continue with "business as usual," and to perform the role of "the good university" (following Schick and St. Denis's (2005, 295) critique of the "good nation").

These are some of the tensions that mark the university in which we teach and research, and the conditions in which students learn, and faculty and staff work. These tensions also give rise to questions: When does business as usual become untenable? What are the limits of revisioning? Are the educational goals of internationalization being realized, and how is internationalization fulfilling the academic mission of the university? These questions bring us back to maintaining a research agenda focused on ethical internationalization when we feel besieged by and crowded out of the internationalization marketplace that is our university.

Internationalization and Culture

Student and faculty mobility resulting from intensified internationalization has led to a significant increase in linguistic and cultural diversity in higher education institutions globally and more so in the Global North. As described earlier in this chapter, conceptualizations of internationalization convey the idea that internationalization promotes intercultural learning and intercultural competence, facilitates education for global citizenship, and seeks to graduate students who have the skills and competencies to be successful in a competitive global market. But how does culture show up in the discourses and practices of internationalization?

Universities rationalize the recruitment of international students as a diversification of the student population. Cultural diversity becomes the default strategy to promote intercultural learning and engagement. In a comparative policy analysis of equity, diversity, and inclusion efforts in research-intensive universities in Canada, Tamtik and Guenter (2019) note that "universities are currently predominantly utilizing recruitment campaigns as mechanisms for achieving greater diversity on campus" (51). This objectification of international students as the bearers of culture brings in an instrumental view of, and objectifies culture itself, as a "thing" to be transmitted, consumed, and acquired as a skill set.

The focus on cultural diversity promotes a celebratory, superficial, and instrumental understanding of culture. As James (2010) reminds us, "culture is not defined strictly by artifacts, clothing, or food but by how group members use, interpret and perceive those artefacts; neither is it a fixed set of customs, languages or rituals" (27). Nevertheless, this surface view of culture is the predominant discourse in Canada embedded in its national policy of multiculturalism. Among the many critiques of multiculturalism is the charge that it misses the important consideration of power relations and cultural difference among groups based on social stratification (James 2010, 29). Multiculturalism welcomes cultural diversity, but that diversity is measured against Whiteness that is equated to being Canadian. Bannerji's (2000) discussion is illustrative of the ways in which this ideology further imposes a deficit discourse imposed on those who are different from the dominant cultural group. She calls multiculturalism a "national imaginary [which] rests on posing 'Canadian culture' against 'multicultures.' An element of whiteness quietly enters into cultural definitions, marking the difference between a core cultural group and other groups who are represented as cultural fragments" (10). A study by Buckner et al. (2021) illustrates how this has become the dominant discourse in internationalization. The authors investigated how institutions in Canada, the United States, and the UK discuss international students in their strategy documents, to understand institutional roles and responsibilities regarding the international students they recruit. One of the main findings was that "while institutions celebrate cultural diversity in their official strategies, their discussions nonetheless frame whiteness as the norm against which cultural diversity is defined" (33).

Another critique of multiculturalism is that it accommodates, celebrates, tolerates and appreciates cultural diversity but leaves out the dominant culture so that it allows "the preservation of the cultural hegemony of the dominant cultural groups . . . [and fails] to deal with the problems of systemic racism" (Henry and Tator 2006, 49). Diversity appears as a neutral, value-free "cultural classification" (Bannerji 2000, 35) leading to the avoidance of cultural difference as a construct of power (James 2010). Difference is ascribed to culture rather than race and results in the erasure of race and racialization (Henry and Tator 2006; James 2010; Simpson, James, and Mack 2011). Multiculturalism erases Indigenous peoples and perspectives by their absence in the policy. It also minimizes the need for an anticolonial approach (Simpson, James, and Mack 2011).

These critiques are important when we try to understand the ways in which international students are culturally Othered. Many of the chapters make reference to the deficit discourses that often frame international students and the diverse forms of knowledge they bring to the institution. Some of the chapters also outline practices that counter these dominant discourses and illustrate ways to begin engaging in ethical internationalization.

Language, Culture, and Internationalization

In this section we address the intersections between language, culture, and internationalization by bringing in current work in several fields within the discipline of applied linguistics. First, we will discuss how the field of applied linguistics has considered language and culture as interwoven for close to half a century now. Next, current understandings around language and linguistic repertoires within the field of critical applied linguistics will be discussed briefly (see also Chapter 2 for a more extensive discussion of this line of thinking). Then we will bring in theorizing around language and internationalization developed in contexts of English as a Medium of Instruction (EMI) by addressing its applicability in Anglo-dominant contexts. The literature briefly reviewed here allows us to address the complexity of the language/culture/internationalization nexus that impacts the experiences of faculty, staff, and students within one internationalizing university, as illustrated in the chapters in this book.

The Language/Culture Interconnection in Applied Linguistics Scholarship

The field of applied linguistics, and especially its subfield of language teaching, has considered language and culture as intricately interwoven since at least the 1970s (Byram and Morgan 1994; Kramsch 1993). Damen (1987) argued that the language culture connection could be conceptualized in terms of systems of classification (in the sense that language enables its users to identify and classify their surroundings and activities), cultural foci (in the sense that points of cultural emphasis are reflected through vocabulary in a language), and worldview (in the sense that language is a powerful tool assisting humans in forming and expressing different ways of coping with their surrounding world). More recently, language and culture have been named an "uncontested duo" (Kramsch 2014, 403) in language education which, in the twentieth century, embraced a positivistic objective link between one language and one culture (2014).

Risager (2020) states that language and culture "are abstract and polysemic ideological constructions, and so are the relationships between them" (626). She points out that while in a general sense "[h]uman culture always includes language, and human language cannot be conceived without culture" (ibid.), in real contexts we engage in a variety of language practices (mono or multilingual, different registers, etc.) and different forms of cultural practices (e.g., various norms, values, symbols, ideologies). Thus, Risager suggests the concept of "linguaculture" which involves three dimensions: "culture in language" (i.e., a semantic dimension), "the culturality of language" (i.e., a poetic or literary dimension), and "the cultural dimensions of language" (i.e., an identity dimension that includes how one positions oneself or is positioned in interactions or society at large) (2020, 627). These dimensions are enacted in language use which has ideological implications in that it is related to power structures operating in a given context. Demuro and Gurney (2018) also view language and culture as fluid and intrinsically linked concepts, with both culture and language "constantly, shifting, evolving and adapting" (256) to the contexts in which they are enacted/performed. They argue for the development of a "deeper awareness of the political and historical contingencies of language" (288) and a broader conception of culture in the field of language education which "acknowledges the relationship between culture, language, and power" (289) signaling that "the omission of critical accounts of language, culture and power—and of their intersections in educational settings—has the potential to reify existing social, cultural, and linguistic inequalities" (2018). The relation between language, culture, and power and their inextricable embeddedness in institutional practices as well as personal views and acts seem evident in the accounts of study participants whose experiences of internationalization in one institution are narrated in the chapters that follow.

Language and Languaging

The idea of "language" as a separate and enumerable entity arose with developments in structural linguistics where the focus was on language as a self-contained semiotic system whose elements are defined primarily in relation to each other, a system that people acquire and use to communicate with each other following established rules for word formation and grammatical structures. This idea has been debunked in the last several decades with Makoni and Pennycook (2007), and others, arguing that language is a myth because it does not exist as a natural phenomenon, but rather is a human construction emerging with the sociopolitical and historical processes of nation-building and colonialism to codify practices of human interaction. Such codification is the result of language ideologies/metadiscursive regimes which paved the way for continuously taken-for-granted concepts like standard languages that underscore preoccupations with correctness of language use and the hierarchization of language practices (Demuro and Gurney 2018).

In contrast, the view endorsed (and convincingly argued) by critical applied linguists, which we espouse, is that language needs to be understood and described primarily as a social practice, emergent in particular sociopolitical and cultural contexts of interaction and involving a repertoire of linguistic resources at the disposal of interactants (García 2009; Gurney and Demuro 2022; Lin 2020; Makoni and Pennycook 2007; and others). The notion that speakers draw on a repertoire of linguistic resources rather than discrete languages in order to communicate is linked to the idea of translanguaging (e.g., Lin 2020) and builds on the notion of languaging (García 2009; Gurney and Demuro 2022). As Gurney and Demuro explain, the term languaging "shifts language from a noun to a verb (Bloome and Beauchemin, 2016), originating not in abstract systems with an arbitrary relationship to sounds and signs, but grounded within idiolectical, cultural and experiential approaches to communication and interaction" (2022, 310). Such a position highlights that languaging "is a set of situated and territorialised social practices belonging to users" (2022) and challenges normative understandings of language. As it will become evident in the chapters in this book, such a view of language/languaging as a dynamic cultural practice involving a range of linguistic resources is not commonly embraced by participants in the studies discussed here and may explain to an extent some of the uneasy lived experiences of internationalization shared here.

Language and Internationalization in EMI Settings

While the English language plays a key role in internationalization given its status in the academic discourse community (Jenkins 2013; Murray 2016; Phillipson 2010), research has not engaged sufficiently with the linguistic implications of internationalization processes in higher education institutions worldwide (Dafouz and Smit 2016, 2020; Murray 2016). Moreover, while much research is being conducted on the consequences and challenges related to the role of EMI in non-Anglophone countries, especially in Europe, (e.g., Lasagabaster 2018; Kuteeva and Airey 2014; Dafouz and Smit 2020), the role of English in discussions of internationalization in Anglo-dominant contexts like Canada or the UK is often assumed or overlooked (Byrd Clark, Haque, and Lamoureux 2013; Jenkins 2013). We contend that conceptual work around English and internationalization done in EMI contexts can be informative in attempts to theorize the connections between language (or we might say "languaculture") and internationalization in settings like the one where the studies discussed in the book took place—an Anglo-dominant university in Western Canada. The work of Dafouz and Smit (2016, 2020) is particularly helpful in guiding us to consider the multidimensionality of the language and internationalization linkages in university contexts.

Dafouz and Smit (2016, 2020) find the term EMI inadequate to encapsulate the phenomenon of education *through* English in twenty-first-century superdiverse higher education institutions where English is an additional language for most stakeholders, and propose that it be replaced by English-medium education in multilingual settings (EMEMUS) or (EME in brief). In addition, they propose a six-dimensional framework, represented by the acronym ROAD-MAPPING, to conceptualize English in higher education given the diversity and complexity of specific settings where EMI/EME takes place. Drawing on developments in sociolinguistics, ecolinguistics, and language policy research, the framework encompasses the Roles of English (RO) in relation to other languages; Academic Disciplines (AD) associated with specific genres and disciplinary literacies; (language) Management (M), that is, implicit and explicit policies; Agents (A) that may be individuals, collectives, or institutions; Processes and Practices (PP) of teaching and learning; and Internationalization and Glocalization (ING), that is, global and local forces driving change in higher education. The framework is multilayered as the dimensions overlap and intersect with each other. Discourse is placed at the center as the access point through which each of these dimensions can be examined, "reflecting the centrally discursive nature of the social practices that construct and are constructed dynamically" (Dafouz and Smit 2020, 46) in EME/EMI.

We see Anglo-dominant contexts as somewhat different from EMI/EME contexts in that in these settings, English is the language in which most societal institutions function. In this reality, where English plays a role as both the default language of wider communication and as the core academic language of teaching and learning, its dominant/hegemonic position entails different power dynamics for universities, their faculty, staff, and students in higher education settings. We value the multidimensionality of ROAD-MAPPING and the importance of placing "discourse" at the core/center of the frame. It seems to us that ROAD-MAPPING can be even more helpful in making sense of language and internationalization in Anglo-dominant contexts if we add "power" to the core, thus indicating the intricate power/discourse ensemble that impacts university internationalization in universities like ours. We invite the reader to engage with the chapters in the book by considering the multidimensionality of language/languaculture and internationalization as outlined in the ROAD-MAPPING framework held together by a discourse/power dynamics nexus.

We now turn to a brief description of some of the main themes in the individual chapters in the book as they illustrate internationalization on the ground.

The Chapters

This book is a polyphonic text, exemplifying the multidimensionality of experiences with internationalization as the authors zoom in on various facets of the language/culture/internationalization relationship enacted by participants in their studies or as they design interventions to alleviate challenges they face in their own work or in supporting others in the institution. The book, we believe, is distinctive in featuring three major stakeholders in the higher education sector and their perspectives in one collection. Before outlining the focus of the various chapters comprising the book, we note that different terminologies may be used in different higher education contexts to refer to the various groups. The group we call faculty members, a term common in North America, is also known as lecturers, university teachers, or academic staff in some countries. The group we refer to as staff may, in some countries, refer to both faculty and nonacademic staff; in this book, the term refers to nonacademic or professional employees of the university.

The collection begins with two chapters on the teaching experiences of faculty members across the university: Beck writes about faculty engagement with cultural diversity and difference in their classrooms, and Ilieva writes about how faculty deal with challenges relating to English language matters. **Beck** employs curriculum theory, which is not commonly applied in the Internationalization of Curriculum literature within international higher education scholarship, to frame her discussion on how faculty in a variety of disciplines recount their intercultural teaching experiences and cultural difference. Curriculum theory supports the notion of culture and intercultural engagement as fluid, unpredictable, unknowable, and embedded in power relations. This approach to curriculum requires faculty to be open, flexible, and willing to drop their own assumptions and positions. The lived experiences of faculty illustrate their risk-taking, creativity, and invisible labor in their diverse classroom encounters with cultural difference. Faculty are also limited in their understanding of culture and difference and could fall into deficit thinking and judgments about international students, in particular, regarding language. *Ilieva* examines the tensions that disciplinary faculty face in engaging with language matters in their daily work with the linguistically diverse students in their classrooms. Drawing on critical applied linguistics scholarship, she argues for the need to dispel fixed notions of language in the internationalizing university and consider shifting to an understanding of languaging as one way to engage in ethical and equitable relations that could perhaps open up space to begin imagining international higher education in Anglo-dominant contexts otherwise.

The next four chapters feature student encounters with cultural difference: the first two from the perspective of international students, and the others on study abroad experiences. ***Zhihua (Olivia) Zhang*** offers accounts of the traumatic experiences of two Chinese students with writing a language proficiency test (IELTS) that serves a gate-keeping purpose for university acceptance. She highlights its negative impact on their identities beyond linguistic abilities and invites universities to rethink the value of standardized language tests in admission and underscores the coupling of language (and more specifically so-called standard English) and internationalization currently reigning in institutions of higher education. **Ravindran and Ilieva** invite us to move beyond deficit views of international students often discussed as a homogenous group in scholarly literature, and speak to students' agency in navigating transcultural spaces via the acquisition and application of intercultural capital. The chapter illustrates how internationalization can be lived on one's own terms in relation to cultural and linguistic repertoires that international students draw on, developed in this case partially through studies in a program uniquely designed for international students.

Uppal-Hershorn and Beck write about a cohort of pre-service teachers recounting their teaching practicum in India. The chapter is informed by a theoretical framework on multiplicity and interstitial space that makes it possible to gain insights into the pre-service teachers' engagement with cultural difference. These findings challenge simplistic notions of intercultural learning and suggest that pre-service teachers' dwelling in discomfort and experiences of vulnerability may support them to take risks, be more flexible, and grow in their understanding of intercultural relations. These are important implications for teacher education in pluralistic communities. *Marshall and Amburgey*'s chapter outlines how teacher professional development in the Global North is taken up and implemented by teachers of English in their local context. Outlining activities in the program and the in-service teachers' negotiations of new knowledge in their schools back home highlight the importance of engaging in international collaborations in teacher education that move beyond Western paradigms and recognize teachers' fluid professional identities.

Research on higher education staff is rare, and the next two chapters focus on staff experiences. *Laird and Beck* focus their attention on the daily work experiences of staff, and draw on a higher education framework on Third Space Professionals to make sense of their experiences. They discuss how neoliberal internationalization has created conditions in which staff have to do more, improvise, and be more efficient. Staff are at varying points of "becoming" Third Space Professionals. *Miranda and Ilieva* discuss the language experiences of staff who are often the frontline workers in the international activities in their departments or units. The views of staff illuminate how language, culture, and internationalization are interwoven, and help us think about recognizing staff as having a significant yet unrecognized role in the internationalizing university. They echo Laird and Beck's call for professional development opportunities for staff around cross-cultural encounters and flexibility in communicative practices.

The final three chapters of the book feature collaborative efforts of faculty in designing and implementing classroom strategies in response to various challenges of multilingual classrooms. **Wallace and Sjoerdsma** lead us into the world of practical challenges that faculty and departments face in addressing expectations for communication skills accreditation within a discipline (in this case, engineering) with a linguistically diverse student body. Highlighting the importance of collaborations between discipline and language experts, the chapter outlines the design of a post-entry language assessment aimed to identify the needs for supporting multilingual students in internationalizing universities to become successful members in their disciplinary community.

Spiliotopoulos's chapter also delves into practical challenges that departments with a large number of linguistically diverse students face when caught in neoliberal discourses of increasing accountability while attempting to implement approaches to disciplinary instruction (i.e., engaging with the AD or academic discipline dimension in the ROAD-MAPPING framework) that build disciplinary academic literacy in all business students regardless of their linguistic resources. The newly designed course strengthens business communication skills in English in inclusive ways and shows some possibilities to move toward systemic change.

Wallace, Singh, and Shaw conclude the trio of works in the book that offer concrete ways to engage with linguistic and cultural diversity in the internationalizing university. Detailing the goals and outcomes of a seminar series designed to support faculty in working with multilingual students in their courses, the chapter illustrates a promising pathway to establishing learning environments that draw on the creativity of faculty to foster linguistically inclusive, and thus, more equitable, class activities. Such seminars allow us to begin reimagining patterns of engagements in contexts of internationalization that may lead us to think about alternatives in doing education in the twenty-first century.

This collection offers perspectives on language, culture, and internationalization of higher education from faculty, language experts, and doctoral students who have been grappling with these topics. The unbridled growth of internationalization has led to complex problems and issues that cannot be resolved with simplistic responses and solutions. We hope this volume offers ways to think about, reimagine, and approach complex issues differently. Our intention is to engage scholars, researchers, instructional staff, practitioners, and administrators in ongoing discussions on mitigating the harms of internationalization and make attempts to realize a different internationalization.

References

Andreotti, Vanessa, Sharon Stein, Karen Pashby, and Michelle Nicolson. 2016. "Social Cartographies as Performative Devices in Research on Higher Education." *Higher Education Research & Development* 35, no. 3: 84–99. https://doi.org/10.1080/07294360.2015.1125857.

Appia, Veronica. 2021. "Timeline: This Is Canada's History of Anti-Asian Racism that COVID-19 Has Amplified." Retrieved June 15, 2022, from https://www.toronto.com/news-story/10349793-timeline-this-is-canada-s-history-of-antiasian-racism-that-covid-19-has-amplified/.

Association of Canadian Deans of Education (ACDE). 2014. *Accord on the Internationalization of Education*. Ottawa: ACDE. https://csse-scee.ca/acde/wp-content/uploads/sites/7/2017/08/Accord-on-the-Internationalization-of-Education.pdf

Bannerji, Himani. 2000. *The Dark Side of the Bation: Essays on Multiculturalism, Nationalism and Gender*. Toronto: Canadian Scholars' Press.

Beck, Kumari. 2021. "Beyond Internationalization: Lessons from Post-Development." *Journal of International Students* 11, no. S1: 133–151.

Beck, Kumari, and Roumiana Ilieva. 2019. "'Doing' Internationalization." *SFU Educational Review* 12, no. 3: 18–39. https://doi.org/10.21810/sfuer.v12i3.1031.

Beck, Kumari, and Michelle Pidgeon. 2020. "Across the Divide: Conversations on Decolonization, Indigenization and Internationalization of Higher Education." In *International Education as Public Policy in Canada*, edited by Roopa Desai Trilokekar, Merli Tamtik, and Glen Jones, 384–406. Montreal: McGill-Queen's University Press.

Bloome, David, and Faythe Beauchemin. 2016. "Languaging Everyday Life in Classrooms." *Literacy Research: Theory, Method, and Practice*, 65, no. 1: 152–65.

Brandenburg, Uwe, and Hans de Wit. 2011. "The End of Internationalization." *International Higher Education* 62: 15–16.

Buckner, Elizabeth, Punita Lumb, Zahra Jafarova, Phoebe Kang, Adriana Marroquin, and You Zhang. 2021. "Diversity Without Race: How University Internationalization Strategies Discuss International Students." *Journal of International Students* 11, Special issue 1: 32–49.

Byram, Michael, and Carol Morgan. 1994. *Teaching-and-Learning Language-and-Culture*. Clevedon; Philadelphia: Multilingual Matters.

Byrd Clark, Julie, Eve Haque, and Sylvie Lamoureux. 2013. "The Role of Language in Processes of Internationalization: Considering Linguistic Heterogeneity and Voices from Within and Out in Two Diverse Contexts in Ontario." *Comparative and International Education (Ottawa, Ont.)* 41, no. 3. https://doi.org/10.5206/cie-eci.v41i3.9212.

Canada Bound Immigrant. n.d. "It's Challenging Being an International Student in Canada." https://www.canadaboundimmigrant.com/top-stories/its-challenging-being-an-international-student-in-canada.

Canadian Bureau for International Education (CBIE). 2022. *Facts and Figures*. Ottawa: Canadian Bureau for International Education. https://cbie.ca/infographic/.

Canadian Bureau for International Education (CBIE). n.d. Downloaded from https://cbie.ca/infographic/.

CISN. n.d. Website. "About." https://criticalinternationalization.net

Damen, Louise. 1987. *Culture Learning: The Fifth Dimension in the Language Classroom*. Reading, MA: Addison-Wesley Pub. Co.

de Wit, Hans. 2014. "The Different Faces and Phases of Internationalisation of Higher Education." In *The Forefront of International Higher Education: A Festschrift in Honor of Philip G. Altbach*, edited by Alma Maldonado-Maldonado and Roberta Malee Bassett, 89–99. Dordrecht: Springer.

de Wit, Hans, and Philip G. Altbach. 2021. "Internationalization in Higher Education: Global Trends and Recommendations for its Future." *Policy Reviews in Higher Education* 5, no. 1: 28–46. https://doi.org/10.1080/23322969.2020.1820898.

de Wit, Hans, and Fiona Hunter. 2015. "The Future of Internationalization of Higher Education in Europe." *International Higher Education* 83: 2–3.

Dafouz, Emma, and Ute Smit. 2016. "Towards a Dynamic Conceptual Framework for English-Medium Education in Multilingual University Settings." *Applied Linguistics* 37, no. 3: 397–415. https://doi.org/10.1093/applin/amu034.

Dafouz, Emma, and Ute Smit. 2020. *ROAD-MAPPING English Medium Education in the Internationalised University*. Cham: Springer International Publishing.

Demuro, Eugenia, and Laura Gurney. 2018. "Mapping Language, Culture, Ideology: Rethinking Language in Foreign Language Instruction." *Language and Intercultural Communication* 18, no. 3: 287–299. https://doi.org/10.1080/14708477.2018.1444621.

Dey, Sreyoshi, and Erin Williams. 2021. "Anti-Asian Racism in Canada: Where Do We Go from Here?" Asia Pacific Foundation of Canada. https://www.asiapacific.ca/publication/anti-asian-racism-canada-where-do-we-go-here.

Dolby, Nadine, and Aliya Rahman. 2008. "Research in International Education." *Review of Educational Research* 78, no. 3: 676–726. https://doi.org/10.3102/0034654308320291.

Foreign Affairs, Trade and Development Canada (FATDC). 2014. *Canada's International Education Strategy: Harnessing Our Knowledge Advantage to Drive Innovation and Prosperity*. Ottawa: FATDC.

García, Ofelia. 2009. "Education, Multilingualism and Translanguaging in the 21st Century." In *Social Justice through Multilingual Education*, edited by Tove Skutnabb-Kangas, Robert Phillipson, Ajit K. Mohanty, and Minati Panda, 140–158. Bristol, Blue Ridge Summit: Multilingual Matters. https://doi.org/10.21832/9781847691910-011.

Government of Canada (GAC). 2019. "Building on Success: International Education Strategy 2019–2024." Ottawa: Government of Canada. Retrieved June 2022, from https://www.international.gc.ca/education/strategy-2019-2024-strategie.aspx?lang=eng#:~:text=The%20Trade%20Commissioner%20Service%20of%20Global%20Affairs%20Canada.

Gurney, Laura, and Eugenia Demuro. 2022. "Tracing New Ground, from Language to Languaging, and from Languaging to Assemblages: Rethinking Languaging through the Multilingual and Ontological Turns." *International Journal of Multilingualism* 19, no. 3: 305–324. https://doi.org/10.1080/14790718.2019.1689982.

Henry, Frances, and Carol Tator. 2006. *The Colour of Democracy: Racism in Canadian Society*, 3rd edn. Toronto: Thomson Nelson.

Henry, Frances, and Carol Tator. 2009. *Racism in the Canadian University*. Toronto: University of Toronto Press.

Hudzic, John K. 2011. *Comprehensive Internationalization: From Concept to Action*. Washington, DC: Association of International Educators (nafsa).

Houshmand, Sara, Lisa B. Spanierman, and Romin W. Tafarodi. 2014. "Excluded and Avoided: Racial Microaggressions Targeting Asian International Students in Canada." *Cultural Diversity and Ethnic Minority Psychology* 20, no. 3: 377. https://doi.org/10.1037/a0035404.

Ilieva, Roumiana, Kumari Beck, and Bonnie Waterstone. 2014. "Towards Sustainable Internationalisation of Higher Education." *Higher Education* 68, no. 6: 875–889. https://doi.org/10.1007/s10734-014-9749-6.

James, Carl. 2010. *Seeing Ourselves: Exploring Race, Ethnicity and Culture*, 4th edn. Toronto: Thompson Publishing.

Jefferess, David. 2008. "Global Citizenship and the Cultural Politics of Benevolence." *Critical Literacy: Theories and Practices* 2, no. 1: 27–36.

Jenkins, Jennifer. 2013. *English as a Lingua Franca in the International University: The Politics of Academic English Language Policy*. Abingdon: Routledge.

Johnstone, Marjorie, and Eunjung Lee. 2017. "Canada and the Global Rush for International Students: Reifying a Neo-imperial Order of Western Dominance in the Knowledge Economy Era." *Critical Sociology* 43, no. 7–8: 1063–1078. https://doi.org/10.1177/0896920516654554.

Jones, Elspeth, Betty Leask, and Hans de Wit. 2021. "Global Social Responsibility and the Internationalization of Higher Education for Society." *Urban Education* 25, no. 4: 330–347.

Knight, Jane. 1994. *Internationalization: Elements and Checkpoints.* Ottawa: Canadian Bureau for International Education.

Knight, Jane. 2008. *Higher Education in Turmoil: The Changing World of Internationalization.* Rotterdam: Sense Publishers.

Knight, Jane. 2014. "Is Internationalisation of Higher Education Having an Identity Crisis?" In *The Forefront of International Higher Education: A Festschrift in Honor of Philip G. Altbach,* edited by Alma Maldonado-Maldonado and Roberta Malee Bassett, 75–87. Dordrecht: Springer.

Kramsch, Claire. 1993. *Context and Culture in Language Teaching.* Oxford; New York: Oxford University Press.

Kramsch, Claire. 2014. "Language and Culture in Second Language Learning." In *The Routledge Handbook of Language and Culture,* edited by Farzad Sharifian, 403–416. New York, NY: Routledge.

Kuteeva, Maria, and John Airey. 2014. "Disciplinary Differences in the Use of English in Higher Education." *Higher Education* 67, no. 5: 533–549. https://doi.org/10.1007/s10734-013-9660-6.

Lasagabaster, David. 2018. "Fostering Team Teaching: Mapping Out a Research Agenda for English-Medium Instruction at University Level." *Language Teaching* 51, no. 3: 400–416. https://doi.org/10.1017/S0261444818000113.

Lin, Angel M. Y. 2020. "Introduction: Translanguaging and Translanguaging Pedagogies." In *Translanguaging in Multilingual English Classrooms,* 1–9. Singapore: Springer Nature Singapore. https://doi.org/10.1007/978-981-15-1088-5_1.

Luke, Allan. 2010. "Educating the Other: Standpoint and Theory in the Internationalization of Higher Education." In *Global Inequalities in Higher Education: Whose Interests Are We Serving?,* edited by Elaine Unterhalter and Vincent Carpentier, 57–65. London: Palgrave Macmillan UK.

Makoni, Sinfree, and Alastair Pennycook. 2007. *Disinventing and Reconstituting Languages,* edited by Sinfree Makoni and Alastair Pennycook. Clevedon: Multilingual Matters.

Marginson, Simon 2006. "Dynamics of National and Global Competition in Higher Education." *Higher Education: The International Journal of Higher Education and Educational Planning* 52, no. 1: 1–39.

Murray, Neil. 2016. *Standards of English in Higher Education: Issues, Challenges and Strategies.* Cambridge: Cambridge University Press.

Naidoo, Rajani, and Ian Jamieson. 2005. "Knowledge in the Marketplace: The Global Commodification of Teaching and Learning in Higher Education." In *Internationalizing Higher Education,* edited by Peter Ninnes and Meeri Hellstén, 37–51. Dordrecht: Springer.

OECD. 2020. "Education at a Glance 2020: OECD Indicators." Paris: OECD Publishing. https://doi.org/10.1787/69096873-en.

Phillipson, Robert. 2010. "English in Higher Education, Panacea or Pandemic?" In *Linguistic Imperialism Continued*, 203–244. Routledge. https://doi.org/10.4324/9780203857175-13.

Risager, Karen. 2020. "Language, Culture, and Context." In *The Concise Encyclopedia of Applied Linguistics*, edited by Carol Chapelle, 625–31. Hoboken, NJ: John Wiley & Sons.

Rumbley, Laura. 2015. "'Intelligent Internationalization': A 21st Century Imperative." *International Higher Education* 80, no. Spring: 16–17.

SFU International. n.d. Website. http://www.sfu.ca/international/index.html.

Shahjahan, Riyad A., and Kirsten T. Edward. 2022. "Whiteness as Futurity and Globalization of Higher Education." *Higher Education* 83, no. 2: 747–764. https://doi.org/10.1007/s10734-021-00702-x.

Schendel, Rebecca, and Tristan McCowan. 2015. "Higher Education and Development: Critical Issues and Debates." In *Education and International Development: An Introduction*, edited by T. McCowan and E. Unterhalter, 275–293. London: Bloomsbury Academic.

Schick, Carol, and Verna St Denis. 2005. "Troubling National Discourses in Anti-Racist Curricular Planning." Canadian Journal of Education 28, no 3: 295–317.

Simpson, Jennifer S., Carl E. James, and Johnny Mack. 2011. "Multiculturalism, Colonialism, and Racialization: Conceptual Starting Points." *Review of Education, Pedagogy and Cultural Studies* 33, no. 4: 285–305.

Smith, Dorothy E. 1996. "The Relations of Ruling: A Feminist Inquiry." *Studies in Cultures, Organizations and Societies* 2, no. 2: 171–190. https://doi.org/10.1080/10245289608523475.

Smith, Dorothy E. 2005. *Institutional Ethnography: A Sociology for People*. Lanham: AltaMira Press.

Smith, Dorothy E., and Alison I. Griffith. 2022. *Simply Institutional Ethnography: Creating a Sociology for People*. Toronto: University of Toronto Press.

Statistics Canada. 2021. "Prior to COVID-19, International Students Accounted for the Growth in Postsecondary Enrolments and Graduates." *The Daily* 11-001-X. November 24.

Stein, Sharon. 2019. "Critical Internationalization Studies at an Impasse: Making Space for Complexity, Uncertainty, and Complicity in a Time of Global Challenges." *Studies in Higher Education*. https://doi.org/10.1080/03075079.2019.1704722.

Stein, Sharon, Vanessa Andreotti, Judy Bruce, and Rene Suša. 2016. "Towards Different Conversations about the Internationalization of Higher Education." *Comparative and International Education* 45, no. 1. Article 2: 1–18.

Stein, Sharon, and Dale McCartney. 2021. "Emerging Conversations in Critical Internationalization Studies." *Journal of International Students* 11, no. S1: 1–14.

Tamtik, Merli, and Melissa Guenter. 2019. "Policy Analysis of Equity, Diversity and Inclusion Strategies in Canadian Universities – How Far Have We Come?" *Canadian Journal of Higher Education* 49, no. 3: 41–56.

Trilokekar, Roopa Desai. 2010. "International Education as Soft Power? The Contributions and Challenges of Canadian Foreign Policy to the Internationalization of Higher Education." *Higher Education* 59, no. 2: 131–147.

Trilokekar, Roopa Desai, and Zainab Kizilbash. 2013. "IMAGINE: Canada as a Leader in International Education: How Can Canada Benefit from the Australian Experience?" *Canadian Journal of Higher Education* 43, no. 2: 1–26.

1

Faculty Experiences of Teaching With/in Cultural Difference in an Internationalizing University

Kumari Beck

Introduction

Faculty play a key role in campus internationalization through teaching, program development, research, and service (Friesen 2013; Leask 2015). As a scholar with extensive experience in international education in the Canadian university context, I have deeply considered the tensions in internationalization for more than two decades. On the one hand, I work in a university that is firmly committed to the profitability of recruiting international students to balance their budget. I have also been part of innovative international program development and teaching that has demonstrated the enrichment and deep learning that international and intercultural classrooms can bring to students and teachers. This somewhat bifurcated experience informed my own interests into a team research project on critical internationalization, where we sought to understand the internationalization experiences of students, faculty, and staff at our university. In this chapter, I share my exploration of faculty experiences of internationalization, their perspectives on the intercultural dimension of their work, and how they viewed and approached cultural difference.

Internationalization of higher education is integrally connected to culture and intercultural learning. Some of the early Canadian scholarship on international education refers to Canada's "multicultural reality [as] the stage for internationalization" (Frances 1993, 5). Influential definitions of internationalization conceptualize it as bringing in an intercultural, international, and global dimension into higher education (de Wit and Hunter 2015; Knight 1994). In the popular imagination, internationalization is associated with cultural diversity, and the expectation that international students from diverse cultural backgrounds will bring even greater diversity to Canadian educational institutions. In this context, culture and cultural diversity take on significance in the work of faculty members and I sought to understand how faculty members engaged with this dimension of their teaching.

I begin this chapter with a brief literature review on internationalizing the curriculum, faculty engagement with internationalization, and faculty experiences of teaching in this context. This is followed by an extended discussion on scholarship from curriculum studies that inform my analysis and discussion. The key ideas and concepts that have influenced my own thinking on teaching and cultural difference over the years, in my view, could enhance the current theorizing of the internationalization of curriculum (IoC) in international higher education. By "curriculum" I am not referring to the "how" of developing curriculum and syllabi, which the term commonly implies. I am using the term as conceptualized in curriculum studies where it reflects the context, the theories, the thinking behind the design, the approach, the engagement with students, the teaching, and most importantly, the relations (Pinar 2019). In seeing curriculum internationalization through this lens, I want to understand what could be described as the "being" of teaching, rather than the "doing." For this purpose, I have selected Ted Aoki (Pinar and Irwin 2005), David G. Smith (2006), and Hongyu Wang (2004, 2006) whose scholarship opened up new possibilities for me in thinking about cultural difference and curriculum and pedagogy in internationalization contexts. I will also elaborate on my choice of title for this chapter. Next I will provide a brief overview of the methodology, and then the data from interviews with faculty. Following a summary discussion of the data, I will conclude with some reflections on faculty teaching in internationalization contexts.

Literature Review

IoC has been identified as one of the essential elements of internationalization (Bond, Qian, and Huang 2003; Knight 1994; Leask 2009). "Curriculum is the backbone of the internationalization process" (Knight 1994, 6). Knight's (1994) early conceptualizations of curricular internationalization refer to "formal curriculum elements… that are primarily international in nature" (6), understood as infusion of international content into programs and courses. The leading scholar on IoC, Betty Leask, extends the description to mean "the incorporation of an international and intercultural dimension into the content of the curriculum as well as the teaching and learning processes and support services of a program of study" (Leask 2009, 209). She argues that this definition links international with intercultural in both the formal and informal curriculum and "provides a direct focus on international and intercultural learning outcomes as well as teaching and learning processes" (2009). She makes a distinction between the process of internationalizing curriculum and the product, which is the internationalized curriculum (Leask 2015, 9–10). Intercultural competence is a key component of IoC (Deardoff 2006), and there is an extensive body of literature on defining it (e.g., Deardoff 2006; Spitzberg and Changnon 2009), training for it (e.g., Landis, Bennett, and Bennett 2004), using specific models for developing intercultural competence (Nawaz 2018), and assessing it (e.g., Deardoff 2009).

Over the past decade, higher education institutions have been increasingly emphasizing the importance of IoC (de la Garza 2021; Fragouli 2020; Osakwe 2017). Developing discipline-specific IoC has been a significant trend with studies centering faculty roles in leading the IoC process (de la Garza 2021; de Wit and Leask 2015; Leask 2013; Suwinyattichaiporn and Johnson 2018). Much of the literature on IoC and intercultural competence focuses on the "hows" of developing internationalized curriculum elaborating on frameworks, models, and strategies, with goals of encouraging intercultural learning and competencies (Ji 2020) and/or global citizenship and awareness (Sawir 2013). Research on intercultural dialogue has also been an area of interest among researchers (Schuessler 2019).

Relative to the importance of faculty to the internationalization imperative, research on faculty engagement and experience in internationalization is less prolific. There are some studies on the need for professional development for academics (Wimpenny et al. 2020), including preparing faculty to teach transnationally (Nawaz 2018), and course development and revisioning (Osakwe 2017). Studies on faculty perspectives about teaching are few and mostly relate to the notion of IoC and related faculty experiences of teaching international students (Clarke and Hui Yang 2021; Coryell et al. 2022). Friesen's (2013) Canadian study on faculty engagement, aimed at understanding the motivations and rationales for Canadian faculty engaged in international work, revealed that faculty engage internationally because they are committed to advancing intercultural understanding for their students and themselves. An important finding was the "relational perspective" that faculty found meaningful: "internationalization stems from personal relationships" (221).

It is surprising that perspectives from the field of curriculum studies are not common in IoC literature (within mainstream internationalization of higher education) although it informs the internationalization of teacher education literature (Koh et al. 2022; Amsler, Kerr, and Andreotti 2020) (see Chapter 6). A related article, Stein's (2017) article on the epistemic dominance of Western-Euro-centered curriculum, although not situated in curriculum studies per se, highlights the questions, concerns, and issues that are relevant to my inquiry. Stein describes the challenges associated with internationalizing curriculum in a colonial imaginary and traces how Western knowledge systems have become entrenched in education institutions globally. She argues that the curriculum, then, must take on the task of challenging and disrupting this imaginary and describes four possible approaches to taking up this challenge. "Thin inclusion" incorporates diverse scholars and texts into programs and courses but doesn't change the structures and still addresses issues from a Western perspective. "Thick inclusion" interrogates the power structures of the colonial framework and asks questions about the process of knowledge production. However, this reordering, she argues, "is directed toward the same ends" (S35). Institutionalized "interdisciplines" seek to center marginalized knowledges although this approach leaves the burden of unlearning and reeducating to marginalized peoples. "Alternate institutions," of which there are a few examples, can operate outside of Western institutions with a goal of revitalizing non-Western knowledges and practices, but they are isolated and lack access to resources among the limitations imposed on their ultimate influence. Stein concludes with recommendations to depoliticize internationalization, by "adequately addressing the history of the present, and considering the deeply embedded power differentials and politics of knowledge that have structured Western universities' curricula" (S39). She further recommends reflecting on and thinking differently about epistemic difference and considering the task of internationalizing curriculum as an ongoing and multipart process, cautioning, it is "messy, contested, [and] nonlinear" (S42).

It is in this intersection of epistemic difference and cultural diversity and difference that I locate my inquiry and will now turn my attention to theorists in curriculum studies to provide a conceptual basis for the analysis of faculty data, and to illustrate the contributions they can make to the conceptualization of curriculum internationalization.

The Contribution of Curriculum Scholars

I begin with Canadian curriculum scholar Ted Aoki. From his extensive body of work, I have selected three concepts that are salient for the present discussion:

diversity, multiculturalism, and multiplicity. Aoki (2005e) questions the "conventional imaginary" (306) of diversity as a collection of national cultures that are often exoticized. Referencing Homi Bhabha (1990, 1994) who argues that cultural diversity is only accommodated within the norms and frames of dominant culture, Aoki observes that such a view masks difference: "such an imaginary . . . produces, in its seemingly liberal openness and tolerance of other, a silent form that contains and constrains differences on the underside of diversity" (Aoki 2005e, 307). He theorizes multiculturalism as a multiplicity rather than the notion of multiple identities. A "multiplicity is not a noun" (Deleuze 1987 cited in Aoki 2005c, 269), meaning it is dynamic and is in a constant state of movement. "In a multiplicity what counts are not the elements, but what there is between, the between, a site of relations which are not separable from each other. Every multiplicity grows in the middle" (Deleuze 1987, cited in Aoki 2005c, 269). This notion of multiplicity, argues Aoki, invites us to move away from a "thing-oriented view of multiculturalism" to placing ourselves "in the midst, between and among the cultural entities" (269), allowing us to understand multiculturalism "in the language of AND . . . AND . . . AND" (271). This theme of "the between" runs through much of Aoki's work and opens up the notion of cultural difference as engaging the space between.

Aoki is best known, perhaps, for his articulation of "curriculum as plan," and "curriculum as lived" where the notion of the "between" arose (Aoki 2005a). Referring to the K-12 classroom, Aoki describes curriculum-as-plan as the outcome of planners who are disconnected from the world of learners and teachers, reflecting their own assumptions, interests, and approaches. Teachers become the instrumental "installers of the curriculum" (160). The other world of curriculum is the curriculum-as-lived—curriculum that is deeply embedded in the lives of students and the teacher, "not the curriculum as laid out in a plan, but a plan more or less lived out" (Aoki 2005b, 201). The teacher is pulled by both worlds and is in tension between them. Teaching, then, is the "in-dwelling" between these two curriculum worlds, in "the Zone of Between" (Aoki 2005a, 163). Rather than considering these tensions as being negative, Aoki says "to be alive is to live in tension" (162); "this tensionality . . . is a mode of being a teacher" (162). Aoki (2005a) recognizes that the openness required to live in this tensionality has its own risks, including the willingness to be vulnerable, but also possibilities: "teaching as a leading out to new possibilities to the 'not yet'" (163).

The theme of becoming and the "not yet" appears in David G. Smith's (2006) discussion of what it means to teach in times of globalization and empire. He draws our attention to how conditions of economic globalization influence and shape teaching, arguing that "teachers and teaching are caught in the middle of both a political and an epistemological crisis" (8). By political, he refers to the "hardline economistic interpretations of life" (8) and the subsequent dominance of economic thinking in education that has arisen from economic globalization. Following a thought-provoking analysis of the "globalization phenomenon," Smith proceeds to explore the tensions between these conditions and teaching, asking "what might constitute an appropriate teacherly response to globalization in the midst of its unfolding complexity?" (24). It is this parallel to faculty immersed in conditions of economic internationalization of their institutions that make Smith's theorization suitable for my purposes.

An important element of Smith's argument is David Loy's (2000 cited in Smith 2006, 25) concept of frozen futurism, where education is in the service of a future that is already known. "[B]uilt into the anticipations of teaching is a mask of the future that freezes teaching in a futurist orientation such that in real terms there is no future because the future already is" (25).

This orientation, argues Smith, leaves teachers disconnected from human and nonhuman relations that are a key element of knowledge production and susceptible to the discourses of global competitiveness and the marketplace. To counter this delocalization, Smith recommends first a "living Now" that leads to a "pedagogy of the Now" (28) which he articulates as involving "*personal truth, truth as shared* and *finding truth as finding home*" (29 emphasis in original). The recovery of personal truth, for Smith, means "a way of living in the world that is attuned to the way of the world's actual unfolding" (30), which gives insight into the notion of teaching in the Now. It involves being present and stepping into the unknown in terms of letting go of an expected future outcome and "a letting go as well as embracing" (31). The classroom is considered a place of truth seeking, discovery, and sharing. Truth as shared, then, is based in relations, which are integrally connected to the recovery of personal truth and a leading to finding truth as finding home or being at home in the world. This latter involves the work of reconnecting with the world from which teachers are disconnected. Living Now and teaching in the Now require that we are alive to the complexity of, and dissonances in, the worlds we occupy, leading to enhancing our capacities to both embrace and let go, or, in other words, become adept at living and teaching with/in uncertainties, unpredictability, ambiguities, and complexity.

Hongyu Wang (2006) theorizes third space curriculum from her experiences of teaching in spaces of cultural difference. Speaking as a Chinese woman teaching a class of American (mostly White) students, Wang offers a beautifully articulated account of third space curriculum. "A third space I am interested in is a space in which both parts of a conflicting (cultural, gendered classed, national or psychic) double interact with and transform each other so that multiplicity of the self gives rise to a new realm of subjectivity in new areas of negotiation" (101–2). Curriculum in third space "signals mutual transformation and creation" (111) and arises from interactions, engagement, and negotiation with students and between cultures. She observes further,

> The cross-cultural space I attempt to dwell in is a space full of ambiguities and paradoxes, and my efforts in the classroom are uncertain in terms of consequences since I never really know I am doing the "right" thing. . . . This uncertainty itself, though, encourages us to take the responsibility of constantly starting all over again. . . . In such an ambiguous encounter, my own cultural identities are questioned and transformed as I travel along with the students. The space I intend to create for myself constantly changes as a result of this teacher-student interaction. A third space does not stay with itself. (115)

This dynamism means that both teacher and student, across cultural differences, enter into a process of negotiation, mediation, and transformation. Neither remains unchanged. Wang argues that in this process of negotiation, neither differences nor contradictions should be resolved, and it is in this process that newness emerges. Similar to the process of embracing and letting go that Smith (2006) refers to, Wang speaks to "the necessity of both distance and engagement" (121) in the pedagogical relationship. Drawing on bell hooks's (1994) engaged pedagogy, Wang discusses the call for professors to be vulnerable in sharing their own experiences with students, asserting that this does not mean giving up on a teacher's responsibility to guide students. An engaged pedagogy, she says, "must be coupled with a provocative pedagogy which questions students and asks them to think beyond, feel the unspeakable, and act differently" (122).

Aoki's Zone of Between, Smith's Pedagogy of the Now, and Wang's third space curriculum are all based on pedagogical relations. The notion of culture and intercultural engagement is fluid, unpredictable, unknowable, and difference is embedded in power relations. Relationality, creativity, and multiplicity are common themes, as are becoming attuned to, and being at home with, uncertainty and ambiguity. Occupying the Zone of Between (Aoki 2005a) is akin to third space curriculum (Wang 2006), anticipating the emergence of something new. The dynamism of multiplicity and the newness of third space suggest possibilities to counter frozen futurism (Smith 2006) that results from the commodification and preset outcomes of internationalization. These curriculum theorists offer a way of understanding teachers' "being-ness" in the world, which, they would argue, is the pedagogical entry point to cultural difference in the classroom. These lenses open up possibilities to see faculty in a web of relations and alive to the tensions, ambiguities, and contradictions inherent in a transnational classroom that is marked by cultural difference.

This brings me to the title of this chapter—"teaching with/in cultural difference." Aoki (2005f) explains the "/" as "a space marked by differences neither strictly vertical nor strictly horizontal, a space that may allow generative possibilities" (420). "It is a space of doubling, where we slip into the language of both this and that, but neither this nor that" (Pinar and Irwin 2005, 73). The "/" in this chapter denotes the spaces between "teaching with" and "teaching in," and I employ this framework of "between" spaces of cultural difference, multiplicities, third space curriculum, and Pedagogy of the Now to better understand faculty experiences of cultural difference.

Methodology

Several of the authors in this book participated in a research project on the internationalization of the university, funded by the Social Science and Humanities Research Council of Canada. Our study sought to gain a deeper understanding of the experiences of students, faculty, staff, and administrators who are engaged in internationalization activities. As with the other groups, a survey of faculty across the university was followed by qualitative interviews. We interviewed twenty-six faculty members from the Faculties of Education, Arts and Social Sciences, Science, Health Science, and Business. All of the participants had five or more years of teaching experience in higher education and had participated in international activities and programs in the university. To maintain anonymity and protect the identity of our participants, I am not identifying their disciplinary background, home department, and other identifying personal information.

To begin the interview, we sought faculty perceptions of internationalization followed by questions that covered topics such as the impact of having international students in their classes, their approach to teaching in international programs and in classes with international students, their understanding of "international knowledge" and "intercultural learning," their understanding of "an international dimension" in relation to their teaching and research, and their ideas about and experiences of cultural difference. Interview data were first transcribed and sent to participants for verification and elaboration. The revised transcripts were then coded using codes generated from the literature and emerging from the data itself (Miles, Huberman, and Saldaña 2014). The data were analyzed according to the themes from the literature and the theories described above to make sense of faculty views of culture and intercultural engagement, cultural diversity, cultural difference, and their experiences of teaching in an international classroom.

Tales of Teaching amidst Diversity and Difference

The faculty we interviewed were all enthusiastic about sharing their views on internationalization and their experiences of teaching. The data covered many topics and themes but for the purposes of this chapter, I am selecting data that relate to faculty experiences of, and views on, culture and teaching in the international context.

What Internationalization Means

Faculty views on internationalization help to contextualize their approaches to teaching. They all referenced internationalization primarily in terms of mobility. Peter and Kathleen, for example, referred to the inherent international nature of a university through knowledge construction and dissemination. Faculty members had strong concerns, however, about the direction of internationalization in their institution and were explicit about their critiques of the university's approach to recruiting and bringing vast numbers of international students to the university. "[I]t is an unethical means to raise international tuition dollars" is how Craig described it. Samuel exclaimed that "[Internationalization] is one of our vulnerabilities because . . . it demonstrates our worst greed." Sasha too voiced a strong critique: "[We are an] increasingly corporatized university . . . marketing ourselves often to more vulnerable populations, families and students in developing nations and calling it internationalization . . . and [this seems] parasitic." Michel referred to a gap between rhetoric and reality, acknowledging the dominance of financial considerations: "The difference between what we are told we are doing and what we are doing is vast and a lot of it has to do with the difference between money and ideals, frankly." He observed that this tension between educational goals and marketization is "where things start to get a little tangled" (Michel).

Faculty members also recognized the colonial nature of internationalization: "my biggest concern is about the power relations, relations of power that exist in people's engagement with projects that come under the auspices of internationalization" (Sandra). Internationalization was described as "an attempt to hegemonize and colonialize the legitimate educational practices of non-Western traditions" (Sasha). Harrison thought internationalization reflected "a missionary approach"—"You know, it's like, 'whatever my culture is, I'm gonna foist it on everybody else' kind of thing."

Along with the critique, some faculty emphasized the importance of an international experience for students. Peter had a strong if idealistic endorsement of the international experience and difference: "I would say that . . . if all people of the world who have at least to some extent the experience of traveling to parts of the world where culture, language, etc., are different, then we will have probably a more peaceful world."

Faculty views on internationalization confirm the literature on multiple points: the critique of the economic orientation of internationalization (Beck 2013), the reproduction of colonial roots (Beck and Pidgeon 2020), and the valuing of the international experience for all students (Sawir 2013). It demonstrates that faculty are very much aware of the problematics of internationalization and show signs that they recognize the "political and epistemological crisis" (Smith 2006) they are facing. We can see how faculty are teaching in that tension between internationalization as a plan and lived reality (Aoki 2005a). Internationalization is the institutional curriculum-as-plan, with preset outcomes to be achieved regarding teaching and service. This plan clashes with the lived curriculum of faculty, whose values are antithetical to institutional objectives and directions. Peter's idealism arose from his own experience as an international student and the benefits he gained, but it reflects a common ahistorical, romanticized, and uncritical view of internationalization (Buckner and Stein 2020). He thinks that even travel to a place that is culturally different will give students the insight they need to become culturally aware. This simplistic view is in contrast to his own very complex experiences of internationalization as a former international student, reflecting the internationalization space as one of ambiguities and paradoxes (Wang 2006).

Cultural Diversity and Difference

Faculty were all very cognizant of the cultural dimension in international education. Many were of the view that cultural diversity was important: "we are all improved by exposure to people different from ourselves" (Sarah). Daniel observed that internationalization involves "interactions that cross boundaries, that cross national, and more commonly, cultural boundaries." He believes that it is important to have different perspectives in the class, and having international students in the classroom contributes to the diversity that is necessary for this to occur.

> [P]eople from, you know, everywhere, whatever will focus on different aspects, and it is very enlightening for the students to say, "I didn't see that!" ... And so having those different things, those different cultures involved, makes it much easier to teach because then you just say to the student, "Explain that, tell us what you were feeling, what you were thinking about when you did that." And the other people just be recognizing that people can see things differently than you is a tremendous revelation to some people. It's like, "Hey, if they can be right about it does that mean I'm wrong about it?" And so confronting that is a tremendous learning experience so having a culturally diverse class helps with that.

For Daniel, having students from diverse cultural backgrounds makes teaching easier, rather than challenging.

> In fact, this [referring to the Lower Mainland of BC] is one of the easiest places to teach intercultural. I also teach regularly in France where the students are all French and it is much more difficult there, right, because they don't have the intercultural—they don't have the mix, the cross-cultural mix, so they can't interact in such a way.

His own experience of, and comfort with, discomfort led Daniel to invite his students to enter that space. "I have sent students out to go into different subcultures in the community and push themselves out of their comfort zone, keep a diary of that, come back and report on what *they* felt and how *they* interacted and that sort of stuff." Being confronted with a different perspective leads to the kind of dissonance that prompts learning. "It's the inter—I teach about the interactions of individuals who are culturally different in organizational settings so that is the essence of the course."

Having a "cross-cultural mix" generates the "multiplicities" (Aoki 2005b) that lead to learning. Daniel is aware of the possibilities of the between spaces, the "inter," and designs activities for his students to step out of their comfort zones. He is not looking to resolve or harmonize differences, but uses the discomfort that difference produces to facilitate personal awareness, which is the entry point for intercultural understanding. His classroom becomes a place of truth seeking, discovery, and sharing (Smith 2006).

Sharad expressed a similar approach to diversity. He reported that 5–10 percent of his students, and often more, were international students from all over the world, and admitted that there were challenges with those numbers but that it was also why he loved these classrooms. He remarks to his students at the beginning of the course: "I'm here to learn from you and I'm here to also teach you. Look around, look to your left, look to your right. People from different parts of the world, and some may be born here, some elsewhere, but they come with a perspective that may be different." Difference for Sharad is what made the ideal learning environment. It is important, he said, to be open to other ways of thinking, especially when dealing with ethical or societal issues, and to understand why and how people arrive at their way of thinking. "[T]he same questions or issues discussed in the class may bring up different results or different answers and different responses and it is really interesting, because through that diversity of thinking you learn a lot, I learn a lot and, you know, you challenge your own thought process".

For Peter, it was not just the diversity of the hosting university that was important, but the mix of international students. Speaking from his own experience of having been an international student in three different countries, he said,

> [t]he places where I learned the most was where there were people who were from a different country from my own, a different culture from my own, but they were not from the country where I was living at. Why? . . . They were as isolated as I was and as a result, they were willing to make an effort to understand where I was coming from and not judge me immediately through their old lenses.

Peter's own lived experience, his experience of taking risks, influenced his teaching. It was not just difference but connecting with those who have had a similar experience of being *rendered* different. There is a subtle critique here of those in the dominant culture, who, by implication, judge others through their old lenses and don't make the effort to understand culturally different others. This lack of relationality and engagement between those who are different does not result in the kind of learning that Peter himself wants to promote. Those personal insights inform his pedagogy as seen below.

> So, if I wanted people to open up their mind I would try to provide a very diverse group where in some way acceptance for diversity will be encouraged and rewarded and so that people have no choice but to open up and by opening up then you learn and learning is painful and costly and, therefore, people have learning inertia, right, so you have to try to make it easy, you have to try to reduce the cost of learning at least at the beginning so that people don't even

realize they are learning until it is too late and they are learning—and I apply that concept when I lecture.

The idea that learning is painful is a theme that ran across his interview. "If you want to be in a Canadian university you have to accept that you have to grow and learn, and it is going to be painful and pain is the only way to grow." Pain here referred to encountering discomfort, and stepping into the unknown was a way to open up to growth and new ways of thinking. "I always tell my students that I would rather make them uncomfortable than make them sleep, so I'm constantly, constantly provoking and I try to be as respectful as I can. It is not always easy. You know, it is intentional—let me shake you up and let's see how you react." He continues: "so if they have to feel uncomfortable there is an uncomfortable silence, and I let it be."

Peter provokes his students, refusing to let them rest in their comfortable place—he shakes them up and they have no choice but to open up. He recognizes that entering into that way of thinking amounts to risk-taking and he rewards it. He encourages his students to participate by recognizing those who respond to questions, even if they make mistakes, and through this process creates "cultures of engagement." He does not try to resolve uncomfortable silences and uses them to invite his students into a relational space. His description of "pain" in the learning process illuminates his pedagogical process, the movement back and forth between his plan, and the realities in the classroom, attuned to the way things unfold.

Faculty recognize and value diversity, even with the challenge of high numbers of international students in their classrooms and the multiplicities of difference they bring. In fact, they rely on that diversity to advance learning, which they identify as encompassing multiple perspectives and curiosity about difference. The presence of students from different cultural backgrounds offers a good starting point, but it is an in-depth encounter with difference that cultural diversity generates that faculty like Daniel, Sharad, and Peter seek to have. When faculty talk about multiple perspectives, they are preparing the space for encounters with cultural difference. This recognition of difference, diversity of thought, and avoidance of the instrumentality of "right and wrong" leads to the experience of multiplicity and the "AND . . . AND . . . AND" (Aoki 2005).

Relationality Supports Pedagogical Risk

For Sharad, encountering difference is a fundamental element of the learning environment and that foundation is created through relationality. Sharad takes great effort to connect with his students and to encourage mutuality. Sharad mentioned this was a priority for him: "one thing I notice in every one of my classes and a theme that runs across every single class . . . I noticed this . . . mutuality between myself and students. I am interested in them. That mutuality is that I don't come just to teach; I learn from them." Sharad's pedagogy is based on the mutuality of relationships, "truth as shared" (Smith 2006).

If Peter came across as being harsh in his approach to teaching, he also had great empathy for international students and understood, for example, their need to stick together in their own cultural groups. He slipped into vulnerability as he recounted his own time as an international student: "I mean I still remember feeling—I still feel inadequate—culturally inadequate very, very often." His experience led him to value deeply the opportunities for encountering difference, and he provided them to his students.

> If I'm your teacher and you are my student and we need to go through this process, I want to respect you, but on the other hand the only way I know how to do this is the way I know how to do this, so in both the teacher and the student, . . . the student and the teacher have to crack their own epistemologies.

Peter had insider understanding of the struggles faced by international students and he empathized with them, but did not see them as victims, and rather, encouraged them to be agentic. He provoked them to think critically, to be creative, and to step into discomfort in challenging habitual ways of thinking. As with Sharad, he recognized that both student and teacher entered a process of change. This is the process of transformation that his third space curriculum generates (Wang 2006).

Michel shared a story from one of his classes that further illustrates this relationality, mutuality of engagement, and opportunities for transformation. The example is worth quoting extensively as it well illustrates the complex engagement that intercultural difference prompts. Michel chooses texts for his (English Literature) class that include immigrant experiences because, as he said, "unless you are aboriginal, in which case we are having a different conversation, . . . we are all from everywhere else." This particular text was an interview narrative of Japanese immigrants to San Francisco, set in pre–World War II. He explains:

> M: From a Western point of view, it was clearly a story about a domineering father, and nine abused children trying to get out from under his thumb. There was a student in the room who happened to be from China, . . . who looked at it and said, "Well clearly the problem is that this child has not been obedient enough." And there was just a complete disconnect between what I had assumed the story was about and what this student was seeing it as. And the look on

his face was clearly, "Why don't you get that that's the problem?" He didn't understand how there was—I mean both of us were going, "What?!" That's a really productive moment, as much as it turned my soul to jelly, like how do you see that—but it was a moment of saying, "Okay, what are your assumptions, what are my assumptions, where are the assumptions coming from?"

KB: It's like challenging your certainty about something, isn't it?

M: Oh God, yeah. And that's the fun part; I mean scary fun! But, yeah, that's the moment when a student can come in and say, "You are teaching it from this particular perspective, but that doesn't match a perspective that I'm familiar with" and then you can negotiate those two things and say, "Okay, why are we coming at these things from these points of view?" So, yeah, the big one is multiple perspectives.

Michel concluded that inviting "multiple perspectives" results in this kind of sharing. What is of greater interest than the teaching strategy he used in this instance is the "scary fun" that Michel experienced, the "productive moment" that "turned [his] soul to jelly". The instance where both student and teacher experienced the "What?!" moment could be described as incommensurable, but Michel looked at it as a point of negotiation. Michel took a pedagogical risk—uncertain of how the negotiation could turn out, and where the conversation would go in the face of such difference. Multiplicities can grow in the middle.

Contradictions and Dissonance

Much as faculty see the possibilities in valuing diversity and teaching *with* cultural difference, there was a range of experience and views among faculty in their stories about teaching both *with* and *in* cultural difference. There were contradictory views expressed, sometimes by the same faculty member. Daniel admitted that teaching in this way is difficult. Referring to open classroom discussions and experiential assignments, he said "it's not easy and some students won't do it.... So you just encourage it because we are not going to change our method here where we are just lecturing and they are sitting there taking notes, right." Michel reflects that "on a practical level they are here to get a certain kind of cultural capital" and so between the practical and the ideal "is where things get paradoxical, contradictory and a little bit bifurcated."

Not all faculty members were enthused with cultural difference when it came to linguistic diversity. This is one area of difference that commonly causes stress, frustration, and impatience among faculty (see Chapter 3 in this volume).

Diversity is good if everyone were to speak and write English fluently. Kathleen saw the problems arising from a lack of fluency in the language of instruction. She believed that speaking the language of the host country is important for all immigrants, and especially important for international students to participate in classroom activities such as discussions.

> I've always thought the mosaic was a better model because it respected these cultural traditions. But I also see the downside of that mosaic, which is that it is little tiny pieces of glass everywhere and they touch on their border, you know, on the edges, but they don't actually fuse and I see that on campus. I see that on campus with the Asian kids that are here, and I see how they come into my class, they write poorly, some of them actually speak poorly.

Along with many other faculty, she is frustrated with the lack of participation and engagement of international students. She falls into the common expectation that everyone should be fluent in English and misses the fact that her international students would be very fluent in other languages. This is the most common example of how international students are valued for their cultural diversity, but their cultural difference is contained (Bhabha 1990) as they are expected to conform to institutional rules on language and academic literacy. Her analysis of the situation, however, is less judgmental and more understanding: "it's not culturally comfortable for a lot of these kids coming from other places to challenge the professor, to participate in sort of the Socratic method of teaching, to engage in group discussion." She believed that the university should provide more support for international students to understand academic literacy and conventions in Canada, but she also felt that international students should work harder to learn the language.

On the other hand, Kathleen values what students bring to the university: "I think that students are enriching all of us—I mean, all what those cultures bring to all of us . . . I mean we are much richer for it and much more able to understand the world." She provided examples of how she would incorporate lived experience of her students as well as diverse texts and materials. She did not connect this richness with linguistic diversity, however, although she was a big advocate of developing awareness and sensitivity of cultural others among students. "If we are this one global community, then we need to accept that there is more than one way. Our way is not necessarily the right way for everybody." Her approach to curriculum could be described as thin inclusion (Stein 2017), including diverse authors and texts, but she was stepping closer to teaching in the Zone of Between (Aoki 2005a) by recognizing and inviting the lived experiences of her international students. "What's your experience? . . . I've only read about it and studied it but you have lived it, so tell me what that it's like to live it."

The Value of Study Abroad

In her study abroad classes with Canadian students, Kathleen emphasized cross-cultural awareness and sensitivity. For her, this meant that they should learn to "be reflective of who they are and who they are in the context of the rest of the world and to, you know, bring that reflexivity into their practice." This also involves critical thinking, "to see how other people might see the world in a way that's different from how you would see the world." She observed, "I think it is actually very hard to teach this—I think you actually have to live this." With this perspective, she strongly advocated for having an international experience, "to go out into the world," and that experience teaches students more about cross-cultural understanding than what can be taught in a classroom.

Sandra was critical of her department's study abroad program where students went overseas on a practicum that had fixed outcomes, "and encouraged to come up with fixes." She was referring to the main assignment for the students, to develop a project for a Ugandan community.

> [T]here is an assumption that you can arrive at an endpoint, right, as opposed to engaging with the process and you are actually not sure where you are going to end up. Engaging meaningfully with people that you don't know, in places that you are unfamiliar with, you know, you don't speak the language, you don't understand the politics, religion, anything—you don't actually know where you are going to end up so to have a preset outcome—it's fake, it's fake from the beginning.

She continued, "[W]e are not training people to work with context—we are training them to focus on outcomes. You almost need to be subverting the dominant paradigm." Sandra believed that this kind of in-depth experience with cultural difference needs to be approached with the mind-set of an anthropologist, meaning, being trained to first observe without interpretation. Sandra applies this thinking to most of her courses, where she sends her students off to a location on campus: "you just sit there, right, and you just watch. And that is going to freak some people out in some cultures but that is what we do." Following that, she engages students in a discussion about what they observe, and what they bring from their own biases and worldviews on interpreting what they observe. This is the first step, she said, about engaging meaningfully with a community. "You go hang out, you ask questions, you just are curious." Sandra's teaching arises from her disciplinary training which emphasizes openness and also from her awareness of power relations in the international setting and experience of encountering cultural difference. "I hope to give my students the intention and the awareness. You know, we talk about cultural baggage that you are taking with you."

Sandra is practicing thick inclusion (Stein 2017) and recognizes that having preset outcomes set by the dominant cultural group reproduces the status quo of power relations that, in her view, internationalization was supposed to disrupt. Sandra's pedagogy involves embracing difference on the one hand and a letting go of certainty on the other (Smith 2006). Her critique of preset outcomes challenges one of the basic elements of curriculum-as-plan as she advocates for students to step into the unknown, and it also reveals her own approach when anticipating cultural difference. She also problematizes the frozen futurity of the fixed outcomes that are a feature of international programs, even the expectation of cultural competency and global citizenship as desired outcomes. To follow Smith (2006), to be in the Now and to be attuned to the actual unfolding of the world requires an opening up to both complexity and unknowability. Sandra is there, some of the time.

Still on the topic of study abroad, Kalani, who also had many years' experience working outside of Canada, thought that it was "incredibly important" that students are "comfortable in moving about in the world." She talked about having to find a way to connect with communities and individuals that are not from one's own background. She said:

> we need more students that we can train to see the world as not us-and-them, you know, out there where "all this stuff is happening but it doesn't affect me," and the kind of slightly judgemental way of seeing the world, to one where we are all responsible for what happens regardless of [whether] we are sitting here or in Europe or Asia, and that what we do actually impacts the world.

None of the critiques of study abroad that others mentioned, nor "the cultural baggage" and the preparation that Sandra deemed necessary in study abroad programs came up in her conversations about teaching. Going abroad and figuring things out while on site is the way she encouraged her students to gain intercultural literacy.

These are just some of the themes that emerged from views shared by faculty. The data are rich and illustrate the complexity of faculty members' engagement with cultural difference in their teaching in "international" classrooms.

Zone of Between, Truth as Shared, and Third Space Curriculum

Many faculty were already inhabiting the Zone of Between to varying degrees. Sharad is willing to learn from students and to diverge from his plan for the class to follow what his students bring to the discussion. He acknowledges his movement between curriculum-as-plan and lived curriculum, going to "the between" as the place of learning and growth (Aoki 2005).

Kathleen is willing to invite the lived experience of her students, but paradoxically, is critical of what she sees as the "language deficiencies" of students. This illustrates a key point in how international students are valued for the cultural diversity they bring, but how other differences (such as language) are seen as detrimental to both the classroom and to the students themselves. It also illustrates how the focus on culture, in this case, erases linguistic racism (see Chapters 3 and 8 for further insights into language). Kathleen relied on curriculum-as-plan for teaching subjects and topics that she was not expert enough or was not comfortable with. One such topic was cultural competence, which she believed all students on study abroad should be taught. Culture is seen as a "thing" that one acquires competency in, and an add-on element for study abroad students. Kalani appears to be at home in the world in the sense of being familiar and comfortable with complexity and yet she did not share details about how understanding of cultural difference might be facilitated in her classroom except to emphasize the lived experience.

Michel goes to the edge when faced with incommensurable differences, and in negotiating through difference, steps into vulnerability and into a third space of new emerging positions (Wang 2006). Peter demonstrates that the process of stepping into that unknown place and being alive to what arises is to discover newness in what can arise between teacher and students, and newness in one's teacher self. This newness is how Wang (2006) sees third space curriculum. There are some who enter into third space curriculum as a generative pedagogical space, and yet others, such as Kathleen or Kalani, demonstrate critique and reflection, but don't fully step into the unknowns that engaging with cultural difference requires.

The classroom for many of the faculty was a place for truth seeking, discovery, and sharing (Smith 2006), and in some cases a place to invite "polyphonic dialogue across difference" (Wang 2006, 121), where multiplicities grow in the middle (Aoki 2005). These faculty experiences illustrate the contradictions and paradoxes inherent in teaching in the international context. Faculty teach in conditions that are complex and uncertain, and some are comfortable with ambiguity and the unknown with/in cultural difference. No matter the extent of their foray into third space curriculum, the orienting principle for all of these faculty is the relational, and this serves them well. The classroom is also a space where some are willing to take the risk of becoming vulnerable, and vulnerability supports them to occupy the Zone of Between.

These insights are not meant to be recommendations or guidelines for teaching. They are meant to illuminate the possibilities and challenges of teaching with/in cultural difference, where going beyond the boundaries of cultural difference doesn't mean eliminating them, but retaining something that went before to enter the third space of something new. To occupy the Zone of Between, there must be a curriculum-as-plan, even as there is a turning toward the lived curriculum. "Being" in this tensioned space, faculty attempt to find their way to teaching in the Now.

Acknowledgment

This research was funded by a grant from the Social Sciences and Humanities Research Council of Canada.

References

Amsler, Sarah, Jeannie Kerr, and Vanessa Andreotti. 2020. "Interculturality in Teacher Education in Times of Unprecedented Global Challenges." *Education and Society* 38, no. 1: 13–37.

Aoki, Ted T. 1986/1991/2005a. "Teaching as In-dwelling Between Two Curriculum Worlds." In *Curriculum in a New Key: The Collected Works of Ted Aoki*, edited by William F. Pinar and Rita L. Irwin, 159–165. New Jersey: Lawrence Erlbaum Associates.

Aoki, Ted T. 1993/2005b. "Legitimating Lived Curriculum. Toward a Curricular Landscape of Multiplicity." In *Curriculum in a New Key: The Collected Works of Ted Aoki*, edited by William F. Pinar and Rita L. Irwin, 199–215. New Jersey: Lawrence Erlbaum Associates.

Aoki, Ted T. 1992/2005c. "In the Midst of Slippery Theme-Words: Living as Designers of Japanese Canadian Curriculum." In *Curriculum in a New Key: The Collected Works of Ted Aoki*, edited by William F. Pinar and Rita L. Irwin, 263–278. New Jersey: Lawrence Erlbaum Associates.

Aoki, Ted T. 1993/2005d. "Humiliating the Cartesian Ego." In *Curriculum in a New Key: The Collected Works of Ted Aoki*, edited by William F. Pinar and Rita L. Irwin, 291–301. New Jersey: Lawrence Erlbaum Associates.

Aoki, Ted T. 1995/2005e. "In the Midst of Doubled Imaginaries: The Pacific Community as Diversity and as Difference." In *Curriculum in a New Key: The Collected Works of Ted Aoki*, edited by William F. Pinar and Rita L. Irwin, 303–312. New Jersey: Lawrence Erlbaum Associates.

Aoki, Ted T. 1996/2005f. "Spinning Inspirited Images in the Midst of Planned and Live(d) Curricula." In *Curriculum in a New Key: The Collected Works of Ted Aoki*, edited by William F. Pinar and Rita L. Irwin, 413–423. New Jersey: Lawrence Erlbaum Associates.

Beck, Kumari. 2013. "Making Sense of Internationalization: A Critical Analysis." In *Critical Perspectives on International Education*, edited by Yvonne Hébert and Ali A. Abdi, 43–60. Rotterdam: Sense Publishers.

Beck, Kumari, and Michelle Pidgeon. 2020. "Across the Divide: Conversations on Decolonization, Indigenization and Internationalization of Higher Education." In *International Education as Public Policy in Canada*, edited by Roopa Desai Trilokekar, Merli Tamtik, and Glen Jones, 384–406. Montreal: McGill-Queen's University Press.

Bhabha, Homi. 1990. "Interview with Homi Bhabha: The Third Space." In *Identity: Community, Culture, Difference*, edited by Jonathan Rutherford, 207–221. London: Lawrence & Wishart.

Bhabha, Homi. 1994. *The Location of Culture*. London: Routledge.

Bond, Sheryl L., Jun Qian, and Jinyan Huang. 2003. "The Role of Faculty in Internationalizing the Undergraduate Curriculum and Classroom Experience." *Canadian Bureau for International Education. Millenium Series* no. 8: 1–20.

Buckner, Elizabeth, and Sharon Stein. 2020. "What Counts as Internationalization? Deconstructing the Internationalisation Imperative." *Journal of Studies in International Education* 24, no. 2: 151–166. https://doi.org/10.1177/1028315319829878.

Clarke, Marie, and Linda Hui Yang. 2021. "Internationalization: Perspectives from University Faculty in the Republic of Ireland." *Journal of Studies in International Education* 25, no. 2: 136–151.

Coryell, Joellen E., Maria Cinque, Monica Fedeli, Angelina Lapina Salazar, and Concetta Tino. 2022. "University Teaching in Global Times: Perspectives of Italian University Faculty on Teaching International Graduate Students." *Journal of Studies in International Education* 26, no. 3: 369–389.

Deardorff, Darla K. 2006. "Identification and Assessment of Intercultural Competence as a Student Outcome of Internationalization." *Journal of Studies in International Education* 10, no. 3: 241–266. http://jsi.sagepub.com/content/10/3/241.full.

Deardorff, Darla K., ed. 2009. *The SAGE Handbook of Intercultural Competence*. California: Sage Publishing.

de la Garza, Armida. 2021. "Internationalizing the Curriculum for STEAM (STEM + Arts and Humanities): From Intercultural Competence to Cultural Humility." *Journal of Studies in International Education* 25, no. 2: 123–135. https://doi.org/10.1177/1028315319888468

de Wit, Hans, and Fiona Hunter. 2015. "The Future of Internationalization of Higher Education in Europe." *International Higher Education*, no. 83 (December): 2–3. https://doi.org/10.6017/ihe.2015.83.9073.

de Wit, Hans, and Betty Leask. 2015. "Internationalization, the Curriculum and the Disciplines." *International Higher Education* 83: 10–12.

Fragouli, Evangelia. 2020. "Internationalizing the Curriculum." *International Journal of Higher Education Management* 6, no. 2: 18–30.

Frances, Anne. 1993. *Facing the Future: The Internationalization of Post-Secondary Institutions in British Columbia*. Vancouver: Centre for International Education.

Friesen, Rhonda. 2013. "Faculty Member Engagement in Canadian University Internationalisation: A Consideration of Understanding, Motivations and Rationales." *Journal of Studies in International Education* 17, no. 3: 209–227. https://doi.org/10.1177/1028315312451132.

hooks, bell. 1994. *Teaching to Transgress: Education as the Practice of Freedom*. New York: Routledge.

Ji, Ying. 2020. "Embedding and Facilitating Intercultural Competence Development in Internationalization of the Curriculum of Higher Education." *Journal of Curriculum and Teaching* 9, no. 3: 13–19. https://doi.org/10.5430/jct.v9n3p13.

Knight, Jane. 1994. *Internationalization: Elements and Checkpoints*. Ottawa: Canadian Bureau for International Education.

Koh, Aaron, Karen Pashby, Paul Tarc, and Miri Temini. 2022. "Editorial: Internationalisation in Teacher Education: Discourses, Policies, Practices." *Teachers and Teaching: Theory and Practice* 1–14.

Landis, Dan, Janet M. Bennett, and Milton J. Bennett, eds. 2004. *Handbook of Intercultural Training*, 3rd edn. Thousand Oaks: Sage.

Leask, Betty. 2009. "Using Formal and Informal Curricula to Improve Interactions Between Home and International Students." *Journal of Studies in International Education* 13, no. 2: 205–221. https://doi.org/10.1177/1028315308329786.

Leask, Betty. 2013. "Internationalization of the Curriculum and the Disciplines: Current Perspectives and Directions for the Future." *Editorial: JSIE Special Issue* 17, no. 2: 99–102. https://doi.org/10.1177/1028315313486228.

Leask, Betty. 2015. *Internationalizing the Curriculum*. Internationalization in Higher Education series. London: Routledge.

Miles, Matthew B., Michael A. Huberman, and Johnny Saldaña. 2014. *Qualitative Data Analysis: A Methods Sourcebook*. Thousand Oaks: Sage.

Nawaz, Tasawar. 2018. "Internationalisation Strategy, Faculty Response and Academic Preparedness for Transnational Teaching." *Education + Training* 60, no. 9: 1–26.

Osakwe, Nneka Nora. 2017. "Internationalizing Courses: A Faculty Development Process." *International Research and Review* 6, no. 2: 1–31.

Pinar, William F. 2019. *What is Curriculum Theory?* 3rd edn. New York: Routledge.

Pinar, William F., and Rita Irwin, eds. 2005. *Curriculum in a New Key: The Collected Works of Ted T. Aoki*. Mahwah: Lawrence Erlbaum Associates.

Sawir, Erlenawati. 2013. "Internationalisation of Higher Education Curriculum: The Contribution of International Students." *Globalisation, Societies and Education* 11, no. 3: 359–378. https://doi.org/10.1080/14767724.2012.750477.

Schuessler, Melissa. 2019. "The Intersection of Internationalisation: Constructing a Knowledge Framework Grounded in Intercultural Dialogue." In *Educational Approaches to Internationalization Through Intercultural Dialogue*, edited by Ulla Lundgren, Paloma Castro, and Jane Woodin, 27–40. New York: Routledge.

Smith, David G. 2006. "The Specific Challenges of Globalization for Teaching and Vice Versa." In *Trying to Teach in a Season of Great Untruth: Globalization, Empire and the Crises of Pedagogy*, 15–34. Rotterdam: Sense Publishers.

Spitzberg, Brian H., and Gabrielle Changnon. 2009. "Conceptualizing Multicultural Competence." In *Handbook of Intercultural Competence*, edited by Darla K. Deardorff, 2–52. Thousand Oaks: Sage.

Stein, Sharon. 2017. "The Persistent Challenges of Addressing Epistemic Dominance in Higher Education: Considering the Case of Curriculum Internationalization." *Comparative Education Review* 61, no. S1: S25–S50. https://doi-org.proxy.lib.sfu.ca/10.1086/690456.

Suwinyattichaiporn, Tara, and Zac D. Johnson. 2018. "Internationalizing Communication Curriculum: An Assignment Examining Relational Communication Across Cultures." *Journal of Intercultural Communication Research* 47, no. 5: 399–410. https://doi-org.proxy.lib.sfu.ca/10.1080/17475759.2018.1475291.

Wang, Hongyu. 2004. *The Call from the Stranger on a Journey Home: Curriculum in a Third Space*. New York: Peter Lang.

Wang, Hongyu. 2006. "Speaking as an Alien: Is a Curriculum in a Third Space Possible?" *Journal of Curriculum Theorizing* 22, no. 1: 101–116.

Wimpenny, Katherine, Jos Beelen, and Virginia King. 2020. "Academic Development to Support the Internationalization of the Curriculum (IoC): A Qualitative Research Synthesis." *International Journal for Academic Development* 25, no. 3: 218–231. https://doi.org/10.1080/1360144X.2019.1691559.

2

Content Area Faculty Engagement with Language Matters in an Internationalizing University

Roumiana Ilieva

Introduction

Globalization trends and university policies on internationalization have led to a student population that is very diverse linguistically. Yet there is limited literature in applied linguistics (AL) and in international education examining the perspectives of key participants engaged on the ground with language matters in times of internationalization: faculty members across the disciplines. With no language training, disciplinary faculty face daily a "superdiverse" (Blommaert and Rampton 2011) student population in their classrooms.

This chapter features research on faculty experiences of teaching and specifically explores some of the challenges content area faculty face when engaged with the linguistic realities of internationalization. The purpose is to shed light on the perspectives of content area faculty in a Canadian university with regard to language issues in their work with students, with the goal to imagine and work toward implementing ethical internationalization practices (Ilieva, Beck, and Waterstone 2014) that acknowledge and make use of the multilingual resources the linguistically and culturally superdiverse student body bring to the internationalized university of the twenty-first century. The chapter begins with a review of relevant literature and then introduces the theoretical perspectives guiding the analysis; brief methodological considerations follow before faculty interview data is analyzed; the chapter concludes with a discussion and implications of the study.

Literature Review

The focus of much of the academic literature on internationalization has been at the level of institutional strategies, with limited research on how internationalization is taken up within the practices of faculty members (e.g., AUCC 2007; Calikoglu, Lee, and Arslan 2022; Criswell and Zhu 2015; Friesen 2013). Existing literature makes the case that the effects of internationalization on faculty members are profound, tangible, and challenging; that instructors' approaches to internationalization are multifaceted and individualized; and that institutional support for faculty members' efforts is necessary but scant (e.g., Calikoglu et al. 2022; Criswell and Zhu 2015; Friesen 2013). I will briefly outline below recent developments in two strands of academic literature that would benefit from cross-referencing each other more to present a detailed and nuanced picture of how content faculty are involved in internationalization activities, specifically in their response to language matters: (1) internationalization literature on faculty engagement and (2) AL literature on multi/plurilingualism and linguistically responsive instruction (LRI) in higher education.

The internationalization literature that focuses on faculty members' internationalization experiences is varied, but overwhelmingly speaks to the key role of faculty in enacting internationalization. Sawir (2011) reported the results of a study in which eighty faculty members at an Australian university were interviewed about their perceptions on the increasing number of international students on campus and its impact on their teaching. A third of the participants were not making adjustments to their teaching, and a common reason for that was the presumption that all students are to be treated equally. The issue of maintaining academic standards was another reason to deny accommodations. Yet, 66 percent of the participants reported making some kind of accommodation. Given the focus of this chapter, it is notable that the most frequent adjustments made to teaching practices were to address what were perceived as language difficulties for international students. In the Canadian context, Friesen (2013) employed a phenomenological approach to investigate the understandings of five faculty with regard to their involvement with internationalization. Overall findings showed that these faculty held multiple understandings of internationalization that did not always align with the visions of their institutions. In particular, the level of engagement reported by faculty seemed to be directly related to the alignment of institutional and individual values.

Criswell and Zhu (2015) presented data from a survey with faculty from higher education institutions in the United States and Canada on their internationalization priorities. While internationalization was supported by the majority, faculty also identified as problematic the institutions' visions and market-driven priorities on internationalization, as well as a gap in institutional rhetoric and actual support available to implement internationalization activities. The question of language was especially pertinent in the views of faculty who suggested that international students be more "heavily vetted" (34) or provided online language classes prior to arrival to ensure their language skills are adequate for participation in content classes.

Nyangau (2020) focused on personal agency beliefs as a powerful influence on faculty engagement in internationalization, but also made a strong case, touched on in earlier literature as well, for the need for a reward structure in universities within the tenure and promotion review process that recognizes faculty international activities. Most recently, Calikoglu et al. (2022) attempted to offer a comprehensive understanding of faculty internationalization by examining rationales, strategies, and barriers to international activities faculty experience within higher education institutions. The study confirmed the need "for sustainable mechanisms and a consensus between faculty perspectives and institutional priorities" (61), maintained the importance of academic culture and disciplinary identity in impacting faculty motivations to engage in internationalization, and illustrated the lack of supportive tenure and promotion policies.

While internationalization literature is consulted to a limited extent in AL scholarship, the question of a linguistically superdiverse student body in today's internationalized universities is a common theme garnering a lot of research in the last two decades. This body of work also highlights the pervasiveness of raciolinguistic ideologies, which "produce racialized speaking subjects who are constructed as linguistically deviant even when engaging in linguistic practices positioned as normative or innovative when produced by privileged white subjects" (Flores and Rosa 2015, 150). While the data discussed in this chapter do not present direct evidence for faculty reproducing raciolinguistic ideologies, it is important to acknowledge that such ideologies are very much tied to deficit perspectives on the language proficiency of linguistically different speakers (Kubota et al. 2021; Sterzuk 2015). One particular strand of literature that attempts to make sense of multilingualism in higher education settings has also examined the perspectives of faculty members across the disciplines dealing with language matters.

The implications of a linguistically diverse student body for content faculty teaching in the Canadian context are the focus of Marshall and Marr's (2018) study exploring faculty members' understandings of multi/plurilingualism, their pedagogical responses to a linguistically diverse body of students, and their perceptions of their role as instructors. The study revealed various pedagogical dilemmas and conceptual binaries as well as tensions these faculty experienced in relation to their professional identities. The interviewed instructors tended to "construct the multilingualism of their students around traditional binary paradigms (native speaker/ESL, . . . domestic student/international student, fluent and competent speaker/one who is lacking)" (33). The authors argued that such binary views encourage remedial views of multilingual students and recommended that faculty employ a multi/plurilingual lens in their teaching. More particularly, the native/nonnative speaker binary that seems to dominate university discourses needs to be problematized as, given the demographics of both domestic and international multilingual students in the institution, linguistic abilities represent more of a blurred continuum. The instructors' professional identities were challenged as they saw themselves primarily as content faculty teaching classes, which include EAL students who should be seeking additional language support elsewhere.

Given the superdiverse student population in Anglo-dominant settings, questions about approaches that acknowledge and make use of the multilingual/plurilingual resources students bring to higher education are gaining momentum in AL scholarship. A recent special issue of the journal *Language, Culture and Curriculum*, edited by Preece and Marshall (2020), was devoted to exploring plurilingual approaches to teaching and learning in some universities in Canada and the UK. Preece and Marshall make the case that institutional policies in these highly diverse linguistically and culturally settings are commonly informed by an outdated "'monolingual disposition' (Gogolin 1994)" (117), which leads to the framing of linguistic diversity "as a problem to be solved." The authors argue for the need to view "language-as-a resource" (Hult and Hornberger 2016), and linguistic diversity as an asset to be harnessed in university classrooms. Marshall's (2020) article suggests that faculty perceptions and responses to the multilingual practices of students are framed by the deficit discourses circulating in the institution as well as ensuing from a tension between the students' learning process involving the use of multiple languages and the demands to display knowledge solely in English. In the same journal issue, Van Viegen and Zappa-Hollman (2020) offer examples of plurilingual pedagogies in action employed by some plurilingual instructors in two Canadian universities, arguing that such practices can be a key form of pedagogical scaffolding in multilingual university settings that support both content learning and language development.

A similar focus on instruction in higher education that supports content and language learning is present in the scholarship of Gallagher and Haan in the United States who named the approach they advocate LRI (Gallagher and Haan 2017; Haan and Gallagher 2022). This body of literature makes stronger connections to processes of internationalization, but the main focus is developing pedagogies supporting multilingual students. Haan, Gallagher, and Varandani (2017) discuss the ambivalent results of a survey on the perceptions and experiences of faculty with internationalization at a midsized university. Most participants demonstrated an awareness of the value of internationalization, but also "expressed reservations" (46) about working with culturally and linguistically diverse students. Reasons for this reservation revolved around an uncertainty about their role in processes of internationalization, which led to a resistance in changing teaching methods to accommodate multilingual students. In Gallagher and Haan (2017), survey responses from 197 faculty members shed light on content instructors' beliefs about emergent multilingual students' language proficiency and their perceptions on LRI. Results showed that "faculty consistently described [emergent multilingual] students as being deficient, vulnerable, and insufficiently supported" (9), and language proficiency was being compared to cognitive and moral ability. Participants also had negative views on instructional accommodations for multilingual students, seeing these strategies as remedial and having concerns about lowering academic standards and an increase in their already full workload. Further work by Haan and Gallagher and a special issue of the journal *TESOL Quarterly* edited by them offer examples of implementation of LRI across various higher education settings (e.g., Mahalingappa, Kayi-Aydar, and Polat 2021, and others). Haan and Gallagher (2022) reiterate faculty members' questioning the idea of supporting language and maintaining academic rigor at the same time, which for the authors signals the need for increased support and faculty development with regard to working with multilingual students. The authors outline the knowledge base for LRI as including "having an understanding of students as multilingual, multicultural learners; knowing how to apply foundational concepts about the second language and literacy acquisition to teaching; and understanding constraints and affordances of the university as a teaching and learning context" (6).

The recommendations found in scholarship on plurilingual pedagogies and LRI are very important in guiding us in work on supporting content faculty in their work and have been taken up in the chapter by Wallace, Singh and

Shaw in this book. With the work I share here, I suggest that a first step in supporting content faculty development necessitates that applied linguists play a role in their institutions in guiding disciplinary faculty to initially develop an understanding of language as a social practice and as fluid linguistic repertoires, and not a knowable distinct entity (Reagan 2004), ideas that current critical AL scholarship has convincingly argued.

There is limited academic literature that has attempted to connect university internationalization with language matters more closely. It is mostly produced by applied linguists who have found it important to draw on scholarship in the field of higher education internationalization in examining the complex nature of multilingualism dominated by English as well as English as a lingua franca issues. Jenkins (2013) writes about English as a lingua franca in the internationalized university and observes that while many universities globally "are declaring their 'international' and/or 'global' credentials . . . there has so far been no serious attempt in either case to consider the issues in relation to the (English) language in which international universities and programmes operate, and the implications for HE English language policies and practices" (18). Moreover,

> if the aim of an international education is to provide students . . . with the "knowledge, attitudes and skills [they] need in order to be globally and interculturally competent" (Jackson 2010, 11), [the current] sidelining of English language is unacceptable. English can no longer be cast aside in the internationalization literature as though it was merely a practical problem to be "fixed" in university EAP units. (10)

Bond (2020) asserts that to create a truly internationalized university, "language needs to be foregrounded across all teaching and learning in Higher Education. . . . If we do not become aware, and raise awareness, of the importance of language and work towards an intercultural model of communication and learning, it is not possible to claim that Higher Education is either international or inclusive" (176). Bond also maintains that there is an urgent need for universities "to develop a well thought out and nuanced strategy and policy that focuses on language" (194). Diaz (2018), who argues for the importance of paying attention to foreign language education in the internationalized university, makes the following observation: "[t]he unprecedented rise in multilingual, heterogeneous, so called 'super-diverse' societies around the world has been met by an equally unprecedented rise in dominant monolingual ethos, practices and ideologies. This is particularly evident in the current Anglophonic/Eurocentric domination of the knowledge economy which characterises internationalisation of higher education worldwide" (21). She is interested in "ways in which a focus on language and language policies may illuminate different understandings of internationalisation processes and enable us to consider potential reconfigurations of epistemologies" (21). This is an interest I share and pursue with this chapter.

Theoretical Framework

Critical AL work (e.g., García 2009; García and Lin 2018; García and Wei 2014; Makoni and Pennycook 2005, 2007; Reagan 2004) frames the data discussed in the chapter. As it will be evident in later sections, and confirming previous research, the views of content faculty around language issues in the superdiverse university are primarily framed around a native/nonnative language speaker binary and what critical linguists call a "normative" view of language. Thus, a major question for me as an applied linguist, who has been involved in internationalization research for more than a decade, is whether critical AL work can lead the way in supporting content faculty to develop more nuanced understandings of "language" that could form the basis for their engagement with plurilingual pedagogies/LRI practices. According to Makoni and Pennycook (2007), "languages, concepts of languageness, and metalanguages used to describe them are inventions" (1) and are part and parcel of the colonial, Christian, and nationalistic projects that have occurred in various parts of the world. Languages are invented in particular ways because of language ideologies circulating in society as languages do not exist outside power relations. In close relation to the invention of languages, an ideology of language developed which considered languages as separate and enumerable entities, enacted through a metadiscursive regime that treats languages as countable institutions "reinforced by the existence of grammars and dictionaries" (Makoni and Pennycook 2007, 2). Of major significance is that these inventions have had very real and material effects on people and societies since they influence how languages have been understood and how education has been pursued. Such positions reflect a positivistic perspective assuming that language as an abstract and knowable entity exists, which in turn has determined the dominance of technicist views of teaching and learning languages (Reagan 2004). As the literature reviewed here and as the data discussed later in the chapter highlight, the material effects of such positivistic views on language are evident in the ways faculty perceive and often respond to language. Understanding the material effects of our views on language as they guide our responses to language matters in university classrooms is of paramount importance. This is because when we understand the ramifications of our views and the actions they underscore, we can begin to understand the importance of engaging in more equitable ways that make full use of the linguistic repertoires of our multilingual students.

More recent critical work focused on the nature of language expands our understandings of languages as inventions. As Kuteeva, Kaufhold, and Nyninnen (2020) observe, "the view of languages as coherent structural systems which are separate from each other and express territorially bound cultures can be perceived to be in stark conflict with linguistic hybridity in contemporary societies and the experiences of language users" (6). However, language perceptions are not commonly in tune with language practices as they "tend to be more strongly affected by wider circulating discourses and ideologies, such as native-speakerism or purist and standard language ideologies" (11). An important aspect of the view of languages as discrete systems that critical applied linguists draw attention to is the erroneous assumption that languages operate independently of language users who simply access them rather than understanding language use as emergent and involving constant negotiation among interactants (Gurney and Demuro 2022). According to Madiba (2018), the construct of language based on a standard language ideology has been the dominant factor in the development of language policies in university settings. At the same time, he argues that "superdiversity compels us to abandon any preconceived or absolute notion of interaction in universities as comprising stable language systems and to replace them with a more fluid and dynamic notion of linguistic repertoires" (509), that is, "the totality of linguistic resources" (2018) available to members of given communities. Drawing on critical AL, I will highlight in this chapter the importance for applied linguists to prioritize debunking fixed notions of language in the work they do with content faculty in their superdiverse institutions.

Methodology and Research Context

The data presented in the chapter is part of a larger study, which was informed by institutional ethnography (Smith 2005), to understand the social relations of an internationalizing university through the practices and experiences of the people involved, and the discursive contexts that shape their experiences

(Foucault 1972). The study, conducted at a midsized Canadian university, consisted of an institution-wide survey conducted with faculty, staff, students, and administrators, supplemented with in-depth interviews with members of the same groups, and document collection of institutional and department publications around internationalization. The overarching theoretical frame and methodology for the study, institutional ethnography (Smith 2005), is a critical qualitative approach that starts from people's everyday experiences within an institution and probes how these experiences organize their everyday work. The sociologist Dorothy Smith defines work as the way individuals conduct their everyday lives and makes the case that it is coordinated through institutional texts and structures (1987).

The data discussed in this chapter come from qualitative interviews (Kvale and Brinkmann 2009) with faculty members across four faculties (Arts and Social Sciences, Business, Education, and Health Sciences) within the research site of the larger study. Twenty-six faculty members participated in the interviews—thirteen from the Faculty of Arts and Social Sciences, three from Business, six from Health, and four from Education. To maintain anonymity, I use pseudonyms to refer to the study participants, do not indicate their home departments, and may have changed their gender identifications. At the time of data collection, the numbers of international students in these faculties varied significantly and amounted to 3 percent of the undergraduates and 10 percent of the graduates in the Faculty of Education, 11 percent of the undergraduates and 16 percent of the graduates in the Faculty of Health Sciences, 18.5 percent of the undergraduate and 23 percent of the graduate students in the Faculty of Arts and Social Sciences, and 29 percent of the undergradudate and 21 percent of the graduate students in the Business Faculty. As it will become clear in the section below, this variation did not seem to translate into distinct views around language matters with regard to engagement with international students by faculty members from the respective university units. Moreover, the number of multilingual students in the institution was (and continues to be) much higher as students for whom English is an additional language also include students who may have been born in Canada, but started using English upon entry into the school system or who have arrived as immigrants to Canada prior to entering university. The latest numbers available from the institution point that 46 percent of undergraduate students speak both English and another language (languages) in their homes and 11 percent speak no English in their home settings. Thus, faculty members are facing daily in their classrooms a diverse multilingual student body. As the literature review suggests, faculty across Anglo-dominant institutions commonly hold negative views of students who may not be speaking English as the so-called ideal native speaker and, as an applied linguist, one of the questions that I was interested in was whether or how language issues would be present in the way participants in this study experience internationalization.

Faculty Experiences with Language

The data shared here is significant in that none of the survey or interview questions in the larger study on internationalization in the institution mentioned or asked about language as a facet of this phenomenon. Thus, the references to language as an aspect of participants' experiences of internationalization speak to the importance of paying attention specifically to language matters in trying to understand internationalization in Anglo-dominant settings. The findings shared below will address tensions faced by faculty members in relation to language issues, some effective practices in addressing language, and data that speaks to what I see as discrepancies in some faculty members' perspectives around critical scholarship broadly conceived.

Language Matters/Living the Tensions

A quote that exemplifies succinctly some of the experiences study participants shared when asked about internationalization comes from Troy, who stated:

> If you were going to ask me what's the major obstacle to improving internationalization, I would have to say that it's language.

Language was also mentioned without any prompting from the interviewer by other disciplinary faculty from across the four faculties in the institution. Here are a few more representative quotes:

> Sometimes [the mix of students] brought in challenges such as language. Some of those people are not good at expressing their ideas. . . . I am one of those people who always claim that language barrier is not a barrier, but sometimes it is. (Ronda)
> I want to give my instructions to somebody . . . without having to micromanage them, without having to worry that they understood what I've said. (Michael)

These statements suggest that assumptions about what are perceived as language difficulties that some students may have seem to shape to a large extent faculty's perceptions and experiences of internationalization. Evidently, these faculty work in an increasingly multilingual university, and many of their students are not the idealized native speaker who is the traditional content learner. Rather, the large number of EAL students seems to put pressure on content faculty with no special training to meet additional demands.

Particular tensions that content faculty may experience are detailed below:

> If they have a hard time to learn some subject . . . because of the language barrier. . . . I think it's very frustrating . . . in natural science field . . . first thing—capture the concept. Second—try to explain it. . . . If . . . they argue that they have problem only in the expression part, description part, it's very hard to say—if that is true or not. (Minori)

Minori exemplifies the tensions some faculty face in trying to recognize language difficulties some of their students experience, but also having a good sense of whether these students have mastered the content presented to them.

> It's a mandatory course . . . and . . . a lot of students [for whom] English is a second language . . . it's a huge challenge for them . . . I'm curious on what basis are you accepting these students? . . . it's about failing these people who we allow entrance. . . . When they get a passing grade on the [TOEFL or IELTS test] . . . the level of comprehension and reading and writing skills required for that is way different than what is required at a higher-level course at university. . . . It's a big dilemma . . . how do you balance that in teaching and that's the struggle I go through every semester and I have to gauge the class very early on—is this one of those classes where I have to drop something or not? (Sharad)

Another tension is evident in the words of Sharad above: To what extent should an instructor stick to the native speaker ideal versus accommodating students with lower levels of English? The kinds of struggles shared suggest that faculty are caught in asymmetrical relations of power among institutions, themselves, and the students and face serving a gate-keeping function when working with multilingual students.

> This is an English-speaking university; . . . It is painful sometimes reading assignments. . . . You can always tell the ones by international students, there is a language gap. . . . [Internationalization] is one of our vulnerabilities because . . . it demonstrates our worst greed . . . albeit our excuse could be, "Well, governments were underfunding us so we had to find alternate sources of money." . . . Certainly, it is great to get different perspectives from people from different countries, but . . . to be completely frank, it has resulted in a profound lowering of standards. (Samuel)

Samuel expresses a common conviction that one should maintain native speaker standards in assessment and a common concern over declining standards. There also seems to be a resentment toward institutional and national policies leading to such outcomes. Within the linguistic realities of internationalization in today's globalizing world, particular expectations of English proficiency seem to reign. Like in the research discussed in the "Literature Review" section, instructors in this study tend to draw on traditional binaries—deficit/asset. It is interesting that none of the study participants entertained a notion of other possibilities than language for their students to display understanding and knowledge of disciplinary content. Overall, faculty assumptions align with a "language-as-a-problem" orientation (Hult and Hornberger 2016), which sees multilingualism as a disability associated with low academic achievement and can also pose a threat to academic standards.

I Am Not There to Take Care of the Language

Another theme commonly discussed in the literature is consistently mentioned by the faculty here—the refusal to consider themselves as potentially involved in supporting the language development of their students.

> If you have a significant portion of your student body [with] English as a second language to a point where they need extra help, there is only so much help you can give . . . it is really easy if you are teaching language to suddenly be both a poetry teacher and an ESL teacher—and I'm not trained for that. (Michel)

> their marks don't reflect [their abilities] because they are challenged in English. . . . And I'm not there to teach them English; I'm there to teach them . . . [my discipline]. Sharad

> [the courses I teach are] all about communications. If they can't communicate, they shouldn't be in my class. (Samuel)

These quotes indicate the sense of professional frustration that some of the study participants experience and show the impact of tensions they encounter on the professional identity of these disciplinary faculty. They also point to the delegitimation of multilingual students and the seeming lack of interest in considering specific pedagogical methods that might be useful in working with EAL students. For example, Samuel, quoted above, refuses to alter his essay assignments because the disciplinary courses he teaches are heavily centered on communication.

As mentioned in the review of existing literature, the maintenance of Western academic standards was also brought up by participants in other studies as a reason not to make classroom accommodations. It is my contention that the refusal of some participants in this study to make language accommodations, based on the perceived need to maintain idealized linguistic standards, can be associated with the limited discussions on the important role of language in processes of internationalization (Bond 2020; Byrd Clark, Haque, and Lamoureux 2013; Jenkins 2013).

Effective Practices: Engaging with Language Matters

While frustrations around dealing with language matters in the internationalized university abound in the views of the participants in this study, there were also some who spoke about accommodations they attempted to make in their classrooms. Interestingly, as exemplified in the words of Sharad below, the tensions and doubts around some students' language issues prompt the proactive attitude of some of the disciplinary faculty interviewed here.

> I confront [the language] issue right off the bat . . . I'll say, "I don't want those who have facility with a language disrespecting the ones who don't have facility with a language and I don't want the ones who don't have facility with the language feeling intimidated by those who talk all the time" . . . I have had to slow down and I would skip some particular subcategory of [my discipline]. . . . Because my philosophy is I'd rather not finish all fast, and leave some people behind—they will get 90% of what I meant to teach. (Sharad)

Other examples of practices of accommodation are shared by other participants below:

> I've simplified my own language usage. I allow translation devices/English dictionaries for the first 15 minutes of tests. . . . I am not testing them on their language. I tell them if they don't understand what a word is to stick their hand up and I will give them an alternate word. (Ann)

> [When] I teach . . . [my] undergraduate course . . . [I would say], "What are the linguistic resources in this classroom?" and . . . frame the multilingualism that many students bring that is a resource to all of us. (Kathy)

> My classroom [time] is so limited, . . . but what I do is . . . hook up my students with ESL students on campus and they will do their own thing outside of my classroom . . . one helps the other one with English, the Chinese student helps my student with Chinese. (Niku)

These examples indicate that some faculty members are creative and often improvise in their teaching to address language issues with their students. However, these quotes also seem to suggest that faculty are using a variety of homegrown strategies (mainly on an individual level) to deal with language issues and thus indicate that institutional support around language is not readily available. As Gallagher and Haan (2017) point out, "favourable attitudes towards serving emerging multilinguals" (2) are as important as teaching techniques. However, it is important to make the case as well that there is a need for more focused institutional support for faculty, as well as articulation between individual and institutional resources.

Faculty Labor

The data shared so far also seems to suggest that disciplinary faculty are facing systemic issues where the internationalization of higher education creates new forms of labor for instructors who seem to expend much time and effort with limited institutional support to navigate institutional demands while attempting to engage meaningfully with students of diverse linguistic resources. That this is the case is further illustrated by the following quotes:

> There isn't actually any particular support on how to use the experience and knowledge of international students or returning Canadian students in the classroom. I think everybody just kind of figures it out. (Keith)

> I think there's an awful lot that goes unrecognized in the tenure and promotion process. . . . So I think there is a complete lack of recognition of pastoral work done by academics, that's for students at any level. . . . And for some international students there is more pastoral work to be done. (Ann)

Overall, the data shared in this chapter reinforces some of the findings around faculty and internationalization noted by Beck et al. (2013) who state that "faculty members work on their own initiative, do not enjoy institutional support [and] are concerned about the neoliberal ideologies that drive institutions to embrace internationalization" (90). Nevertheless, it is important to state as well that the creative and efficient practices that some faculty members employ in their daily work with linguistically diverse students reflect possibilities for more equitable university internationalization.

Endorsement of Critical/Postcolonial Thought versus Positivistic Conceptualizations of Language

Of particular significance for the focus of this chapter is what I perceive as conflicting epistemological views shared by a few participants in this study. I was struck by what would be considered an endorsement of critical/postcolonial perspectives within the social sciences when it comes to some of the work around teaching and research that these faculty spoke about and the lack of alignment with critical/postcolonial perspectives on language in the field of AL. Below are some views that I found quite intriguing. Michel made the following comments at various times during the interview:

> On a practical level my approach to teaching language itself is always that I'm teaching particular kind at particular place. . . . When it comes to more abstract texts, looking at issues of colonialism and the racism that arises from it—"Why are we here studying this particular language and this particular literary tradition?" . . . the reason that English is the lingua franca is because of the last two empires who have spoken it.

> [Students] are being pushed through their language tests, arriving here really ill-equipped. . . . They . . . can't possibly do well in first year English let alone pass half the time. . . . I love having people from 12 different countries in the room—it's when language breaks down that's the problem . . . when I look at the first two sentences of a paper and I think, "Aw, Cantonese speaker. Okay, this is going to take longer."

The first quote indicates Michel's approach to teaching his disciplinary content. The references to issues of colonialism and racism that he makes reflect a critical and postcolonial understanding of the nature of English and English literary traditions resulting from the power of English steeped in relations subjugating various peoples as a result of economic and political dominance historically. The second quote reflects Michel's views on language as a means of communication and a tool for learning content. One way to look at it would be through the lens of critical AL scholarship around the nature of language, as discussed in the "Theoretical Framework" section. It is evident that the second quote indicates the endorsement of a view of language as a knowable fixed entity that one either possesses or doesn't. This quote also illustrates that instructors seem to view language acquisition and use as an individual student's problem that might be gone if only students came to the institution "better" prepared.

Another set of quotes I want to draw attention to comes from Keith, a faculty member who works with students engaging in global initiatives. Keith states:

> One of those skills [taught in the practicum preparation class] is cross-cultural awareness . . . and this translates into the safety training we do as well—under the theme of know thyself. If you know who you are, you are a much safer person in

> the world and you are a much more effective practitioner . . . if you know . . . that you are white, educated, and privileged and you are working with an aboriginal community or an immigrant community that is not. . . . It is important . . . to understand . . . who you are and who they are.
>
> The reputation of the university is at risk when we send students out to the world who can't put together a paragraph. . . . I have heard from others, they . . . sort of cut them some slack because they are not speaking English as their first language. . . . I tend not to . . . you should be able to perform commensurate with the degree that you earned.

It is clear from the first quote that Keith endorses in his teaching a view on the importance of one's positionality and the impact of privilege on marginalized groups. Such views are common in critical scholarship in the social sciences. However, the second quote seems to marginalize a specific group in the institution, that of speakers of English as an additional language, whose evaluation is to be conducted by validating a somewhat narrow view of educated English as per scholarship in critical AL I referred to earlier. Institutional requirements endorsed here seem to reflect an assumption of a homogenous language that all students need to be equally competent in.

Steve talks passionately about research with an Indigenous community he is engaged with:

> So we've taken a bottom up approach that is based on community-based participatory research, as well as a critical theory orientation where we are constantly adjusting our methodology as things unfold.

Yet, criticality as understood in terms of addressing power dynamics in contexts of interaction and learning is not evident when he discusses the impact of having multilingual students in his classrooms:

> there is the issue of for many of those English is a second language and so you end up with classroom situations where a number of people who can be very, very intelligent, don't have the means to communicate effectively, and that can unintentionally have an effect on those native English speakers who are not receiving the attention that they would otherwise have.

What seems to be in operation as reflected in the above quote is an "us/them" mentality guided by a perceived deficiency in language proficiency among EAL students. Overall, the data shared in this section suggests that disciplinary faculty overwhelmingly espouse normative perspectives on language and language issues, even those who are critically oriented and embrace diversity in their research and teaching.

Discussion and Conclusions

What can we make of the experiences with internationalization of content faculty in relation to language matters? Overall, the data shared here suggests that there are inherent tensions in the complex ways faculty experience internationalization on the ground. Besides, beliefs and assumptions about language often shape faculty's perceptions and experiences. The standard language ideology seems present in faculty's accounts mainly through the idealized assumption of linguistic academic standards. Indeed, one of the negative consequences of internationalization identified by some faculty is the perceived lowering of academic standards, which they regard as resulting from the increase in the number of international students at the university. It also seems evident that institutional support to equip faculty to meet student needs is insufficient. In addition, the question of linguistic accommodation is fraught with ambivalence in the narratives of many of the study participants.

The chapter discussed challenges content area faculty face in serving a gate-keeping function when working with international students, whose somewhat difficult socialization in the norms of a North American academic institution is commonly perceived as a deficiency in language proficiency. Jenkins (2013) advocates the "need for a change of mind-set so that the accommodation of international students' English language needs is ... [seen] as the incorporation of a genuine international perspective" (202). As far as language is concerned, such an attitude is not prevalent among faculty participants in this study. According to Reagan (2004), viewing language from a positivistic perspective leads to the objectification of language and a focus on constructs such as grammar, native speakers, and proficiency. These are the dominant views in the data shared here.

What possibilities are out there to dispel homogenous notions of language? Critical AL scholarship abounds with ideas to embrace to subvert dominant language ideologies. For example, lacking understanding of the complexities of language and language use may lead to the simplistic conclusion that international students are the only ones responsible for effective communication (Canagarajah 2011). Thus, the first thing would perhaps need to be to shift from thinking about languages to thinking about languaging, that is, viewing language as a dynamic process and practice, rather than a product. As Gurney and Demuro (2022) explain, "in opposition to the term 'language,' as static and fixed, *languaging* is defined as action, and has been linked to a praxis 'in and through which language events are achieved and recognized in culturally saturated interactivity between persons' (Thibault 2017, 76)" (309). When we no longer view languages as separable and countable, but instead as interacting in fluid and complex ways (García 2009; García and Wei 2014), we would be more in tune with considering the linguistic repertoires of our multilingual students. Languaging after all "is a set of situated and territorialised social practices belonging to users and interactants" (Demuro and Gurney 2022, 311) and thus indicates the responsibilities of all in acknowledging difference in communication and in negotiating understanding within interactive events. It is this kind of understanding that I believe would allow content faculty to fully embrace and engage in multi/pluri/translanguaging pedagogies (Lin 2020; Preece and Marshall 2020) that tap into the full range of students' linguistic resources. Indeed, AL faculty have an important role to play to have our professional voices heard in our institutions (Millar 2009) with regard to sharing currents views around language/languaging. Critically oriented applied linguists need to proactively offer professional development opportunities for other faculty, specifically around conceptualizations of language with incentives provided for participation as well as acknowledgment possibly through the tenure and promotion process. Such opportunities should not only engage with the construct of language, but also prompt self-reflections on disciplinary identity among content faculty that promote the view that language/languaging be considered in everyone's pedagogies regardless of content area. As Bond (2020) observes, "[m]aking the choice to consider or ignore language, which is perhaps the most evident discursive practice in which privilege and prejudice are woven into our everyday lives, is . . . a political decision" (200). Such a massive undertaking, of course, necessitates the development of institution-wide language policies that acknowledge the primary role of language/languaging in knowledge construction and assessment. Thus, there is a need for a multidimensional conceptual approach to theorizing internationalization that attends properly to language (Bond 2020; Byrd Clark et al. 2013; Jenkins 2013). One step toward that goal might be building bridges across critical and postpositivist frames by working toward coalition building with like-minded content faculty endorsing critical perspectives within their own disciplines. Ethical internationalization would not be possible unless and until "a view of internationalisation . . . that acknowledges languages' central role in knowledge (and imaginaries) production and reproduction" (Diaz 2018, 26) becomes commonplace in Anglo-dominant universities. In this endeavor, the goal should be for institutions to view linguistic heterogeneity as the "norm," undermine monolingual views of language, be critical of "White English" (Kubota et al. 2021), and consistently consider languaging as the dynamic practice all university stakeholders are involved in.

Acknowledgment

This research was funded by a grant from the Social Sciences and Humanities Research Council of Canada.

References

Association of Universities and Colleges of Canada. 2007. *Internationalizing Canadian Campuses: Report on Findings of the 2006 Survey on Internationalization*. Ottawa: Association of Universities and Colleges of Canada. http://www.aucc.ca/_pdf/english/publications/aucc-scotia_web_e.pdf.

Blommaert, Jan, and Ben Rampton. 2011. "Language and Superdiversity." *Diversities* 13, no. 2: 1–22.

Beck, Kumari, Roumiana Ilieva, Ashley Pullman, and Zhihua Zhang. 2013. "New Work, Old Power: Inequities Within the Labor of Internationalization." *On the Horizon* 21, no. 2: 84–95. https://doi.org/10.1108/10748121311322987.

Bond, Bee. 2020. *Making Language Visible in the University: English for Academic Purposes and Internationalisation*. Bristol, Blue Ridge Summit: Multilingual Matters.

Byrd Clark, Julie, Eve Haque, and Sylvie Lamoureux. 2013. "The Role of Language in Processes of Internationalization: Considering Linguistic Heterogeneity and Voices from Within and Out in Two Diverse Contexts in Ontario." *Comparative and International Education (Ottawa, Ont.)* 41, no. 3. https://doi.org/10.5206/cie-eci.v41i3.9212.

Calikoglu, Alper, Jenny J. Lee, and Hasan Arslan. 2022. "Faculty International Engagement: Examining Rationales, Strategies, and Barriers in Institutional Settings." *Journal of Studies in International Education* 26, no. 1: 61–79. https://doi.org/10.1177/1028315320963508.

Canagarajah, Suresh. 2011. "Translanguaging in the Classroom: Emerging Issues for Research and Pedagogy." *Applied Linguistics Review* 2, no. 2: 1–27.

Criswell, John R., and Hao Zhu. 2015. "Faculty Internationalization Priorities." *FIRE: Forum for International Research in Education* 2, no. 2. http://preserve.lehigh.edu/re/vol2/iss2/3.

Diaz, Adriana. 2018. "Challenging Dominant Epistemologies in Higher Education: The Role of Language in the Geopolitics of Knowledge (Re)Production." In *Multilingual Education Yearbook 2018*, edited by Indika Liyanage, 21–36. Switzerland: Springer International Publishing AG. https://doi.org/10.1007/978-3-319-77655-2_2.

Flores, Nelson, and Jonathan Rosa. 2015. "Undoing Appropriateness: Raciolinguistic Ideologies and Language Diversity in Education." *Harvard Education Review* 85, no. 2: 149–171. https://doi.org/10.17763/0017-8055.85.2.149.

Foucault, Michel. 2002. *Archaeology of Knowledge / Michel Foucault*; Translated by A.M. Sheridan Smith. London and New York: Routledge.

Friesen, Rhonda. 2013. "Faculty Member Engagement in Canadian University Internationalization." *Journal of Studies in International Education* 17, no. 3: 209–227. https://doi.org/10.1177/1028315312451132.

García, Ofelia. 2009. "Education, Multilingualism and Translanguaging in the 21st Century." In *Social Justice through Multilingual Education*, edited by Tove Skutnabb-Kangas, Robert Phillipson, Ajit K. Mohanty, and Minati Panda, 140–158. Bristol, Blue Ridge Summit: Multilingual Matters. https://doi.org/10.21832/9781847691910-011.

García, Ofelia, and Angel M. Y. Lin. 2018. "English and Multilingualism: A Contested History." In *The Routledge Handbook of English Language Studies*, edited by Philip Seargeant, Ann Hewings, and Stephen Pihlaja, 77–92. London; New York: Routledge, Taylor & Francis Group.

García, Ofelia, and Li Wei. 2014. *Translanguaging: Language, Bilingualism and Education*. London: Palgrave Macmillan Pivot.

Gallagher, Colleen, and Jennifer Haan. 2017. "University Faculty Beliefs about Emergent Multilinguals and Linguistically Responsive Instruction." *TESOL Quarterly*: 1–27. https://doi.org/10.1002/tesq.399.

Gogolin, Ingrid. 1994. *Der monolinguale Habitus der multilingualen Schule [The Monolingual Habitus of Multilingual School]*. Münster, Germany: Waxmann.

Gurney, Laura, and Eugenia Demuro. 2022. "Tracing New Ground, from Language to Languaging, and from Languaging to Assemblages: Rethinking Languaging through the Multilingual and Ontological Turns." *International Journal of Multilingualism* 19, no. 3: 305–324. https://doi.org/10.1080/14790718.2019.1689982.

Haan, Jennifer E., and Colleen Gallagher. 2022. "Situating Linguistically Responsive Instruction in Higher Education Contexts: Foundations for Pedagogical, Curricular, and Institutional Support." *TESOL Quarterly* 56, no. 1: 5–18. https://doi.org/10.1002/tesq.3087.

Haan, Jennifer E., Colleen Gallagher, and Lisa Varandani. 2017. "Working with Linguistically Diverse Classes Across the Disciplines: Faculty Beliefs." *The Journal of Scholarship of Teaching and Learning* 17, no. 1: 37–51. https://doi.org/10.14434/v17i1.20008.

Hult, Francis, and Nancy Hornberger. 2016. "Revisiting Orientations in Language Planning: Problem, Right, and Resource as an Analytical Heuristic." *The Bilingual Review* 33, no. 3: 30–49.

Ilieva, Roumiana, Kumari Beck, and Bonnie Waterstone. 2014. "Towards Sustainable Internationalisation of Higher Education." *Higher Education* 68, no. 6: 875–889. https://doi.org/10.1007/s10734-014-9749-6.

Jackson, Jane. 2010. *Intercultural Journeys from Study to Residence Abroad*. Houndmills, Basingstoke: Palgrave Macmillan.

Jenkins, Jennifer. 2013. *English as a Lingua Franca in the International University: The Politics of Academic English Language Policy*. Abingdon: Routledge.

Kvale, Steinar, and Svend Brinkmann. 2009. *InterViews: Learning the Craft of Qualitative Research Interviewing*, 2nd edn. Thousand Oaks: SAGE Publications.

Kubota, Ryuko, Meghan Corella, Kyuyun Lim, and Pramod K Sah. 2021. "'Your English Is So Good': Linguistic Experiences of Racialized Students and Instructors of a Canadian University." *Ethnicities*: 1–21. https://doi.org/10.1177/14687968211055808.

Kuteeva, Maria, Kathrin Kaufhold, and Niina Hynninen. 2020. *Language Perceptions and Practices in Multilingual Universities*. Switzerland: Springer International Publishing.

Lin, Angel M. Y. 2020. "Introduction: Translanguaging and Translanguaging Pedagogies." In *Translanguaging in Multilingual English Classrooms*, 1–9. Singapore: Springer Nature Singapore. https://doi.org/10.1007/978-981-15-1088-5_1.

Madiba, Mbulungeni. 2018. "The Multilingual University." In *The Routledge Handbook of Language and Superdiversity*, 1st edn, 504–517. Routledge. https://doi.org/10.4324/9781315696010-35.

Mahalingappa, Laura, Hayriye Kayi-Aydar, and Nihat Polat. 2021. "Institutional and Faculty Readiness for Teaching Linguistically Diverse International Students in Educator Preparation Programs in U.S. Universities." *TESOL Quarterly* 55, no. 4: 1247–1277. https://doi.org/10.1002/tesq.3083.

Makoni, Sinfree, and Alastair Pennycook. 2005. "Disinventing and (Re)Constituting Languages." *Critical Inquiry in Language Studies* 2, no. 3: 137–156. https://doi.org/10.1207/s15427595cils0203_1.

Makoni, Sinfree, and Alastair Pennycook. 2007. *Disinventing and Reconstituting Languages*. Edited by Sinfree Makoni and Alastair Pennycook. Clevedon: Multilingual Matters.

Marshall, Steve. 2020. "Understanding Plurilingualism and Developing Pedagogy: Teaching in Linguistically Diverse Classes Across the Disciplines at a Canadian University." *Language, Culture and Curriculum* 33, no. 2: 142–156. https://doi.org/10.1080/07908318.2019.1676768.

Marshall, Steve, and Jennifer Walsh Marr. 2018. "Teaching Multilingual Learners in Canadian Writing-intensive Classrooms: Pedagogy, Binaries, and Conflicting Identities." *Journal of Second Language Writing* 40: 32–43. https://doi.org/10.1016/j.jslw.2018.01.002.

Millar, Geoff. 2009. "Working with International Students: Applied Linguistics and the Art of Inclusive Teaching." *TESOL in Context* 19, no. 2: 1–12.

Nyangau, Josiah. 2020. "Faculty Engagement in Internationalization: The Role of Personal Agency Beliefs." *International Journal of Research in Education and Science* 6, no. 1: 74–85.

Preece, Siân, and Steve Marshall. 2020. "Plurilingualism, Teaching and Learning, and Anglophone Higher Education: An Introduction Anglophone Universities and

Linguistic Diversity." *Language, Culture, and Curriculum* 33, no. 2: 117–125. https://doi.org/10.1080/07908318.2020.1723931.

Reagan, Timothy. 2004. "Objectification, Positivism and Language Studies: A Reconsideration." *Critical Inquiry in Language Studies* 1, no. 1: 41–60.

Sawir, Erlenawati. 2011. "Dealing with Diversity in Internationalised Higher Education Institutions." *Intercultural Education* 22, no. 5: 381–394. https://doi.org/10.1080/14675986.2011.643136.

Smith, Dorothy. 1987. *The Everyday World as Problematic: A Feminist Sociology*. Boston: Northeastern University Press.

Smith, Dorothy. 2005. *Institutional Ethnography: A Sociology for People*. Lanham, MD: AltaMira Press.

Sterzuk, Andrea. 2015. "'The Standard Remains the Same': Language Standardization, Race and Othering in Higher Education." *Journal of Multilingual and Multicultural Development* 36, no. 1: 53–66.

Thibault, Paul J. 2017. "The Reflexivity of Human Languaging and Nigel Love's Two Orders of Language." *Language Sciences* 61: 74–85. https://doi.org/10.1016/j.langsci.2016.09.014.

Van Viegen, Saskia, and Sandra Zappa-Hollman. 2020. "Plurilingual Pedagogies at the Post-secondary Level: Possibilities for Intentional Engagement with Students' Diverse Linguistic Repertoires." *Language, Culture and Curriculum* 33, no. 2: 172–187. https://doi.org/10.1080/07908318.2019.1686512.

3

Narratives on IELTS Test Writing, Preparation, and English Learning of Chinese International Students in Canada

Zhihua (Olivia) Zhang

Introduction: The Researcher's Story

Before I came to Canada as an immigrant, I had taken the TOEFL[1] test for academic purposes and earned very good marks. These high English test scores, together with my positive English teaching experiences at a university in China, led me to believe that my English was good enough to pursue my PhD in Canada and tackle the general IELTS[2] test for immigration purposes. Born and brought up in Mainland China, I was imbued with the idea that English tests are effective tools to assess people's language proficiency and potential. If I could earn very high scores in TOEFL, I would definitely be able to do well in the IELTS test and be successful in my doctoral studies. However, my IELTS test score for general purposes was far lower than I had expected, and I struggled with English throughout my doctoral studies.

For quite some time, I had been attributing my unsatisfactory IELTS score to my unpreparedness. After starting my doctoral studies, however, I gradually realized that I had established the connection between test scores and "real" learning potential when I was in China. My seemingly sufficient TOEFL score that gained me admission to Simon Fraser University (SFU) did not secure a smooth learning journey. I was confused and lost, struggling to figure out doctoral studies in a Canadian university.

I observed similar confusion and sense of loss in the international students in the English Bridge Program (EBP)[3] at SFU. This triggered my compassion for their experiences and prompted my doctoral research on the issues these students faced. They were enrolled in SFU conditionally and had to pass the program and achieve a 6.0 in another IELTS test to get official admission to the university. I had believed, based on my own experience, that students could achieve a satisfactory score should they spend enough time and effort in preparation. However, the IELTS test-taking stories I heard from these students contradicted my assumptions. Several of them could not attain an adequate score despite their prolonged preparation and repeated writing of the test both in China and Canada. Those who were finally able to attain the score requested by different institutions and/or academic programs still could not escape "the problem of English" as it haunted them as the most challenging aspect of their university studies.

In this chapter, I present data from my doctoral research that sought to understand the English learning and IELTS test-taking experiences of some Chinese international students before and after coming to Canada; the changes in their understanding and expectations of international education; and their construction, negotiation, and perception of themselves as international students. A brief review will first summarize literature on language learning and test-taking of Chinese international students in relation to their agency, investment, and identities. This will be followed by an articulation of the theoretical framework and methodology. Narratives in this chapter focus on IELTS test preparation, writing experiences, and identity performance of two participants (from among eleven interviewed for the study). The chapter closes with my suggestions and recommendations for stakeholders of international higher education so that the overall learning experiences of international students could be enhanced in their host countries.

Context

The internationalization of an institution is most commonly related to the number of international students recruited and their contribution to the host country economy (Canadian Bureau of International Education 2015). The top source country of international students for Canada had been China until 2018—140,530 Chinese international students studied in Canada, comprising 28 percent of all Canadian international students (CBIE 2018). China was surpassed by India and ranked as the second-largest origin country since then; in 2022, a total of 116,935 Chinese international students came to Canada for international education (Canada International Student Statistics 2022).

The influx of Chinese international students to Western countries is addressed in scholarly literature. Social adjustments, language learning, and identity issues, among others, are topics that have been examined (Ilieva 2010; Ma 2017; Marginson 2014). The literature suggests that Chinese international students have been stereotyped in essentializing terms that negatively impact their image (Heng 2018; Ye and Edwards 2015): they are perceived as silent, passive in learning, and lacking in critical thinking skills. These constructs prevail in the popular discourse even though academics generally agree that such portraits are biased and simplistic.

The construction of Chinese students as problematic learners has been challenged by authors arguing that Chinese learners are complex subjects (Grimshaw 2011; Jin and Cortazzi 1995). In the context of Canadian higher education, Chinese learners have been investigated at various levels of studies (Heng 2018; Ilieva and Waterstone 2013; Zhou, Liu, and Rideout 2017). Most studies focus on a certain period of their learning in Canada with insufficient reference to their past experiences in China and/or expectations for the future. In other words, Chinese international students are not seen and portrayed holistically as whole individuals with past experiences and future aspirations (Zhang 2017; Zhang and Beck 2017). I was motivated, therefore, to conduct a more holistic investigation of Chinese international students to understand their progression from a Chinese to a Canadian learning environment; how their past experiences shape and influence their perceptions of learning and their future, and how their test-taking experiences color their view of education.

Literature Review

Language learning has been identified as a major challenge for international students in academic settings (Huang, Guo, and Zhou 2022; Ilieva and Waterstone 2013; Montgomery 2010; Zhou, Liu, and Rideout 2017) even though they have earned the official gate-keeping scores in standardized English tests such as TOEFL or IELTS to enter Canadian colleges or universities. Their experiences after they passed the test in the university can be "arduous, attenuated and even humiliating at times". In general, how language learners study is affected by their imagined identities and participation in various communities in the future (Yashima 2013). Regarding English learners from China, McKay and Wong (1996) have found that they are complex social beings with agency and their investment in learning English is determined by their needs and desires. Their language learning involves motivation, identity, culture, and investment transformation

(Gu 2008). Their motivations for English learning, according to Gao, Cheng, and Kelly (2008), are complex, and they negotiate identities as learners while imagining the community they intend to join. Chinese international students exert agency and selectively invest in studies that would increase their market value in their envisioned future communities (Y. J. Chang 2011; Wang 2012). In their selective investment in learning, Chinese international students imagine themselves as successful academic English writers (Liu and Tannacito 2013); they negotiate multiple identities and their investment in English learning is informed by their sociocultural background and future aspirations (Y. C. Chang 2016).

English learning for test writing experiences of Chinese international students is not well researched in the literature. As a general practice of postsecondary institutions in Anglophone countries, IELTS and other standardized English tests are used in admitting international students from non-English-speaking backgrounds. The presumption behind this practice is the idea that achieving certain scores in the test would enable international students to succeed in their postsecondary academic studies. An average IELTS score of 6.5–7.0 in all four sections, namely listening, speaking, reading, and writing, is usually required for admission to degree programs.

Test-taking experiences of international students from China have been investigated, though the impacts of IELTS on Chinese learners in the home setting are rarely considered (Fox and Curtis 2010). The efforts of Chinese students to prepare for the IELTS examination at home and abroad are investigated by Yu (2014), for example, focusing on the primary purposes and perception of test-takers scoring 7.0 or higher in IELTS. Literature on the identities of international students as IELTS test-takers is limited as well. Shohamy (2001, 2013) asserts that the field of modern language learning regards test-takers as deficient with subtractive identities and calls for testing methods that could "reflect identities and proficiencies" of test-takers (2013, 235).

Considering the large number of Chinese international students preparing and writing the IELTS test, the scarcity of literature on their IELTS preparation and writing experiences is surprising. In addition, how the identities of students as English learners and test-takers are impacted by these experiences needs to be better understood so that their overall well-being can be supported by instructors, staff, and others in Anglo-dominant institutions. This study intends to bridge this gap.

Theoretical Perspectives

I rely on Bourdieu's notion of economy of practice; Norton's concepts of agency and investment in language learning; and Darvin and Norton's model of investment that takes into account ideology, capital, and identity to ground the analysis of the selected narratives of two Chinese international students at SFU.

Norton's Concepts of Agency and Investment in Language Learning

When examining the identities and experiences of language learners, Norton (2013) questioned the traditional Second Language Acquisition motivation theories and formulated her notions of agency and investment in second language learners by integrating Bourdieu's (1991) concept of "cultural capital" and economic investment. Bourdieu's (1986) notion of *economy of practice* articulates how the social and cultural practices of language learning and use are linked to power and capital. Bourdieu introduced *capital*, *field*, and *habitus* to indicate how social relationships are reciprocally shaped in the complex and practical social environment. The exchange of "capital" is what drives all social interaction within a field; recognized and legitimate capital benefits people who possess it. *Economic capital* can convert into money "immediately and directly" (1986, 143) while *symbolic capital* takes the form of *social* and *cultural capital*. The value of cultural capital is decided by the recognition and status of institutions who grant qualifications, certificates, or credentials; academic qualifications may convert into economic capital through the labor market.

To Norton (2013, 45), how a person relates to the world shows their understanding of "how that relationship is structured across time and space, and how the person understands possibilities for the future." Language learners assume that they will gain a wider range of symbolic and material resources when they invest in learning a target language. In language learning in a community, learners are involved in power relations and develop new ways with the changing social world, a process critically examined through the lens of investment. "[A]n investment in a target language is also an investment in a learner's own social identity" (Norton Pierce 1995, 18). Norton's (2013) concept of investment highlights "the role of agency and identity in engaging with the task at hand, in accumulating economic and symbolic capital, in having stakes in the endeavor and in persevering in that endeavor" (195).

Participants in the study under discussion came to Canada and invested in higher education for qualifications and credentials to gain perceived social and cultural capital that would lead them to more resources and possibilities. English turned out to be a vital tool in the whole process of pursuing international education in Canada. These participants invested heavily in English learning and test writing; their selective investment in and understanding of the linguistic capital of English were informed by the English ideology that shaped them in China, which will be discussed further in this chapter.

Darvin and Norton's Model of Investment: Ideology, Capital, and Identity

To address the changing linguistic landscape, Darvin and Norton (2015) developed a lens "that explicitly calls out ideology and examines the sociopolitical contexts of schools and communities and the shifting values of linguistic capital" and proposed a model of investment involving ideology "as a normative set of ideas" (44). This model encompasses symbolic power, legitimated authority, modes of inclusion and exclusion, learner positioning, and the right to enter a community of language learners. It recognizes ideology "as a site of struggle, of competing dominant, residual, and marginal ideas" so that identity is understood as having both "a certain disposition to act and think a certain way" and "the agency to restructure contexts" (Darvin and Norton 2015, 44). The authors then propose using "ideologies" to complement their understanding of "identity as multiple and fluid, and of capital shifting values in different contexts" (44). With investment lying in the intersection of identity, capital, and ideology, this model creates "a space" for learners to battle their marginalized position by default and develop "an agentive capacity to evaluate and negotiate the constraints and opportunities of their social location" (Darvin and Norton 2015, 47).

This model allows me to understand how learners form their perceptions of the social place they should occupy and decide what to invest in within a given community. The narrative stories I present later in this chapter will demonstrate how the two participants struggled to enter different communities (EBP and the university) using different English test scores, how they positioned themselves in relation to the scores they earned, and how they employed and invested in various approaches to achieve their desired identities.

Methodology and Methods

This study was conducted in the EBP at SFU, a high-ranking medium-sized comprehensive university in Canada. EBP was selected as the research site mainly because I found students were struggling with English learning and IELTS test preparation when I worked as a teaching assistant in the program. I recruited eleven participants through email and word of mouth from different faculties and departments and at various years of university studies.

To achieve my goal of considering Chinese international students as individuals in their wholeness rather than people segregated from their past and future, my research investigated the narrative experiences of Chinese international students before and after they came to SFU, including their English learning and IELTS test writing experiences before and after coming to Canada.

I used narrative interviews in collecting the stories of my participants. Interviews are extensively used as a source of storied narratives in narrative inquiry (Riessman 2008) and are particularly suitable when investigating, as I was, the perceptions, attitudes, and experiences of participants (Gubrium and Holstein 2009). I designed two rounds of in-person narrative interviews with each participant to generate "text" for this study. The interviews were conducted in Chinese and translated into English with participants checking on the interpretation of their narratives. The first interview was conducted in a free-flowing, exploratory, and open-ended format; in this interview, I briefly introduced the design and intention of the study and answered any questions before moving the conversation naturally to the interview questions. Based on the stories emerging in the first unstructured narrative interview, I designed the second semi-structured interview to elicit more stories from the participants. By combining unstructured and semi-structured interviews that kept the information and interpretation a two-way street, I could not only balance the needs of the researcher and that of the participants but also decrease the potential inequality between us. In this chapter, I focus on narrative stories from two participants in order to uncover and understand more deeply their multilayered experiences as test-takers.

IELTS-Related Stories

IELTS-related narrative stories that I collected from the participants fall into three themes: discrepancies between test writing strategies and academic learning in the university, equating learning for test writing with academic learning, and IELTS and identity. In this chapter, I present stories of Kaddy and Zoe on their IELTS test experiences and identities through the lenses of capital, investment, habitus, identity, and power and resistance to test-taking. International students invest heavily in symbolic capital and identities that are desirable to them, and such investment is closely related to their IELTS test writing and preparation experiences before and after they came to Canada. Such experiences offer a lens to view international students as individuals with histories, and they need to be understood holistically as complex subjects with multiple identities. The experiences of international students should be taken into consideration in the internationalization activities and practices of educational institutions hosting international students in Canada.

Test-Coping Strategies and Academic Learning at SFU

All the participants in this study wrote the IELTS test multiple times to achieve the threshold English proficiency requirement to enter the EBP first and eventually SFU. Kaddy was a student in Business and Zoe was seeking her second degree in Economics when the research was conducted. Zoe wrote the test at least ten times in total, and Kaddy five times, in China and Canada. Repeated test writing, together with the preparation for tests, cast long-lasting unpleasant effects on participants in terms of their understanding of academic English learning in university and their concepts of themselves as international students. Kaddy and Zoe's stories showed how IELTS test writing and preparation not only shaped who they were, but also affected them emotionally.

Kaddy—Marked by marks: "Am I not a good girl?": Kaddy was the participant that I met most often during and after my data collection. She recalled how her life had been scheduled around learning English and writing and preparing for the IELTS test. She became emotional almost every time she talked about English learning and IELTS test writing. When she did well in her courses, she would tell me happily that her English was improving. When she was not satisfied with her academic performance, she would relate it to her insufficient English proficiency. I could then see sadness and disappointment on her face. When Kaddy finally passed EBP and entered SFU officially, she felt relieved thinking that her English was good enough for the university. However, her sense of relief did not last long as she found English was still her "biggest problem" and headache. She then questioned herself desperately, saying that although she liked English, English did not like her. Also, she tried what she could to improve her English. For instance, she went to the learning center for international students and met with the learning coaches regularly. However, she still encountered various problems in English at different stages of learning. She would "feel very sad from time to time" whenever she thought about English and even wanted to give up. "But one or two days later, I would tell myself to turn over a page. The next day would be a new day, and I will keep going."

Kaddy wrote the test five times in total. She had to fly to another city in China for the chance to write her first one, in which she got a 5.5. Then she wrote the test for the second time, and the 6.0 score was not sufficient for direct entry to SFU. It was the third time of writing the test that traumatized her and led to her doubting herself as a good daughter.

> It was in November, and I was running a high fever during that week. Before that, I believed that I was very strong-minded and could handle all kinds of difficult situations in my life. But I was wrong. I actually called my parents and told them I couldn't bear it anymore. The IELTS test was hard and I was under great pressure. My dad went to visit me. It was a shame. I shouldn't have made my parents worried as they are always busy with their business. I'm not a good daughter. I took my third test on a Saturday and it was 6 again.

With this score, Kaddy entered the EBP Program at SFU; she needed to pass this program and earn at least a 6.0 by the end of the semester again as per the completion requirement of the program. If she could get a 6.5, she would be able to skip a noncredit writing course. She was under the pressure of learning English, preparing for the IELTS test while taking courses in EBP, and paying high fees for her international education in Canada. Unfortunately, she got 6.0 in her fourth IELTS test which literally made her "collapse":

> I was shocked at the score and kept crying and couldn't stop. I felt hurt and miserable. I'm a good girl and I'm very nice. I would help homeless people on the street and buy food for them.... So why did I have to go through this? It was not that I didn't work hard. If I had been very careless with my study and put little effort in preparing for the test, I would deserve the punishment from the heavens. But I've been so good and hard-working. Why am I punished by not being able to get the extra 0.5? I just want 0.5 more. I was very depressed and frail. I would start crying whenever I thought about IELTS. Then I went to talk with every instructor and asked them where my problems were. I needed their help to find out why I couldn't improve.... I had been working so hard! I cried when meeting them. Then I was awakened up by the words of one instructor. He said, it was your choice to come to Canada for international education, and if you were not ready to face all the problems, why are you here? Then I thought he was right. I began to reflect upon myself, and realized that I didn't work as hard as I had believed. I wasn't as good as I had believed.

Kaddy quivered as she told me her stories, and I could feel her effort to hold back her tears. Though she felt better and thought she was not "that bad" after she got her 6.5 score the fifth time she took the test, her good feeling did not last long because the challenges around English in her SFU content classrooms followed.

I admired her questioning of her unfair experiences in taking IELTS, but she reflected that it must be her own problem that she did not get a higher score. When an instructor told her that she had to face and solve all the problems by herself as it was her decision to come to Canada for an international education, she agreed immediately and believed the source of her problems was that she herself did not work hard enough. What she did after that was to work even harder by spending longer hours in IELTS preparation.

Zoe—"I'm a loser!": Among all the participants of this study, I have known Zoe the longest. I was working in an IELTS preparation school as a part-time instructor when I met her. It was a year before we met again in EBP. Zoe could not even remember exactly how many times she had written the test and she said ten times at least. She sarcastically said that the IELTS test organization and IELTS training schools owed her "a medal" for the time and money she spent in preparing and writing the IELTS test. When talking about the test, Zoe made an implicit connection between the score and academic studies at SFU. While she knew an English test score may enable international students to start their learning in a Canadian educational institution, she did not believe the grade could help them to "survive academic studies" in the university, nor "guarantee success." She borrowed a metaphor that an instructor in EBP used comparing writing IELTS repeatedly and standing on a scale:

> You stand on the scale today and it shows 6.0; if you do it again the next day, it probably would become 6.5. So if you get a higher score in writing IELTS repeatedly, it doesn't mean that your English proficiency has improved. It is your IELTS writing strategies that have improved.

In addition to equating IELTS test scores to real learning, she related these experiences back to who she was. Writing the test for "more than ten times" was not "the most painful part"; it was "the pressure and the loss of hope" that cast doubt on herself as an international student.

> I know without an English test score, it would be difficult for international students to survive academic studies in the university. . . . Without the score I can't see any hope. I can't get enrolled at SFU to start my dream of graduate studies. I can't see any future. . . . Sometimes I think it's a mistake for me to come to Canada. I could have lived comfortably with my parents and earned a good salary in my job in China. But I can't go back, right? I don't want to give up and go back without getting my degree as planned. Or I'm a loser. I didn't come to Canada to become a loser. But I think I am a loser anyways because I can't get

that score. I need the score to move on, and I need the score to show that I'm not inferior to other people. So I have to keep working on IELTS until I get it.

The following excerpt was from a meeting with Zoe after she enrolled in a Second Degree Program in Economics. When we met for coffee, she told me that she eventually became a "loser" in writing IELTS.

> Looking back, I don't think I should have spent that much time and money (on writing IELTS).... I didn't think of anything else except taking IELTS preparation courses. I registered for all the IELTS tests that a test-taker is allowed to write in a certain period. It was not only about time and money. It was more about how I felt. There was only one thing in my mind: prove that you're not a loser by gaining a higher IELTS score. Then I was forced to give up my plan of getting an MA in Communications because I couldn't get the desirable score in IELTS.

Although she felt happy that she gave up writing more IELTS tests for a better score, she later took a different path by going to college and entering the second degree program in Economics. She said she "came to terms" with herself.

> I decided to take a different way—I was forced to. I went to a college for a year, and then I applied for a second degree without an IELTS score. It was a hard decision to make, but later I came to terms with myself. Moreover, my learning in the college was very satisfactory. In fact, I found I could make greater progress in English while taking courses in a content area. Only then did I realize that I was probably not a loser. It was only that writing IELTS repeatedly under great pressure didn't work out well for me. Now I just regard all the time and money spent on IELTS as part of the growing pain in seeking an education in a foreign country.

Discussion and Findings

In proposing an expanded model of investment, Darvin and Norton (2015) intend to make use of it as "a normative set of ideas" that is "constructed by symbolic power or world-making power" (43). Such power creates different models of inclusion and exclusion in which learners are judged and positioned. By integrating ideology, this model can not only enable the examination of power, but also how power is structured so that the entry to a certain space may be prohibited to certain people. I employ this model to explore the structure of power in the space of the IELTS test system my study participants seem to have experienced.

Identity, Power, and Resistance

All the participants in this study wrote IELTS tests multiple times, and they felt they should put all the blame on themselves for failing to gain satisfactory scores as required by different levels of study in Canada. In Kaddy and Zoe's cases, they perceived their academic identities and who they were as learners based on the scores they earned in writing IELTS tests, demonstrating the power of the tests. Kaddy's perception of herself as a good daughter was shattered when she sought help from her father and did not earn a better score on one test. Another 6.0 in IELTS on her fourth try caused Kaddy to mentally collapse; her self-perception as a good and hardworking student was questioned. For Zoe, the unsatisfactory IELTS test scores led to the perception of herself as "a loser," and someone who was "inferior" to other people with higher IELTS scores. Seeing no hope of getting a desirable score to enter her dream MA program as planned, Zoe took a different path: she went to a college and transferred back to SFU for a secondary degree. Her self-perceptions as "a loser" were erased only after she became a successful learner in that college.

Kaddy and Zoe realized the discrepancies between what they learned from writing the IELTS test and the test's relevance to their academic studies in content areas at SFU. The expensive, time-consuming, and painful process of IELTS preparation and writing that my participants went through brought confusion to their learning and doubt about their investment in learning for the purposes of passing the test. Zoe questioned the power of the test as a gate-keeping mechanism used by the university. Her stories confirm Shohamy's (2001, 2013) and Yucel and Iwashita's (2017) assertions that the current application of standardized language tests in deciding the access of international students to tertiary institutions puts international students in disadvantaged positions with barely any space to negotiate. This also exacerbates the already unequal treatment that international students face in host countries. Further, the application of language tests reinforces the internalization by some international students of a self-image as deficient learners. The existing discourse of international students as problematic learners (Heng 2018) is therefore strengthened and perpetuated.

When language tests are used as a filter to determine who has the chance to get into an educational institution, or "as a rite of passage" (Shohamy 2001), what these tests measure is the social, cultural, or linguistic capital of test-takers, but not their academic abilities. As demonstrated above, Kaddy and Zoe had to earn different scores in IELTS for access to different learning communities.

In pursuing the dream identities of international students in the EBP Program and at SFU, Kaddy and Zoe perceive IELTS test scores as tickets without which their pursuit of academic qualifications is impossible. IELTS test scores are transformed into cultural capital that my participants keep seeking. Their entrance into different levels of learning is solely decided by the capital, or the test score, that they possess. The increase of the test score will help accumulate capital, which will lead to attainment of more cultural capital: the admission to university. As Shohamy (2001) proposes, language tests function more than an assessment tool as they decide the learning paths of international students while shaping how they perceive themselves as language learners and test-takers. More importantly, their understandings of themselves as Chinese international students are negatively impacted.

Kaddy and Zoe questioned the function of the IELTS test as the gate-keeping mechanism of the university; to them, when the university adopts such an entrance mechanism, the institution lacks knowledge of the test as a filter and its impacts on international students as test-takers. However, while acknowledging the problems with language tests, they both expressed their helplessness and felt they had no choice but to comply and write the test. IELTS-related narratives also showed how the participants were forced to learn to "play the testing game" (Shohamy 2007, 523) that was not "under their control" at all. They also suffered from the "the detrimental consequences" of unsatisfactory test performance, which transformed them into "winners and losers, successes and failures, rejections and acceptance" (Shohamy 2007, 523). It is evident that the participants as test-takers and international students have internalized the irresistible power of tests and are rendered invisible and voiceless in the hegemonic relationship between tests and test-takers.

Capital, Field, and Investment

Language learners, according to Norton, invest in learning a language to gain symbolic resources (e.g., language, education, and friendship) and material resources, or various forms of capital. All practices that language learners perform as social actors are within the field that they dwell in. Capital or resources in that field will frame power and bring recognition and benefit to the actors. But as capital is fluid, dynamic, and subject to the ideology of a specific field (Darvin and Norton 2015), the capital that language learners invest to gain in one field may not be as valuable in another. Kaddy and Zoe's IELTS test-related experiences before entering SFU are taking place in one field, but SFU classrooms in various disciplines are another field. When they moved into the field of the university after they achieved the satisfactory IELTS scores, those test-coping strategies, or the capital that enabled them to pass the gate-keeping test and gain the power to enter SFU, turned out to be largely irrelevant, if not useless, in the new field of academic study in the university. Whichever academic field they entered, they had virtually no power. Those who control the fields, I argue, are not aware of, nor concerned about, this lack of power.

Kaddy and Zoe's learning paths were predetermined by the different levels of test scores that different academic programs or institutions require: 5.0 to enter EBP and 6.0 on the exit IELTS test plus success in the EBP program to enter SFU, and 6.5 to be exempt from the noncredit language course for international students. A score of 7.0 is needed to enter an MA program. The 5.0, 6.0, 6.5, and 7.0 are different gate-keeping thresholds that stood mercilessly along these students' learning paths. More importantly, the test requirements framed the participants' understanding of their IELTS scores.

Kaddy and Zoe's IELTS stories showed that as language learners they invested immensely in preparing for and writing IELTS tests across borders in China and in Canada. Their investment included lengthy preparation (ranging from one to four years), costly expenses in taking preparation courses, and writing the test multiple times in different locations. The great impetus behind their investment was their belief that a certain score in IELTS would lead them to certain capital they desired and allow them access to the communities they wanted to enter. In working hard to achieve IELTS marks, they in fact considered these IELTS scores as symbolic resources which would enable them to enter SFU as legitimate students with increased symbolic power. Norton (1995, 2001) has written about how language learners invest in their social identity when investing in a target language. What Kaddy and Zoe worked hard to achieve went beyond the score itself. They were hoping to get the "ticket" to a desired college or university, where they could gain and increase their symbolic resources and get the credential.

Imagining who they would become in different communities also drove them to invest in learning for different purposes. Before they were conditionally enrolled at SFU, they imagined their identity as an SFU student. While in the EBP, they yearned for the status of an official SFU student. While in different programs at the university, they looked forward to their future identities as successful university graduates, legitimate working visa holders, and eventually permanent residents and even Canadian citizens. To achieve the desirable identities at different stages of study always involved English learning and sometimes test writing (they need to write a general IELTS test to become a

Canadian citizen). How and how much they exerted effort and invested in learning was affected by who they would become in the next stage of learning. This aligns with the research studies showing that international students are complex social beings with agency whose investment in learning English was decided by their desires and needs (McKay and Wong 1996; Yashima 2013). It also proves that the language learning of international students is complex and involves motivation, identity, investment transformation (Gu 2008), and future identity negotiations. Participants of this study exerted agency and selectively invested in studies that would increase their capital in their envisioned future communities (Y. C. Chang 2016; Y. J. Chang 2011; Liu and Tannacito 2013).

Kaddy and Zoe came to the university with the expectation that their English proficiency as demonstrated by the IELTS test scores was sufficient to make them successful university students. To achieve this goal, they strategically invested in different learning settings (EBP, test preparation classes, various programs at SFU, and the college transfer program) and invested considerable effort to gain legitimate access to and participate in different communities. Their selective investment confirms Norton's view that investment underscores how agency and identity work when language learners are engaged with the task at hand, which, in this case, was preparing for the IELTS test (Darvin and Norton 2015). Also, their strategic investment shows that the investment of language learners could be "complex, contradictory, and in a state of flux" (Norton 2013, 159). Such strategic investment also confirms Y. J. Chang's (2011) suggestion that international students used their agency "to fight their academic battle" (228).

Conclusion and Pedagogical Implications

In this chapter, I presented IELTS test-related stories of two participants, Kaddy and Zoe. Their English test writing and preparation experiences shaped their perceptions of test writing, English learning, and their identities. In doing so, I wished to highlight some of the voices of test-takers that were muffled in writing the test. I argue that individual test-takers fumbling alone in writing English tests suffer from great pressure that may lead to their undervaluation of themselves as whole and complex beings. Meanwhile, these accounts also offer stakeholders in the field of testing an opportunity to become aware of the impacts of the tests on test-takers. These accounts can offer test designers, test delivery organizations, and those who rely on test results a lens to understand the impacts of the tests on people who take them, thus allowing stakeholders in testing to develop expanded perspectives on test features and their impact. I am not hopeful, however, in this outcome given the profitable business this field has become. What I am hopeful for is that professors and language instructors could become aware that satisfactory English test scores that earn international students their university admission but do not transfer to academic English proficiency needed in the university classrooms automatically. They need support for the transition to happen. Institutions should take these considerations into account in their internationalization practices.

For decades, there has been much literature on the challenges and difficulties faced by nonnative English-speaking international students in English-speaking host countries. Developing coping mechanisms to survive these challenges and difficulties has become normalized for these students in order to achieve success. To support them, activities, programs, and socialization initiatives should be offered throughout the entire learning process in a university, starting from the initial orientations that support their transition to the university, to workshops that facilitate their transition from the university to the workplace, for example. Many test-takers who have invested a lot to enter the university need specific support to transition from learning English for test-taking purposes to developing academic English that is relevant to the disciplines they are pursuing their degree in. Considering the diversity and complexity of international students, host colleges and universities should think outside the box of general admission requirements and search for more inclusive and adjustable criteria.

It is my hope that this chapter will inspire educational institutions hosting international students speaking different native languages to reconsider the practice of accepting international students based on high-stakes language test results. Institutions that use high-stakes English tests are participating in the creation and perpetuation of the inequality of languages while promoting the marketization of such English tests (Shohamy 2013). Additionally, English as a language with more desirable capital is perpetuated and the inequality of languages is reproduced. Therefore, I would conclude this chapter by inviting higher education institutions to consider and act on the following questions: How can institutions hosting international students recruit eligible international students without relying on such high-stakes English tests? Is it possible to create approaches and procedures taking into consideration individual applicants while reviewing their qualifications? These and other questions will continue to guide my research and practices with international students in Canada.

Notes

1 TOEFL: Test of English as a Foreign Language, a standardized English ability test for nonnative English speakers who wish to enter English-speaking institutions for academic studies, is another one of the major English language tests in the world that is designed and administered by the Educational Testing Service.
2 IELTS: The International English Language Testing System, an international standardized test of English language proficiency for nonnative English language speakers, is one of the major English tests widely used by many educational institutions in the world to assess the English proficiency of international students.
3 The EBP was an academic English program designed for international students whose English proficiency did not meet the requirement of SFU. Students were conditionally admitted to SFU when they enrolled in this program. The program has since been canceled.

References

Bourdieu, Pierre. 1986. "The Forms of Capital." In *Handbook of Theory and Research for the Sociology of Education*, edited by John G. Richardson, 241–258. New York: Greenwood Press.
Bourdieu, Pierre. 1991. *Language and Symbolic Power*. Cambridge: Harvard University Press.
Canadian Bureau for International Education (CBIE). 2015. "A World of Learning: Canada's Performance and Potential in International Education." Canadian Bureau for International Education (CBIE). http://net.cbie.ca/download/A%20World%20of %20Learning%202015%20-%20high%20res.pdf.
Canadian Bureau for International Education (CBIE). 2018. "International Students in Canada." https://cbie.ca/wp-content/uploads/2018/09/International-Students-in -Canada-ENG.pdf.
Canada International Student Statistics. Erudera 2022 (October). https://erudera.com/ statistics/canada/canada-international-student-statistics/.
Chang, Yu-Jung. 2011. "Picking One's Battles: NNES Doctoral Students' Imagined Communities and Selections of Investment." *Journal of Language, Identity & Education* 10, no. 4: 213–230. https://doi.org/10.1080/15348458.2011.598125.
Chang, Yueh-Ching. 2016. "Discourses, Identities and Investment in English as a Second Language Learning: Voices from two US Community College Students." *International Journal of Education and Literacy Studies* 4, no. 4: 38–49.
Darvin, Ron, and Bonny Norton. 2015. "Identity, Investment, and Pedagogy in Transcultural Cosmopolitan Times." Literacy in Transcultural, Cosmopolitan Times, Calgary, Canada. https://werklund. ucalgary.ca/ltct/files/ltct/darvin-norton.pdf.

Gao, Xuesong, Huiman Cheng, and Peter Kelly. 2008. "Supplementing an Uncertain Investment?: Mainland Chinese Students Practising English Together in Hong Kong." *Journal of Asian Pacific Communication* 18, no. 1: 9–29. https://doi.org/10.1075/japc.18.1.02gao.

Grimshaw, Trevor. 2011. "Concluding Editorial: 'The Needs of International Students Rethought–Implications for the Policy and Practice of Higher Education.'" *Teachers and Teaching* 17, no. 6: 703–712. https://doi.org/10.1080/13540602.2011.625147.

Gu, Mingyue. 2008. "Identity Construction and Investment Transformation: College Students from Non-urban Areas in China." *Journal of Asian Pacific Communication* 18, no. 1: 49–70.

Gubrium, Jaber F., and James A. Holstein. 2009. *Analyzing Narrative Reality*. London: Sage.

Heng, Tang T. 2018. "Different Is not Deficient: Contradicting Stereotypes of Chinese International Students in US Higher Education." *Studies in Higher Education* 43, no. 1: 22–36. https://doi.org/10.1080/03075079.2016.1152466.

Huang, Ju, Haojun Guo, and Qiutong Zhou. 2022. "A Narrative Inquiry of Three Chinese International Students' Academic Adjustment Experiences at Canadian universities." *Journal of Teaching and Learning* 16, no. 2: 107–122.

Ilieva, Roumi. 2010. "Non-native English–speaking Teachers' Negotiations of Program Discourses in their Construction of Professional Identities within a TESOL Program." *Canadian Modern Language Review* 66, no. 3: 343–369. https://doi.org/10.3138/cmlr.66.3.343.

Ilieva, Roumiana, and Bonnie Waterstone. 2013. "Curriculum Discourses Within a TESOL Program for International Students: Affording Possibilities for Academic and Professional Identities." *TCI (Transnational Curriculum Inquiry)* 10, no. 1: 16–37.

Jin, Lixian, and Martin Cortazzi.1995. "A Cultural Synergy Model for Academic Language Use." In *Explorations in English for professional communication*, edited by Paul Bruthiaux, Tim Boswood, and Du-Babcock Bertha, 41–56. Hong Kong: City Publication.

Liu, Pei-Hsun Emma, and Dan J. Tannacito. 2013. "Resistance by L2 Writers: The Role of Racial and Language Ideology in Imagined Community and Identity Investment." *Journal of Second Language Writing* 22, no. 4: 355–373. https://doi.org/10.1016/j.jslw.2013.05.001.

Ma, Junqian. 2017. "Cooperative Activity as Mediation in the Social Adjustment of Chinese International Students." *Journal of International Students* 7, no. 3: 856–875. https://doi.org/10.5281/zenodo.570038.

Marginson, Simon. 2014. "Student Self-formation in International Education." *Journal of Studies in International Education* 18, no. 1: 6–22. https://doi.org/10.1177/1028315313513036.

McKay, Sandra Lee, and Sau-Ling Cynthia Wong. 1996. "Multiple Discourses, Multiple Identities: Investment and Agency in Second-Language Learning among Chinese Adolescent Immigrant Students." *Harvard Educational Review* 66, no. 3: 577–609.

Montgomery, Catherine. 2010. *Understanding the International Student Experience*. London: Macmillan International Higher Education.

Norton, Bonny. 1995. "Social Identity, Investment, and Language Learning." *TESOL Quarterly* 29, no. 1: 9–31.

Norton, Bonny. 2001. *Identity and Language Learning: Gender, Ethnicity and Educational Change*. Boston, MA: Allyn & Bacon.

Norton, Bonny. 2013. *Identity and Language Learning: Extending the Conversation*. Toronto: Multilingual Matters.

Peirce, Bonny Norton. 1995. "Social Identity, Investment, and Language Learning." *TESOL Quarterly* 29, no. 1: 9–31.

Riessman, Catherine Kohler. 2008. *Narrative Methods for the Human Sciences*. Thousand Oaks: Sage.

Shohamy, Elana. 2001. *The Power of Tests: A Critical Perspective on the Uses of Language Tests*. Harlow: Longman.

Shohamy, Elana. 2007. "The Power of Language Tests, the Power of the English Language and the Role of ELT." In *International Handbook of English Language Teaching*, edited by Jim Cummins, and Chris Davison, 521–531. Boston: Springer US.

Shohamy, Elana. 2013. "The Discourse of Language Testing as a Tool for Shaping National, Global, and Transnational Identities." *Language and Intercultural Communication* 13, no. 2: 225–236.

Wang, Yina. 2012. "Transformations of Chinese International Students Understood through a Sense of Wholeness." *Teaching in Higher Education* 17, no. 4: 359–370.

Yashima, Tomoko. 2013. "Imagined L2 Selves and Motivation for Intercultural Communication." In *Language Learning Motivation in Japan*, edited by Matthew T. Apple, Dexter Da Silva, and Terry Fellner, 35–53. Bristol, UK: Multilingual Matters.

Ye, Lily, and Viv Edwards. 2015. "Chinese Overseas Doctoral Student Narratives of Intercultural Adaptation." *Journal of Research in International Education* 14, no. 3: 228–241. https://doi.org/10.1177/1475240915614934.

Yu, Yuqing. 2014. "A study on Chinese Learners' IELTS Preparation Efforts." *HKU Theses Online (HKUTO)*. Retrieved from https://hub.hku.hk/bitstream/10722/209680/1/FullText.pdf.

Yucel, Megan, and Noriko Iwashita. 2017. "The IELTS Roller Coaster: Stories of Hope, Stress, Success, and Despair." In *Narrative Research in Practice: Stories from the Field*, edited by Rachael Dwyer, Ian Davis, and Elke Emerald, 209–223. Singapore: Springer.

Zhang, Zhihua. 2017. "Past Expectations, Current Experiences, and Imagined Futures: Narrative Accounts of Chinese International Students in Canada." PhD diss., Simon Fraser University.

Zhang, Zhihua, and Kumari Beck. 2017. "Seeking Sanctuary: Chinese Student Experiences of Mobility and English Language Learning in Canada." *International Journal of Chinese Education* 6, no. 2: 176–209. https://doi.org/10.1163/22125868-12340080.

Zhou, George, Tian Liu, and Glenn Rideout. 2017. "A Study of Chinese International Students Enrolled in the Master of Education Program at a Canadian University: Experiences, Challenges, and Expectations." *International Journal of Chinese Education* 6, no. 2: 210–235. https://doi.org/10.1163/22125868-123400.

4

Internationalization as Intercultural Capital or "I Feel I Am a Cultural Transformer"

Aisha Ravindran (posthumous manuscript) and Roumiana Ilieva

This chapter, completed by Roumi, aims to keep true to Aisha's powerful scholarly voice and writing style. An incredible intellectual and a wonderful friend, Aisha was my supervisee and a research assistant on the study discussed here. The chapter is based on work Aisha did as the first author on several conference proposals and presentations on the project. In completing the chapter, I have kept most of her own words and see my contribution primarily as updating some of the literature and making sure that the overall thread of developing/enacting "intercultural capital" as the main construct guiding the analysis comes across in a coherent way.

Introduction and Context

The development of English as a language of global significance in the last several decades is an important factor motivating an increasing number of students to seek academic and professional credentials in Anglo-dominant universities (Chowdhury and Phan 2014; Lin and Motha 2021; Park and Wee 2012; Ravindran and Ilieva 2020). The growing influx of international students in higher education settings in Britain, Australia, and North America (BANA) is seen as a vital source for increasing economic capital in these countries (De Vita and Case 2003; Global Affairs Canada 2016; Sabzalieva et al. 2022, and others).

This study was conducted in the context of increased interest at the federal government level to attract a significant number of international students to Canada and specifically the government policies that position international students as an economic resource. The first education strategy of the Government of Canada (DFATD 2014) aimed to attract 450,000 students by the year 2022 and create new jobs and opportunities for Canadians through international education. More specifically, the goal was to create 86,500 net new jobs for a total of 173,100 jobs in Canada, see international student expenditures in Canada rise to over $16.1 billion, generate approximately $910 million in new tax revenues, and provide an annual boost to the Canadian economy of almost $10 billion.

The most recent numbers provided by the Canadian Bureau for International Education indicate that in 2022 there was a total of 807,750 international students in Canada across all levels of education (CBIE 2023), a number suggesting that Canada surpassed the anticipated increase well ahead of 2022. Even though there has been a decrease of 17 percent in the number of international students from 2019 to 2020, most likely attributed to the significant impact of the COVID-19 pandemic on student mobility, statistics in 2022 point to an overall growth of 43 percent over the previous five years and nearly 170 percent over the last decade (CBIE 2023). In the most recent Canadian Strategy for International Education (2019–24), the discourse of the economic benefits of internationalization continues to dominate the document with international education viewed as "an essential pillar of Canada's long-term competitiveness" (Global Affairs Canada 2019) where "[c]ompetitor countries in this sector . . . have upped their game, and to remain competitive, we upped our game too" (GAC 2019). Thus, the currently operating strategy builds on the first one and continues to prioritize international education as a commodity for economic gains. In this context, a key question to address might be the extent to which this economic impact compares with less tangible aspects of mobility in Canada like the experiences of international students settling in the country postgraduation.

The Ambivalent Position of the International Student

Despite their economic value, the position of international students postgraduation remains ambivalent as discussed in academic literature. Simmons (2010) uses the term "designer immigrants" to designate international students, as with the academic credentials acquired at higher education institutions, and the acquisition of linguistic proficiency and the skills to maneuver within the social and cultural contexts in Canada, they appear to be "custom designed" to seamlessly integrate into the host country meeting the criteria "of a neoliberal nation" (85). The objective is the creation of "ideal candidates for economic immigration" (Belkhodjia and Esses 2013, 3). However, according to Erika Gates-Gasse (2010), and as can be presumed from the government statistics shared above, their status is equivalent to goods and services, as they are commodified and somewhat dehumanized. Current research literature on international students provides us with data on various academic, social, cultural, and workplace challenges they face in Canada and other BANA contexts. Scott et al. (2015) share data from focus group interviews with international students in higher education institutions in Ontario and conclude that participants' integration into the labor market is impeded by difficulties in adjustment with regard to language abilities, limited connections to the host communities, and perceived discrimination by employers toward international students. A recent study by Sabzalieva et al. (2022) argues that international students are subjected to paradoxical discourses as while they are potentially selected as ideal immigrants, they are vulnerable to shifting immigration policies that might cause them to "fail" in achieving immigration status. In addition, while being perceived as ideal candidates to fill in national economic shortages, they commonly face difficulties in the labor market. Last, but not least, while international students "help build national reputation[,] . . . [they] have been known to be exploited and subject to discrimination" (178).

Overall, government and institutional policy documents and targeted marketing strategies routinely construct international students as somewhat of a homogenous group with regard to their linguistic and academic competences or social abilities to navigate the cultural expectations within a host country. This is also reflected in much of the literature on international students in Canada, where their experiences around academic, social, or professional socialization are constructed in relation to overcoming deficiencies as they are perceived as the Other within a deficit model (Belkhodja and Esses 2013; Huang and Klinger 2006; Nunes and Arthur 2013; Vasilopoulos 2016). In addition, international students are often discursively represented as "individuals trapped by their desires and choices in the host country" (Ravindran and Ilieva 2020, 111; see also Chowdhury and Phan 2014). In this chapter, we would like to move beyond a focus on the difficulties international students face when settling in a BANA country postgraduation and explore their agency in carving productive spaces for their professional lives in their new environment.

Theoretical Perspectives

The theoretical framework that undergirds our study has three major strands. The first is the work of Jonas Stier (2004, 2010), who discusses three ideologies of internationalization, namely those of idealism, instrumentalism, and educationalism, with all three embedding assumptions regarding the goal and objectives of higher education, especially within a globalized context. Idealism refers to a view that internationalization is "good per se" (2004, 88). Its aim is global cooperation through academia with the purpose to contribute to growth in cohesion and harmony; its essential desirability is due to its ability to generate and inculcate values and qualities to address global inequities. Instrumentalism focuses on international mobility between educational institutions for economic and cultural objectives and the development of appropriate skills and competencies to contribute to the economic exigencies of a capitalist global world in creating a highly competitive marketable global workforce. Educationalism values lifelong learning and personal growth and the development of enhanced multicultural understandings through awareness of diverse academic and cultural contexts. Stier presents a balanced perspective by offering critiques of these ideologies, as they also possess characteristics that perpetuate colonial discourses and power hierarchies. Idealism reflects monolithic ethnocentric ideas and Western cultural imperialism. Instrumentalism promotes the commodification of education through standardizing curricula and leading to the homogenization of cultures, and educationalism may result in "academicentrism," which privileges one academic context over others and solutions for global problems ensuing from wealthy countries in the Global North.

As this chapter focuses on the strategies of some TESOL program graduates in their working environments in Canada, following their cross-cultural experiences in a Canadian university, we found very useful the work of Pöllmann (2013, 2016) on intercultural capital, which is said to be acquired through both intra- and interpersonal means. Drawing on Bourdieu's typology of diverse kinds of capital (1991), Pöllmann (2013) states that "[w]hat distinguishes cultural and intercultural forms of capital is their relative degree of field-transcendence" (2). Moreover,

> intercultural capital in the embodied state, . . . may, at first glance, appear as yet another linguistic variant of similar and already well-established terminologies such as intercultural competence, intercultural communication skills, or intercultural sensitivity. In fact, the notion of embodied intercultural capital— . . . expressly entails intercultural skills, competencies, and sensitivities. However, inspired by Bourdieu's work, it does not solely relate to intercultural proficiencies as such, but also to their relative exchange value and the circumstances under which they are more or less likely to be realized. (2)

Of particular importance for making sense of the data that addresses the impact of the TESOL program on our study participants, which we share below, we also find the following line of thought: "[i]ntercultural capital can be realized in terms of (a combination of) awareness, acquisition, and application" (Pöllmann 2013, 2).

Other theories we draw on are those related to the enactment of agency within "third spaces." Bhabha's (1994, 2009) concept of third space is engendered through cultural hybridity and cultural translation where the individual, carrying traces of past traditions and present changes, is also enunciating the possibilities of occupying other spaces of change and agentive action. In the meeting of cultures and different educational practices at the interstices of internationalization in the contexts of globalization, hybridity is enacted and "gives rise to something new and unrecognizable, a new era of meaning and representation" (Bhabha 2009, 211). Thus, hybridity or third space entails new possibilities, "new signs of identity" (Bhabha 1994, 1) and "new structures of authority" (Bhabha 2009, 211). In the context of language education, Kramsch (2011) views third place as the enactment of symbolic competence, "a process of positioning the self both inside and outside the discourse of others" (359). As symbolic competence, third place "involves a dynamic interplay between competing cultural (local and global) discourses and the act of cultural translation becomes a central activity in it" (Ilieva, Li, and Li 2015, 5). These are the processes being enacted at the threshold of intercultural capital acquisition and application.

Research Site and Methodological Notes

As mentioned in our discussion above on the ambivalent position of international students, our study is placed within a context where competing discourses communicate contradictory messages to the international student who, not completely unwittingly, subscribes to, as Andreotti, Stein, Pashby, and Nicolson (2016) have elucidated, a "global imaginary" embedded within a Western-centered capitalist and neocolonial agenda. The data for this chapter is drawn from a study entitled "International students as designer immigrants: Exploring the experiences of graduates of the TEF/SL program residing in Canada," which entailed conducting in-depth individual qualitative interviews with eleven graduates of a TESOL Master's program designed only for international students at a university in Western Canada. Study participants were originally from China, Korea, and Taiwan, but stayed in Canada postgraduation.

This TESOL program is housed within the Faculty of Education of a midsized university and is funded entirely through student fees. Thus, it is a cost-recovery program reflecting the dominance of neoliberal orientations in the context of higher education internationalization in BANA institutions. Instructors in the program have documented dilemmas they face in their attempts to navigate the commodification of international education at the same time as engaging in ethical practice with their students (Beck et al. 2007; Ilieva and Waterstone 2013). The program runs for four terms and consists of coursework, "fieldwork" including observations and practical involvement in Canadian classrooms both within the K-12 system and in adult settings, and a capstone comprehensive examination. The program enrolls around twenty students in a cohort, and its academic culture emphasizes group work, critical thinking, personal relevance, and making links between theory and practice. Housed in a faculty known for offering teacher education programs emphasizing self-reflection as paramount for becoming a professional teacher, the program invites students to engage in self-reflection in a consistent manner. The goal is to open up spaces where students negotiate their preprogram understandings of language teaching and learning with ideas and concepts introduced to them through the program curriculum. The program components that seem to attract applicants the most are the fieldwork opportunity and the cultural and academic literacy support offered throughout the duration of the program.

The main theoretical perspectives engaged with in this TESOL program include critical, sociocultural, and poststructural understandings around language teaching and language acquisition in the context of globalization, multilingualism, and the continued domination of English in a neocolonial world. Given the program's emphasis on self-reflection throughout, many of the readings and activities in program courses ask students to probe their teaching beliefs and aspirations and consider how the broader sociocultural and political contexts in which they live may impact these. As international students aspiring to become teachers of English, the students in the program are inevitably caught in the native/nonnative speaker of English dichotomy that seems to dominate societal as well as institutional settings in Anglo-dominant contexts (Jenkins 2013; Lin 2020, and others) and views so-called nonnative speakers as deficient. Thus, student experiences with the English language become a significant thread in their constructions of their professional identities and enactments in their work settings.

The data shared here comes from graduates from cohorts 2–8 of the program who had employment in Canada linked to educational activities spanning from six months to seven years at the time of the interviews. Many of the graduates were compelled to work at private ESL institutions or other business organizations motivated by objectives of financial profit, as they acquired work experience to enable them to apply for permanent residency in Canada. The presented data is from stories participants share about their experiences when reflecting on the program, their own classrooms, or related interactions in their workplace. The questions that we ponder over across the study participants' narratives (Barkhuzien 2013) are not related to institutionalized representations and processes of internationalization in the institution or the host country, but rather focus on articulations and enactments of internationalization by the students. More specifically, we discuss below the following: How do international students in this master's program respond to the constructs of idealism, instrumentalism, and educationalism, as ideology, "manifested as an unconscious frame for the individual" (Stier 2004, 85)? How does the graduate program create spaces for emergent subjective and personal ideologies to enable empowering engagement with dominant discourses, which frame international students through a deficit lens? How is internationalization redefined as intercultural capital through the self-perceived roles of the students as "cultural transformers"?

The transcribed interviews were coded for recurrent themes or patterns across the narratives following Saldaña's (2013) thematic analysis procedures. Offering valuable insights into "people's private worlds" (Pavlenko 2007, 164), narratives are considered "a powerful tool for self-reflection and exploration" (Reis 2015, 38), representing eloquently the ways in which these graduates make sense of their experiences and of themselves as agents in their academic and professional lives in Canada. The data excerpts below reflect succinct articulations of themes that appeared in the data.

Living Internationalization as Cultural Transformers

The data we share in this section attempts to outline what we consider our study participants' agentive redefinition of internationalization as they live it as "cultural transformers" in the TESOL program and beyond and not as the homogeneous group subjected to dominant discourses that construct them as deficient, which scholarly literature commonly refers to. Thus, the theoretical perspectives discussed above will be used to analyze the themes that reflect what we consider articulations of internationalization as intercultural capital as seen in excerpts from the interviews across the following three aspects:

intercultural relativity, hybridity in contextualized spaces, and performative identities.

Intercultural Relativity

In sharing her experiences in the TESOL program, Dawn appreciated the opportunity to be regularly involved in group work:

> while you are discussing, you can learn so much . . . from different people and something you've never even realized before. That's why we have to be aware of all those possibilities. You just have to learn to think by yourself and for yourself, because for me at least I feel the way I was taught before was to be fed with all those . . . perfect answers; you are not thinking; you are just accepting. . . . Awareness was the word repeated thousands of times throughout the program.

Being able to add to individual funds of knowledge commences with the instrumentalism generated through the activities in the program (e.g., engaging in class discussions), but it is the awareness one develops of such possibilities, and is persistently reminded of ("thousands of times"), that allows making sense of intercultural relativity and the expansion of one's repertoire of strategies to navigate cultural differences in educational practices and understandings. This awareness translates into conceptual awareness for maneuvering within culturally unmapped territories.

Intercultural literacy can be acquired through "interactions with culturally different others, the curriculum, or by learning in a foreign place" (Beck et al. 2013, 87). Our contention is that the same can be said about intercultural capital. Certainly, one way to learn about cultural difference and also gain intercultural capital to be employed in other contexts is to be involved in an enculturation process, like the one Jessica reflects on in sharing her thoughts on some content she came across in the program:

> Those were really social ideas and social concepts in the Canadian culture, because education is something really deeply rooted in a society. . . . I started to know how to communicate with Canadian friends, because all those ideas like multiculturalism and anti-racism, . . . after I understood those ideas, I could communicate with my Canadian friends much better. I started to understand the way they think and the way they perceive others, the way they perceive the outside environment.

Yet, as Jessica reflects on her experiences as an English textbook consultant in her workplace in Canada below, it looks like intercultural capital is not derived solely from enculturation.

Sometimes I didn't know, I just express myself, still with my Chinese cultural identity. Sometimes my manager told me that "Oh, Jessica, you have to be more firm, more aggressive and more direct about what you want." But it's interesting for me to also find that they really appreciate the soft power that you can demonstrate. . . . We can also negotiate or talk or communicate in a very soft polite way, in a very Chinese way. So we can achieve our goal. I think that's also part of international communication, we say internationalization today is more and more learning from each other.

Thus, there are opportunities to affirm one's own mode of interpersonal communicative behavior, despite diverging from the existing norm in the new cultural context. Together with gaining capital within the Canadian context, is the middle ground of intercultural relativity, where agentive choice resists the imposition of systemic structures around patterns of cultural behavior.

We would like to end this section with a quote from Melissa that speaks to the value and maneuverability associated with gaining and applying intercultural capital:

> I cannot move my social capital here and also my cultural capital. But what I can do is to expand my cultural and social capital here in Canada. . . . It's not like "oh, you always stay in your own culture. You don't observe any Canadian culture" or you are totally westernized. It's not that. I think it's a compromise.

Hybridity in Contextualized Spaces

The students in the program come with academic and professional qualifications from their home countries, but seek to increment their pedagogical repertoire and academic knowledge in Canada, reflecting an instrumental orientation. However, in the excerpts in this section, the participants share their experiences of hybridized spaces they dwell in in Canada as they acquire and apply intercultural capital. Kris reflects on how the program impacted her in being able to navigate Canadian work environments postgraduation.

> It was a self-discovery and the program doesn't just impose or tell you "This is the way we believe teaching should be." They don't use the word "should." The program was more like "So this is what people say about it and this is what other people say about it. What do you think about it?" So they kept on getting us connected to . . . new insights, connecting to yourself. . . . I think if the program [taught] "this is how you teach, this is what we do here, this is how I want you to teach," maybe it would have been more useful to get employment, but it won't

necessarily help you ... navigate the new context and the whole discourse of this new place.

Kris speaks about how the program did not impose goal-directed prescriptive understandings or meanings on the students, but created a space for agentive flexibility to develop, acknowledged difference, and allowed discursive interpretations of culture and agentive choice. This is also an example reflecting participants' awareness of some of the professional constraints within the discursive field of private ESL schools, which Kris and others were able to navigate successfully.

Elizabeth teaches IELTS courses in a language training school, which she describes as follows: "my job is to teach them like the test skills and improve their language level in a short period of time. So I wouldn't call it a school. It's more like an education industry, so very goal-oriented for profit." Yet she realizes skillfully her intercultural capital in this context, observing that:

> The IELTS test is just a one-time thing. After they get into the college, they have more difficulties and challenges to face. So they might have difficulties in writing academic essays and they might have difficulties communicating with their TAs and instructors. So these are the things I like to prepare them for. For example, I will tell them what it feels like to be a college student, because I had the experience. And I will tell them how could you negotiate with your classmates or team mates when there is a disagreement, because I had that before.

Thus, Elizabeth is creating a third space in her classrooms while she complies with institutional objectives and conforms to the school's financial and academic goals. She also brings in content that she considers important: "I think it's the balance between the institution['s] goals and my own teaching style. Because my school just wanted their students to pass. But I wanted my students to learn." In that manner, Elizabeth enacts her symbolic competence (Kramsch 2011) and establishes a new structure of authority (Bhabha 2009) in the IELTS classes she teaches.

Below, Jessica dwells on her hybrid place in Canada as she sees herself as contributing to the culture of her new environment and being able to think critically about the educational systems she has experienced because of how she has lived internationalization on her own terms within the TESOL program.

> So if you would like to demonstrate your cultural identity and find your place in Canada, you have to share your own culture, ... your own cultural background, which can contribute to the Canadian culture. So that is how internationalization happens. ... I wouldn't say that Chinese education is better than the Canadian

education. No, but there are advantages and some weaknesses in both, but we have to learn to find those strengths from both systems and try to combine them together. So I would think critically on both systems, which I couldn't do before, before I came here.

As seen in these interview excerpts, the participants generate new personal spaces, discursive convergences, and intercultural transactions that speak to their agency in living in hybridity.

Performative Identities

Our final theme reveals the various performative events where study participants' subjectivities emerge to challenge the existence of uncontested assumptions within widely circulating dominant discourses. Sarah, originally from Taiwan, relates some of her experiences in teaching English in Canada postgraduation.

> I encountered a few students, they would challenge you . . . They see you as . . . Oh, you don't look as I expected . . . they just judge me, you know, . . . So . . . I present myself professionally and then . . . I would tell them that I've been through the same experiences as you all. . . . A lot of my Taiwanese students actually see me as a model, they see me as "Okay, if she can speak as fluently as other people, then I can do that too." So that for me is a plus.

The excerpt above illustrates how Sarah was assessed on the basis of her physical appearance, and as some of her students connected teachers of English with specific racial characteristics, she was seen as being deficient. Sarah speaks about how her strategies overturned the existing dichotomy around who could be an English teacher so that she would emerge as a model to her students. In this process, she seems to be applying the intercultural capital she has acquired in performing the identity of a capable English teacher regardless of raciolinguistic ideologies circulating in her workspace, according to which racialized bodies are ascribed with linguistic deficiencies unrelated to linguistic practices (Flores and Rosa 2015).

Melissa shares how her students lack confidence in their abilities to speak English and makes connections to ideas around linguistic identities she was introduced to in the program.

> Because when we studied . . . there was an article about how we see ourselves, imagined identity, imagined community, and to see the value of bilingualism. So I really see now I'm bilingual and that's what I can do. . . . I always tell my students "Don't think that your English is bad. At least you can

speak English. . . . And you're educated." So I always tell my students to be confident in their own identity.

Melissa encounters the dominant discourse of native speaker/nonnative speaker dichotomy that positions her students as deficient, a discourse that is reflective of her own experiences and has been addressed in this TESOL program. Using concepts from the program that foregrounded her bilingual identity as one of empowerment, she shares with her students the counter-discourses that she developed to dismantle this hierarchy. In this process, she is able to apply the intercultural capital she acquired in living through the tensions of native speakerism (Holliday 2006) as an international student and as an English teacher in an Anglo-dominant context.

The question of identity, and its enactments, is constantly discussed throughout the program these graduates completed. The extracts from both Emma and Anita below represent their identities as emergent and dynamic, constituted and generated by social and cultural contexts and discursive processes (Norton 2013).

Anita speaks to the primordial role of engaging with program curriculum and related interactions in shaping who she is in her work life in Canada.

> I think the program has empowered me. I became more strong, strong and powerful than before . . . every discussion and every interaction with classmates and the professors shaped my new identity. It's hard to describe.

Emma articulates very clearly how she understands the importance of performing her identity in ways that serve her purposes in her teaching context in Canada.

> identity; it [the program] was a journey of discovery of myself and more importantly . . . I have to know who I am in terms of different context[s]. . . . It's the issue of how to better change your identity a little bit to fit perfectly in that context. It's a kind of identity shift. You have to know exactly what position you are in . . . to, you know, work things out. For example, before I started working, I've been . . . picturing some of my future teaching scenes, but in reality, it's totally different. . . . I think the most important thing for me now is like I said, is knowing my identity. But I have to go beyond that . . . and I have to be flexible. Because I'm dealing with different kinds of students, so I have to . . . have a lot of images in my teaching. . . . It's always about context and identity. That's very important.

Emma's words exemplify the combination of awareness, acquisition, and application of intercultural capital in relation to performance of the self (which is field-transcendent) that she was able to develop in the program.

Similarly, Muriel is performing her professional identity in ways that take into account the expectations about high grades that Chinese parents hold for their children, whom Melissa advises, to be able to apply to Ivy League universities in BANA. However, she believes it is very important to "give them more sense about the culture" and feels she is "a cultural transformer" in translating cultural expectations around activities like volunteering or the development of team skills for university applications. We conclude this section with a final excerpt from Muriel that emphasizes the enactment of theoretical perspectives introduced in the program. Despite admitting the need to conform to existing structures to become an immigrant in Canada, she also reiterates the possibilities of the performative value that membership in a community of practice (i.e., the program cohort she was a part of) promises in order to alter structural constraints with respect to educating other international students:

> So if we want to earn a living or survive here . . . we have to follow . . . their [private language schools] philosophy. But when my classmates and me . . . When we have like a party or we have . . . dinner together, we always think that after we get the PR [permanent resident] status, we will run our own school and we will do something that we have learned in our program. . . . And we [will] do it just for education, not for making money . . . we will run our own school to help the students . . . to learn for themselves, not for others' expectations.

Discussion and Implications

The data we shared above across three themes reveals that the graduates of this TESOL program are not unaware of the place that has been created for them in immigration policies and some workplace discourses, a place that they tend to legitimize by accepting the lure of education in the West. But it is interesting to note that once they encounter authoritative discourses and constraints that marginalize, they use the skills and knowledge they have acquired to contend with and counter them through counter-discursive strategies that display agentive choices and actions. While the TESOL program did not directly prepare the students for the challenges they face in integrating in Canada, they are well aware of various professional and social constraints within the discursive fields they maneuver in in the host country.

In a context where "educational actors are preoccupied with different aspects of internationalisation" (Stier 2004, 93), international students confront divergent and often contradictory perceptions of internationalization.

As the international graduates reflect on the impact of this TESOL program in affecting their transition to settlement in Canada, we see agentive individuals and subjects who take control of their discursive fields and navigate various economic, sociocultural, academic, and professional contexts through the creation of "third spaces" (Bhabha 1994). Such spaces of emergent intersubjective and personal ideologies intersect and transcend the broader discourses dominating internationalization in BANA contexts, with the redefinition of internationalization becoming an assertion of choice and agency.

In addition, our study participants visualize themselves as having a big stake in the new country of settlement. Having acquired the skills and competencies that grant them greater economic, symbolic, and intercultural capital, they straddle two worlds, seeking to conjoin the best in both within the various spaces they generate and inhabit. The students have the choice of returning home with broader and authentic experiences and capital, or settling within the host country. Their value lies in the cultural hybridization and intercultural translations they have realized. They perceive themselves as capable of enacting these processes in diverse contextualized spaces in academic, professional, social, and personal arenas, whether in the home or the host country as "cultural transformers."

Our study attempts to alter existing perceptions of international students as a homogenous group and suggests the need to validate their articulations of internationalization vis-à-vis theoretical and institutionalized representations as students redefine internationalization as intercultural capital through strategies for navigation and dialogue in multiple intercultural spaces. This allows for an expanded understanding of their position in the contexts of employment, settlement, and processes of immigration in Canada.

We also contemplate the broader implications this study has for program design so that international students are supported by the affordances of academic spaces that encourage the development of agentive identities capable of utilizing conceptual content from their programs in transformative ways. Given the focus on the development of intercultural capital, our recommendation is for higher education settings to "create learning environments that value a wide range of processes of intercultural capital realization" (Pöllmann 2016, 2). This would mean to consider programs attended by international students as spaces for the development of intercultural capital in terms of awareness, acquisition, and application. After all, "[t]he relative exchange value of individually embodied reservoirs of intercultural capital depends fundamentally on the realities and potentialities of their objectification and institutionalization within pertinent educational, sociocultural, and political fields" (Pöllmann 2016, 5).

References

Andreotti, Vanessa, Sharon Stein, Karen Pashby, and Michelle Nicolson. 2016. "Social Cartographies as Performative Devices in Research on Higher Education." *Higher Education Research & Development*. https://doi.org/10.1080/07294360.2015.1125857.

Barkhuizen, Gary Patrick. 2013. *Narrative Research in Applied Linguistics*. Cambridge: Cambridge University Press.

Beck, Kumari, Roumiana Ilieva, Ashley Pullman, and Zhihua Zhang. 2013. "New Work, Old Power: Inequities Within the Labor of Internationalization." *On the Horizon* 21, no. 2: 84–95. https://doi.org/10.1108/10748121311322987.

Beck, Kumari, Roumi Ilieva, Anne Scholefield, and Bonnie Waterstone. 2007. "Locating Gold Mountain: Cultural Capital and the Internationalization of Teacher Education." *Journal of the American Association for the Advancement of Curriculum Studies* 3. https://doi.org/10.14288/jaaacs.v3i0.187666.

Belkhodja, Chedly, and Victoria Esses. 2013. *Improving the Assessment of International Students' Contribution to Canadian Society*. Retrieved July 18, 2019, from http://p2pcanada.ca/wp-content/uploads/2014/02/International-Students-Contribution-to-Canadian-Society.pdf.

Bhabha, Homi. 1994. *The Location of Culture*. London: Routledge.

Bhabha, Homi. 2009. "In the Cave of Making: Thoughts on Third Space." In *Communicating in the Third Space*, edited by Karin Ikas and Gerhard Wagner, ix–xiv. London: Routledge.

Bourdieu, Pierre. 1991. *Language and Symbolic Power*. Cambridge: Harvard University Press.

Canadian Bureau of International Education. 2023. *Facts and Figures*. https://cbie.ca/media/facts-and-figures/.

Chowdhury, Raqib, and Phan Le Ha. 2014. *Desiring TESOL and International Education: Market Abuse and Exploitation*. Bristol: Multilingual Matters.

Department of Foreign Affairs, Trade and Development. 2014. *Canada's International Education Strategy: Harnessing Our Knowledge to Drive Innovation and Prosperity*.

De Vita, Glauco, and Peter Case. 2003. "Rethinking the Internationalisation Agenda in UK Higher Education." *Journal of Further and Higher Education* 27, no. 4: 383–398. https://doi.org/10.1080/0309877032000128082.

Flores, Nelson, and Jonathan Rosa. 2015. "Undoing Appropriateness: Raciolinguistic Ideologies and Language Diversity in Education." *Harvard Education Review* 85, no. 2: 149–171.

Gates-Gasse, Erika. 2010. *International Students as Immigrants: Literature Review and Good Practices*. Toronto: World Education Services.

Global Affairs Canada. 2016. *Economic Impact of International Education in Canada – 2016 Update*. Retrieved July 18, 2019, from http://www.international.gc.ca/education/report-rapport/impact-2016/references.aspx/lang=eng?lang=eng.

Global Affairs Canada. 2019. *Building on Success: International Education Strategy 2019–2024*. https://www.international.gc.ca/education/strategy-2019-2024-strategie.aspx?lang=eng.

Holliday, Adrian. 2006. "Native-speakerism." *ELT Journal* 60, no. 4: 385–387. https://doi.org/10.1093/elt/ccl030.

Huang, Jinyan, and Don Klinger. 2006. "Chinese Graduate Students at North American Universities: Learning Challenges and Coping Strategies." *Comparative and International Education (Ottawa, Ont.)* 35, no. 2. https://doi.org/10.5206/cie-eci.v35i2.9080.

Ilieva, Roumiana, Aojun Li, and Wanjun Li. 2015. "Negotiating TESOL Discourses and EFL Teaching Contexts in China: Identities and Practices of International Graduates of a TESOL Program." *Comparative and International Education (Ottawa, Ont.)* 44, no. 2. https://doi.org/10.5206/cie-eci.v44i2.9274.

Ilieva, Roumiana, and Bonnie Waterstone. 2013. "Curriculum Discourses Within a TESOL Program for International Students: Affording Possibilities for Academic and Professional Identities." *Transnational Curriculum Inquiry* 10, no. 1: 16–37.

Jenkins, Jennifer. 2013. *English as a Lingua Franca in the International University: The Politics of Academic English Language Policy*. United Kingdom: Routledge.

Kramsch, Claire. 2011. "The Symbolic Dimensions of the Intercultural." *Language Teaching* 44, no. 3: 354–367. https://doi.org/10.1017/S0261444810000431.

Lin, Angel M. Y. 2020. "From Deficit-based Teaching to Asset-based Teaching in Higher Education in BANA Countries: Cutting through 'Either-or' Binaries with a Heteroglossic Plurilingual Lens." *Language, Culture and Curriculum* 33, no. 2: 203–212. https://doi.org/10.1080/07908318.2020.1723927.

Lin, Angel M. Y., and Suhanthi Motha. 2021. "'Curses in TESOL': Postcolonial Desires for Colonial English." In *Rethinking Languages Education: Directions, Challenges and Innovations*, edited by Ruth Arber, Michiko Weinmann, and Jillian Blackmore. Abingdon, Oxon; New York: Routledge.

Nunes, Sarah, and Nancy Arthur. 2013. "International Students' Experiences of Integrating into the Workforce." *Journal of Employment Counseling* 50, no. 1: 34–45. https://doi.org/10.1002/j.2161-1920.2013.00023.x.

Norton, Bonny. 2013. *Identity and Language Learning: Extending the Conversation*. Bristol, Blue Ridge Summit: Multilingual Matters.

Park, Joseph Sung-Yul, and Lionel Wee. 2012. *Markets of English: Linguistic Capital and Language Policy in a Globalizing World*. New York: Routledge.

Pavlenko, Aneta. 2007. "Autobiographic Narratives as Data in Applied Linguistics." *Applied Linguistics* 28, no. 2: 163–188. https://doi.org/10.1093/applin/amm008.

Pöllmann, Andreas. 2013. "Intercultural Capital: Toward the Conceptualization, Operationalization, and Empirical Investigation of a Rising Marker of Sociocultural Distinction." *SAGE Open* 3, no. 2: 1–7. https://doi.org/10.1177/2158244013486117.

Pöllmann, Andreas. 2016. "Habitus, Reflexivity, and the Realization of Intercultural Capital: The (Unfulfilled) Potential of Intercultural Education." *Cogent Social Sciences* 2, no. 1: 1–12. https://doi.org/10.1080/23311886.2016.1149915.

Ravindran, Aisha, and Roumiana Ilieva. 2020. "Affective Affordances, Desires, and Assemblages: A Study of International Students in a TESOL Program in Canada." In *Deterritorializing Language, Teaching, Learning, and Research: Deleuzo-Guattarian Perspectives on Second Language Education*, edited by Francis Bangou, Monica Waterhouse, and Douglas Fleming, 110–132. Leiden; Boston: Brill Sense.

Reis, Davi. 2015. "Making Sense of Emotions in NNESTs' Professional Identities and Agency." In *Advances and Current Trends in Language Teacher Identity Research*, edited by Yin Ling Cheung, Selim Ben Said, and Kwanghyun Park, 31–43. New York: Routledge.

Sabzalieva, Emma, Amira El Masri, Anumoni Joshi, Melissa Laufer, Roopa Desai Trilokekar, and Christina Haas. 2022. "Ideal Immigrants in Name Only? Shifting Constructions and Divergent Discourses on the International Student-Immigration Policy Nexus in Australia, Canada, and Germany." *Policy Reviews in Higher Education* 6, no. 2: 178–204. https://doi.org/10.1080/23322969.2022.2096106.

Scott, Colin, Saba Safdar, Roopa Desai Trilokekar, and Amira El Masri. 2015. "International Students as 'Ideal Immigrants' in Canada: A Disconnect Between Policy Makers' Assumptions and the Voices of International Students." *Canadian and International Education* 43, no. 3: 1–6. https://doi.org/10.5206/cie-eci.v43i3.9261.

Saldaña, Johnny. 2013. *The Coding Manual for Qualitative Researchers*. Los Angeles, CA; London: Sage Publications.

Simmons, Alan. 2010. *Immigration and Canada: Global and Transnational Perspectives*. Toronto: Canadian Scholars' Press.

Stier, Jonas. 2004. "Taking a Critical Stance Toward Internationalization Ideologies in Higher Education: Idealism, Instrumentalism and Educationalism." *Globalisation, Societies and Education* 2, no. 1: 1–28. https://doi.org/10.10801/14767720420001777069.

Stier, Jonas. 2010. "International Education: Trends, Ideologies and Alternative Pedagogical Approaches." *Globalisation, Societies and Education* 8, no. 3: 339–349. https://doi.org/10.1080/14767724.2010.505095.

Vasilopoulos, Gene. 2016. "A Critical Review of International Students' Adjustment Research from a Deleuzian Perspective." *Journal of International Students* 6, no. 1: 283–307. https://doi.org/10.32674/jis.v6i1.570.

5

Pre-service Teachers' Experiences of Learning with/in Cultural Difference in Study Abroad

Jas K. Uppal-Hershorn and Kumari Beck

Introduction

Along with the intensification of internationalization of higher education globally, study abroad has become more prevalent in higher education institutions. Here in the Global North, study abroad refers to domestic students going abroad for short-term academic programs in another country, whereas elsewhere, the term commonly refers to all academic student mobility, including full-length degree programs in a country outside one's own (Cushner and Karim 2004). International experience is claimed to provide opportunities for intercultural learning, experiential learning, developing global citizenship, supporting career aspirations, and becoming globally and internationally minded (Canadian Bureau of International Education 2016; Tiessen and Huisch 2014). Other reasons for study abroad are to help students shape new perceptions of their identities (Malewski and Phillion 2009), to become more aware of geopolitical networks of privilege and their relation to educational equity (Phillion et al. 2009), to practice self-reflexivity (Sharma 2009), and gain skills to respond competitively to a shifting global market (Study Group on Global Education 2017).

A majority of Canadian universities (97 percent) offer study abroad programs (AUCC 2014) including opportunities for an international practicum. An internationally located teaching practicum is offered in more than half of the fifty-one Canadian teacher education programs (Larsen 2016) and one-third of teacher education programs in British Columbia (BC). The main goal of these programs is to prepare teachers to effectively teach in pluralistic classrooms at home by having a teaching practicum experience in a location that is culturally different (Larsen 2016), assumingly leading to intercultural learning (Vande Berg, Paige, and Hemming Lou 2012).

Given the sparse research on intercultural learning in an internationally located practicum, Jas's interest was in investigating pre-service teachers' (PST) experiences in a practicum setting characterized by significant cultural difference. The research featured in this chapter highlights Jas's study on PSTs' experiences in a teaching practicum in India. The study was guided by the following questions: How does the international experience inform PSTs' understandings of teaching, learning, and cultural difference? How might the PSTs' experiences inform teacher educators' considerations of curricular approaches for international teaching practica?

A brief overview of the literature on study abroad in teacher education is presented first, followed by the theoretical frames used in the study. The data are presented under the themes that emerged from PSTs' predeparture imaginings and expectations, recollections of the international practicum, and reflections on their learning. The chapter concludes with a summary of the findings on intercultural dynamics emerging from the study and implications for study abroad in teacher education.

Study Abroad and Teacher Education

Much of the literature on international practica in teacher education presents a good news story of the PST experience. Some studies find that PSTs learn adaptability, flexibility, and to go with the flow (Babaeff 2017; Cushner 2007; Kulkarni and Hanley-Maxwell 2015). In other studies, PSTs demonstrate resourcefulness (Cushner and Mahon 2009; Maynes et al. 2012) and experience greater tolerance for ambiguity and self-confidence (Ingersoll et al. 2019). These studies confirm the effectiveness and usefulness of the international practicum for PSTs. Some studies, however, identify the limitations of such experiences. Seeing the international practicum only as a one-sided positive experience for the Global North PSTs as a unidirectional benefit (Babaeff 2017; Maynes et al. 2012; Pence & Macgillivray 2008; Tripp et al 2020) conceals the complications of uneven power relations and overlooks the need to address systemic harm (Andreotti 2016). In addition, reductionist views of culture disregard power inequities in intercultural relations (Tarc 2013) as the concept of the "intercultural" tends to focus on "contact" and "exchange" between groups, largely assuming equal power relations between cultural groups (Black and Bernardes 2014).

There has been a growing critique of power relations in study abroad in general, bringing attention to voyeurism, the touristic gaze, and "saving the poor" or "White savior" attitude (Andreotti 2016; Jefferess 2012). The Association of the Canadian Deans of Education supports international practica to build/enhance future teachers' capacities to teach in pluralistic classrooms in Canada (ACDE 2017), but warns there are risks associated with potentially reproducing colonial attitudes and practices in teacher education (ACDE 2014). Inequitable power relations are an inherent feature of the teacher–student relationship within the Canadian classroom, as students mostly identify with minority groups and teachers with the dominant group (Sensoy and DiAngelo 2017). These hegemonic relationships are likely to be reflected in each intercultural encounter within the international context.

These critiques highlight that understanding intercultural learning in study abroad is inadequate without a close examination of power inequities and dynamics in the intercultural encounter. A few studies employ theoretical frames that center power relations (Bernardes et al. 2019; Trilokekar and Kukar 2011) or apply frames that emerge from differing ontological and epistemological orientations (Mwebi and Brigham 2009). There has been little substantive or nuanced analysis, however, of the pedagogical experiences (Larsen and Searle 2017; Smolcic and Katunich 2017) enacted in study abroad contexts. One Canadian study highlights that personal and professional dimensions are interlinked in intercultural encounters (Ingersoll et al. 2019), although even in this study, the nuances of the pedagogical dynamics are not illuminated.

Discomfort is considered significantly pedagogical in the encounter with difference in study abroad (Merryfield 2000; Scholefield 2006; Tarc 2013). Kumashiro (2015) argues that an emotional crisis ensues when one discovers that one's understanding of the world is limited. This discovery is emotionally disruptive, but, as Kumashiro argues, this feeling of discomfort is essential for the learning process. However, only a few researchers explore PSTs' experiences of discomfort. For example, Trilokekar and Kukar (2011) explore discomforting experiences associated with racialization without attending to subjectivity. While Druissi (2019) illuminates the PSTs' emotional-subjective experience of discomfort, the power relations are not examined in depth. Wong (2015) also argues for the need to understand intercultural learning that includes ontological shifts, such as students' capacity to take chances, access their intuition, and trust their creative impulses and inspiration (Wong 2018). In summary, the exploration of the intercultural encounter in teacher education as an experience that illustrates pedagogical dynamics in study abroad has potential to unveil concealed but valuable curricular insights that have not been addressed in the literature to date.

Theorizing Study Abroad

To understand the complex pedagogical dynamics within intercultural encounters that are marked by cultural differences, this study employs several concepts and theoretical approaches: cultural difference from an interstitial perspective (Bhabha 1994; Anzaldúa 1987), curriculum as multiplicity (Aoki 2005), and stop moments (Appelbaum 1995).

Cultural difference is often understood from "superior" versus "inferior" orientations emerging from dualistic thinking, and those whose ways differ from superior practices are positioned as inferior and only accommodated within the frames of the culturally dominant group (Bhabha 1994). Bhabha's (1994) problematization of this view of difference is an important framework to disrupt inherited inequitable power relations. Bhabha (1994) theorizes cultural difference as enunciated in the moment, as a lived relational process that challenges difference as fixed. This objectified way of recognizing difference is characterized by rigid designated categories of culture and race that reinforce a judgmental lens. Bhabha's (1994) conceptualization of interstitial space is an invitation to go beyond a confined way of relating to an encounter with difference. Interstitiality opens up a space "that entertains difference without an assumed or imposed hierarchy" (Bhabha 1994, 5). In this interstitial space, there is a sense of disorientation, disturbance of direction, a restlessness, a movement of neither here nor there; in other words, it is inherently uncertain, unpredictable, and contested.

Two related concepts support the discussion of learning with and in cultural difference. Similar to Bhabha's notion of interstitiality, Anzaldúa discusses cross-cultural encounters as involving literal or figurative borders crossed and describes them as a "vague and undetermined place created by the emotional residue at an invisible boundary" (Anzaldúa 1987, 25). Anzaldúa's scholarship is complementary to Bhabha's work, bringing attention to a social space "in constant state of transition," the place in which cultures meet, interact, and emotions are experienced (Anzaldúa 1987, 25). Another concept that informs the data analysis below is Appelbaum's notion of the "stop moment." Appelbaum's (1995) stop moment is explained as those instances in which one is taken aback; they are abrupt moments when one is confronted with what cannot be avoided. These stop moments are disruptive spaces that create both emotional and cognitive confusion because common sense cannot be accessed, but disorientation opens possibilities to go beyond a binary understanding of the encounter.

Curriculum scholar Aoki (Pinar and Irwin 2005) conceptualizes curriculum as a human experience of constant negotiation which decenters an instrumental approach to teaching and learning and advances the notion of cultural difference as a dynamic process. The "curriculum-as-plan" (Aoki 2005a) concept reflects an instrumentalist perspective, which emphasizes attempts to control, predict, and create certainty. The "curriculum-as-lived" (Aoki 2005a) notion highlights the complex realities of intercultural encounters that, when discussed in relation to PSTs in a study abroad situation, exemplify the situation they may find themselves in during their practicum. Aoki employs the Deleuzian notions of "multiplicities that grow in the middle" (Aoki 2005b) to theorize the constant shifting dynamics and the generative space between curriculum-as-planned and curriculum-as-lived (Aoki 2005b). Multiplicity points to the "sites of relations" (Aoki 2005b, 205) that exist between worldviews, people, and events and draws attention to the relational, dynamic, and generative site of "and" (Aoki 2005c, 271). The space between a familiar world including the environment, daily living, work, and the unfamiliarity of new surroundings, practices, and orientations is rife with tensions, that is, a "tensioned space," and in terms of cultural difference is a pedagogical opportunity (Aoki 2005b). This embodied experience of discomfort illuminates the subjectivity that is often overlooked in study abroad, as is Aoki's (2005b) argument that this experience is alive with possibilities that could offer PSTs opportunities to become more fully human, a corequisite to becoming a teacher.

The concepts of multiplicity, lived curriculum, tensioned space (Aoki 2005), interstitiality (Bhabha 1994), invisible boundary (Anzaldúa 1987), and stop moments (Appelbaum 1995) frame this study and bring to light the pedagogical dynamics of cultural difference and intercultural learning in all its complexity.

The Study Design

The experiences of PSTs were investigated using a qualitative case study research design (Merriam 2009; Stake 1995, 2005; Yin 2014). The case was the South Asian Module (SAM) in a teacher education program in a Canadian university. The aim was to highlight/examine/explore PSTs' encounters with intercultural difference in an international setting—northern India/Tibet. Eleven out of sixteen PSTs enrolled in SAM participated in the study, with ten female participants and one male participant. Most of the participants were in the 22–24 age group with two between 28 and 29. Eight identified as Christian. Prior international experience for the majority was limited to leisure travel, with most having traveled to Europe, and only four to South Asia.

Semi-structured interviews were conducted with the participants in three phases, pre, during, and post-practicum experience, over the duration of twelve months of their program. The interview transcripts were double coded, themes were identified, and data was interpreted through categorizing themes and making connections to the theoretical frames (Miles, Huberman, and Saldaña 2014). Some limitations of the study are that the participants were from one cohort, and six could not participate in all three interviews. The trustworthiness of the study was increased by the researcher's sustained involvement in the program, member checking of transcripts, triangulating the data with literature, the collection of sufficient data to understand contextual factors, and the process of double coding (Miles, Huberman, and Saldaña 2014).

Going Abroad

The PSTs' accounts of their experiences begin with their expectations and motivations for embarking on the practicum located in India, which they undertook in the very first semester of their teacher education program. This is followed by their recollections of their practicum experience after they return from India, and finally, they reflect on what they have learned from their practicum experience, from the perspective of their classroom practicum back in BC (Canada).

Imagining the Experience

The participants looked forward to the opportunity to practice and learn in India. Their motivations for selecting this international program ranged from getting a job more easily upon completion of their program, seeking a novel travel adventure to India, and learning to better navigate cultural differences. They also anticipated that they would be out of their comfort zone and hoped to grow from the experience.

The participants' minimal experience of, and engagement with, cultural difference prior to the program was evident, in spite of the fact that many lived in a culturally diverse community. Most participants admitted that their initial knowledge of the host community started in the program. Some claimed their knowledge about India was from TV shows expressing stereotypical images of Indian people and Buddhist traditions. PSTs also looked forward to experiencing Indian culture. For example, Beth desired to return from overseas and to share with others how she "embraced all of these new cultures that [she] was thrown into." Jen hoped to become less fearful and less judgmental about working with students culturally different than her. Gabby anticipated that "feel[ing] like the minority and the immigrant" in India would serve her well in diverse classrooms back home. Another common view held by participants was that they imagined themselves as helpful Canadians and their presence as beneficial for the Tibetans.

There was one PST who questioned the program and the rationale for having to go somewhere else to engage in hands-on cultural learning. Jackie stated that viewing *Schooling the World* (Black 2010), a documentary that critiques the imposition of education from the Global North on the Global South, left her with great discomfort with her desire to participate in a study abroad program. She comforted herself, however, by indicating that she intends to not harm the Tibetans but rather do good work through which she hoped to convey her belief in them. "It inflicts all sorts of strange things in one's head about what is the value in going overseas and educating people, and so I hope through these connections I give back my caring sense and my faith in them" (Jackie).

The PSTs expected the unknown to evoke contradictory emotions of fear and excitement. Hilary expected "to feel uncomfortable like a fish out of water." However, she believed the discomfort would be short-lived and eventually greater comfort with the foreignness would occur. Jen's concerns arose as she realized she was being "push[ed] out of [her] comfort zone" and would not be able to predict situations "in the lots of unknowns." Through the experience with unfamiliarity, the PSTs also anticipated an internal change. Beth hoped the challenges she encountered while abroad would teach her better stress management, coping skills, and "to think on [her] feet and plan ahead for things."

The participants' minimal experiences with difference are a reflection of their privileged positionality (Sensoy and DiAngelo 2017). The PSTs imagine the host community from a dominant cultural frame (Bhabha 1994). From this stereotypical perspective, they position themselves as helpful. These views, according to the literature, run the risk of reproducing a White savior mentality (Cole 2012; Jefferess 2012). Many of the PSTs approach their practicum much like their prior experience of preparing for a "fun" travel experience. Most participants seem to view the intercultural experience as a means to an end while viewing cultural difference as something to be learned about (Tarc 2013). However, Jackie's questioning the need to go to India is a glimpse into a possibility for dwelling in the (dis)comfort, showing the value of provoking this discomfort as a pedagogical strategy. Although the PSTs expect personal and professional growth, as noted in Driussi (2019), they feared the uncontrollable and unpredictable nature of the unknown, of being out of their comfort zone. As noted with Jackie, there is a possibility for dwelling in the middle of (dis)comfort (Aoki 2005a), but most PSTs are not quite yet at the point of recognizing its pedagogic value. Rather, they imagine that "problem-solving" their way out of the discomfort is the best way forward. These views compromise the PSTs' understanding of intercultural difference as a process, minimizing the likelihood of movement into the interstitial space, and experiencing the "something new" (Bhabha 1994).

The Immersion Experience

Landing in an unfamiliar place, the PSTs found themselves feeling overwhelmed as they crossed four key undetermined borders: navigation of the "Indian culture," living arrangements, the Tibetans in Exile (TIE) community in northern India, and their new role as teachers in the TIE schools.

The PSTs reported that the vibrancy and frequency of unfamiliar scenes were felt as soon as they landed in Delhi. David expressed the inability to place what was occurring in India, which was like a movie with "humanity in your face," intensifying the experience as a feeling of "sensory overload." Anne stated that the experience left her disoriented:

> It [India] has some of the most delicious smells and some of the most beautiful flowers and a huge sanitation problem and some really unfortunate smells. With sounds you hear some beautiful music, really soothing, kind of meditation, yoga music, and water flowing, it's all lovely; but then you also hear in the larger cities the extreme non-stop honking and the dogs that never stop barking. So, I'd say . . . India is just an overload. (Anne)

The PSTs were jolted at the physical, cognitive, and emotional levels. Beth depicted an unsettling nature of contradicting emotions. The rapid movement of unfamiliar sights and sounds from many directions instigated emotions that felt uncontrollably unfamiliar. She described that at one point "[she] was ready to cry" but not scared. In this unfamiliarity, the PSTs felt that their comforts of routine thinking, being, and doing were inaccessible and disrupted.

Accessing their habitual ways that usually permitted them to predict left them with uncertainty. This new reality left Serena with high levels of insecurity: "we are in the 'middle of nowhere,' we were so far away from our comfort zone." Meanwhile, Anne felt "the ups and downs" of being "thrown into the deep end" was all at once "really good, really stressful, scary and exciting."

For David, it was all about "learning the ropes." "At first, you feel like a fish out of water, you're floundering. I feel like the experience is that you just have to get thrown into it and deal with it and that's part of the beauty."

The PSTs' conditioned common sense was disrupted, which was a discomforting sensation. The comfort of certainty was nudged against, leading them to recognize they have just one worldview. They begin to recognize their knowing of how the world works is partial (Kumashiro 2015). Situating themselves in between the certainty and uncertainty of understanding, their world is a movement toward interstitiality. The meeting point, a space found in-between what is familiar and what is not, is significant. Finding themselves at the edges of what is known to them, their sense of certainty is ruptured, and they find themselves at the edge of a boundary between certainty and uncertainty. Emerging in (un)familiarity is the landscape of "AND … AND … AND, …" (Aoki 2005c, 271).

Reflecting Back on the Experience

The PSTs returned home after this practicum and continued with their program, heading directly into their certifying practicum in BC. During that time, they reflected on their time in India. Among the many topics they touched on, they spoke about the broadening of perspectives, learning to live life in the flow, about personal change and growth including gaining self-confidence in their practice.

Broadening of perspectives: The PSTs noticed that they were becoming critical of things they had not noticed prior to the experience. The PSTs began to question their wealthy lifestyles, their orientation to relationships, and the hidden Eurocentric basis of the curriculum. Jen questioned whether the overaccumulation of taken-for-granted "stuff" in her closet was necessary. Gabby questioned the focus on content versus the lack of emphasis on relationships between teacher–student and student–student in BC classrooms. Jackie, who was unaware of how a curriculum can reflect dominant culture, started to recognize Eurocentrism in the BC curriculum when she returned. Anne's perspective of the Tibetan community changed. She was affected by community members' stories of adversity and how they were capable of surviving and doing well "on their own." With time spent in the community, she shifted her initial response of pity to inspiration and developed a humbler attitude, recognizing she had a lot to learn. "I was humbled by their experiences as I realized I do not need to feel sorry for these people, but understand their struggles and instead appreciate them and love them. I felt truly inspired by the resilience of everyone there" (Anne).

However, deeply entrenched beliefs were not always disrupted. Serena remarked that any time her peers encountered something that was different from home, they would make reference to India's tourism slogan *"incredible India,"* with a teasing attitude that had strong tones of judgment and sarcasm. Being in India had significant appeal for the PSTs, and many of them became more open to considering other viewpoints upon return to BC; however, some PSTs' attitudes to cultural difference suggest deeply held beliefs about difference may not be easy to change and not easily disrupted (Sensoy and DiAngelo 2017).

As noted earlier, the PSTs' encounters with (un)familiarity helped them to gain insight, revealing their common sense is partial (Kumashiro 2015). This enhanced their awareness that differing worldviews existed. This broadened their perspectives, which suggests they may begin to orient themselves to another worldview through which they could interpret events and interactions. This finding is consistent with Mwebi and Brigham (2009) and Bernardes et al. (2019), who note that PSTs may slightly shift their perspectives, but as Wong (2015) notes, significant cognitive changes are not often made through study abroad experiences. These limited cognitive shifts imply that PSTs found it daunting to critically examine their beliefs, assumptions, and assumed privilege. Contending with disrupting one's worldview is complex and may require a longer time duration with sustained commitment. It should be noted, however, that becoming aware of differing worldviews is not equivalent to a process of thoroughly grappling with or dismantling entrenched belief systems.

Living life in the flow: Serena found that making changes instantaneously amidst all the unexpected events was frustrating and made the experience consistently challenging. She stated there "was chaos at times" and they rarely "followed through a plan perfectly." She found that she "just kind of went with the flow, eventually." Similarly, Jackie said that the study abroad experience commanded a way of being that expected "[them to be] jumping into it and going with the flow." They began to let go of the need to control situations. Jen gave credit to taking risks daily in India for her willingness without hesitation to teach a subject she was not comfortable with during her high-stakes practicum in BC. "[India] kind of made me more comfortable, just being out of my comfort zone.

I was more willing to jump into it, take risks and try new things. For example, I had never taught science [and that was] an option they gave me. And I [had] the willingness [to try it]" (Jen). The PSTs' belief that one can plan, structure, and predict future situations was revisited. With these sudden encounters and not being able to figure it out at first, the PSTs surrendered to the given moment and were willing to take risks.

Living life in the flow in India suggests PSTs are opening themselves up to an alive pedagogic encounter with difference. For instance, Serena's not being able to plan or Jen having to "jump into it" and "go with the flow" illustrates how in each moment they were not able to figure out what to do or say next, therefore letting go of their habitual need to control life and expect certainty. For the PSTs, relinquishing what happens next in encounters with difference is quite a radical step. Such letting go demands of them to go beyond the edges of the borders of a boundary, with its fixed ways of being, to dwell in the (dis)comfort inhabited with uncertainty. Accepting this may amount to "jumping" off the edge of the boundary. PSTs surrendering to become more open to receive what confronts them depicts their need for control and certainty being released, even if for a short moment. In this way, opening themselves up to new possibilities of the "not yet" can serve to enhance the quality of pedagogic "beingness" (Aoki 2005a).

This finding is similar to Babaeff's (2017), where "going with the flow" is an important learning in study abroad, but enhances it by describing it as a dynamic and nuanced process. This subjective experience of going with the flow is an alive process of responding to what "is" and realizing an interstitial space. This possibility expands the PSTs' capacity to move beyond the boundedness of an instrumental orientation by letting go of the need for control and certainty, and experiencing life in the flow.

Personal change: The PSTs changed professionally and personally. The difficult but gratifying experience evoked a change process contributing to the PSTs' growth as a teacher and person. The unfamiliarity the PSTs encountered revealed how the compounded experience of intercultural difference changed them. As David described it, "being in a new culture, new language, I was already feeling vulnerable, in the middle of nowhere with a bunch of people and community I know nothing about, with peers so different. So having me be vulnerable in the other areas, made my vulnerability in teaching kind of rise a little bit more" (David). The overwhelming experience of unfamiliarity seemed to awaken something deep within, and going out of his comfort zone brought new possibilities: "[The international experience] is challenging, rewarding, insightful, rich, in the sense of just being, like, whole, in every which way, and conducive to my growth—professionally, and personally, and emotionally" (David).

The PSTs experience encounters that called them forth to live in the middle of (dis)comfort. Reflecting upon their experiences of both practicums, the PSTs begin to deepen an understanding of learning to teach that emerges from experiencing uncertainty. David uses what on the surface appears to be contradictory words, "challenging" and "rewarding," to describe the experience. David practiced dwelling in (dis)comfort with each encounter that he could not understand. He finds himself at the edge of a boundary. The overwhelming (dis)comfort urges David to find another way to live "in the midst of differences" (Aoki 2005c, 269). It provides him with the opportunity to live in-between the comfort of knowing and the discomfort of not knowing in interstitiality. He enters a pedagogical vulnerability with its "ever-present risks" to live an aliveness (Aoki 2005a, 163). Consequently, entering this pedagogical site concealed in (dis)comfort is a generative moment.

The possibility arises at each "stop" moment in the international site. These disruptions of PSTs' comfortable understanding of the world offer pedagogical risks (Fels and Belliveau 2008), and become invitations for PSTs to dwell in a tensioned space (Aoki 2005a) with "all its ever-present risks" (163). Through experiencing vulnerability and recognizing its pedagogic value, David begins to understand "living teaching as a mode of being" (Aoki 2005a, 165) while confronting his prior reductionist view of teaching. This changing relationship with (dis)comfort may expand PSTs' capacity to become more attuned to the nature of cultural difference.

This finding complements Driussi's (2019) work which illustrates the risks that PSTs take that move them beyond their comfort zone. Our findings illuminate the complexity and nuances of inequitable power relations as subjective intercultural dynamics, and in intercultural difference within the Global South (Tarc 2013). The personal and professional "qualities" that Ingersoll et al. (2019) refer to encompass what may be considered a vulnerability, as well as a small indication as to the capacity for living with/in vulnerability that these PSTs might realize in (dis)comfort. The findings in this study may be a valuable starting point to center vulnerability as personal change within the future teacher's professional role. Our extrapolation of Ingersoll et al.'s work demonstrates the importance, from our perspective, of situating vulnerability as an inextricably foundational piece to capture (dis)comfort within the context of the study abroad.

Increase of confidence: The experience with uncertainty paradoxically contributed to a newfound sense of confidence. Many of the PSTs identified a realization of a newfound self-reliance from being out of their comfort zone. For instance, Beth indicated that consistently being out of her comfort zone enhanced her capacity to handle many unpredictable situations while in India. Tiffany described that "being placed outside [her] comfort-zone . . . kept [her] confident throughout the process." David said "when you're really feeling challenged, you just need something to hold on to and you find that strength in yourself." He located an inner strength as he practiced keeping himself firmly situated in uncertainty. The PSTs indicated that their need for comfort when faced with uncertainty required them to access their inner resources.

The PSTs express that "being out of their comfort zone" or "feeling challenged" contributed to an inner strength. The more the PSTs were able to let go and accept the (dis)comfort, the greater the likelihood for them to dwell in uncertainty. This growing acquaintance with uncertainty could be viewed as an exercise in risk-taking into vulnerability that requires a letting go of control, and lessening the need for certainty. Vulnerability invites acts of humility, and humble acts may contribute to the process of deepening an internal trust in the unknown, consequently cultivating confidence. Therefore, in each (un) familiar moment, a possibility to develop confidence exists, resulting from repeated risk-taking into vulnerability. The literature notes PSTs' enhancement of self-confidence (CBIE 2016; Ingersoll et al. 2019) as an important outcome of intercultural contact, however, it does not explore the subjective dynamics nor the process of vulnerability it entails. These pedagogical dynamics contributing to confidence could be letting go of the need for control, humility, risk-taking into vulnerability, and being at ease with dwelling in (dis)comfort.

Conclusion/Implications

This study illuminates the intercultural experience as the emotional-subjective dynamics of being in a tensioned space—body, mind, and soul uniting in an embodied experience of vulnerability (Aoki 2005b). The data show that intercultural experiences are not limited to cognitive experiences or outcomes. Instead, the emotional-subjective perspective provides a possibility to examine the complex and nuanced nature of an intercultural encounter in the outer world as an opening into one's inner world. The opening invites PSTs into a vulnerability to turn inward. At this meeting point, they find themselves at the edge of a boundary. Beyond the boundary is a possibility to humbly surrender to being out of their comfort zone, and instead, dwell in (dis)comfort. What becomes available is more of trusting oneself and being more fully human (Aoki 2005a). Centering pedagogical vulnerability in these disruptive spaces has tremendous possibilities to prepare future teachers to move into interstitial space, which moves them beyond the confines of superior/inferior or an us/them thinking (Andreotti 2016). Therefore, changing the PSTs' relationship with the risk associated with (dis)comfort could be a curricular approach for the immersion in intercultural difference.

The value of the experience itself in study abroad (Wong 2018) is illuminated in this study. The findings highlight the pedagogical dynamics of this emotional-subjective experience through realizing an embodiment of inspirited (dis)comfort. The findings in the landscape of "and" in the international practicum go beyond previous studies, to illuminate a lived curriculum. This lived curriculum is a complex experience of varied configurations of intercultural differences where pedagogical dynamics shift moment to moment and differ for each person with different levels of intensity or duration depending on the person's lived experience. Emerging at the relational sites of difference is a curricular landscape of "and" where the PSTs are provoked to be out of their comfort zone—physically, cognitively, and emotionally—to find themselves at the edge of a boundary. The possibilities and impossibilities at the edge of the boundary could be viewed as (inter)cultural learning.

In this (inter)cultural learning, each site of relations with difference is an "environment [that] ceases to be an environment" (Aoki 2005b, 202) but becomes a "pedagogic situation" (202). At this pedagogic site, the comforts of one's bounded ways could be dissolved, even if short-lived and temporary, by moving beyond the boundary's edge. The PSTs could dwell in the space in-between the comfort of knowing and the discomfort of not knowing. When the initial tensioned space in difference is felt, the embodied experience of (dis)comfort is realized. These tensioned moments, in intercultural difference, signal PSTs to open themselves to a possibility of a life beyond the confines of a hierarchical orientation to the world but rather let go of inherited and contained ways of being, and humbly enter the interstitial space.

A more intimate understanding of immersion in intercultural contexts is illuminated with the lived experience of the PSTs in this study. Curriculum that centers subjective relationships with (dis)comfort moves the learner away from instrumentality. There is less focus on outcomes and the cognitive dimension of learning, centering the "and," opening PSTs to something "growing in the middle" (Aoki 2005b, 211). The newness in the interstitiality that emerges has the potential to point to ways of being "otherwise" (Andreotti 2016). In other words, the interstitial space invites approaches to living differently. The study abroad—particularly within the context of the Global South—offers opportunities to go beyond the fixed categorizations of culture, potentially transcending, rather than reinforcing, dualistic thinking of superiority and deficiency.

The international site centers vulnerability as it unfolds as foundational to (inter)cultural learning. Supporting PSTs to become comfortable with (dis)comfort, thus, is a pedagogical prerequisite in (inter)cultural learning.

In this pedagogic intercultural environment where students' worldviews will likely not be affirmed, vulnerability is a reality, and social–emotional supports must be fostered to effectively support PSTs' learning. Curriculum for supporting PSTs to enter interstitiality requires teacher educators to pedagogically soften themselves (Andreotti 2016). In their classroom, with careful attention placed on the social and emotional conditions, the PSTs can pedagogically experience the concealed vulnerability in intercultural encounters. However, teacher educators must cultivate their own comfort with inspirited (dis)comfort. The teacher educator's greater comfort with vulnerability may help them prioritize and attend to the process of supporting PSTs' dwelling in vulnerability before they are asked to dismantle an inherited dominant worldview. Consequently, teacher educators are pedagogical leaders that can lead PSTs out "to the new possibilities yet unknown" through the process of dwelling in tensioned space (Aoki 2005a, 164). When going beyond inherited and confined ways in the interstitial space, PSTs are invited into living beyond the edge of a boundary. This (dis)comfort, a dynamic process for (inter)cultural learning in teacher education, is a hopeful place.

Acknowledgment

This research was funded by a grant from the Social Sciences and Humanities Research Council of Canada.

References

Andreotti, Vanessa. 2016. "The Educational Challenges of Imagining the World Differently." *Canadian Journal of Development Studies* 37, no. 1: 101–112. https://doi.org/10.1080/02255189.2016.1134456.

Anzaldúa, Gloria E. 1987. *Borderlands/La Frontera: The New Mestiza*. San Francisco: Aunt Lute Books.

Aoki, Ted T. 1986/1991/2005a. "Teaching as In-dwelling Between Two Curriculum Worlds." In *Curriculum in a New Key: The Collected Works of Ted T. Aoki*, edited by William F. Pinar and Rita L. Irwin, 159–166. New Jersey: Lawrence Erlbaum Associates. (Original work published 1986).

Aoki, Ted T. 1993/2005b. "Legitimating Lived Curriculum: Toward a Curricular Landscape of Multiplicities." In *Curriculum in a New Key: The Collected Works of Ted T. Aoki*, edited by William F. Pinar and Rita L. Irwin, 199–218. New Jersey: Lawrence Erlbaum Associates. (Original work published 1993).

Aoki, Ted T. 1992/2005c. "In the Midst of Slippery Theme-Words: Living as Designers of Japanese Canadian Curriculum." In *Curriculum in a New Key: The Collected Works of Ted T. Aoki*, edited by William F. Pinar and Rita L. Irwin, 263–279. New Jersey: Lawrence Erlbaum Associates. (Original work published 1987).

Aoki, Ted T. 1987/2005d. "Inspiriting the Curriculum." In *Curriculum in a New Key: The Collected Works of Ted T. Aoki*, edited by William F. Pinar and Rita L. Irwin, 357–366. New Jersey: Lawrence Erlbaum Associates. (Original work published 1987).

Appelbaum, David. 1995. *The Stop*. New York: State University of New York Press.

Association of Canadian Deans of Education. 2014. *Accord on the Internationalization of Education*. https://csse-scee.ca/acde/wp-content/uploads/sites/7/2017/08/Accord-on-the-Internationalization-of-Education.pdf.

Association of Canadian Deans of Education. 2017. *Accord on Teacher Education*. https://csse-scee.ca/acde/wp-content/uploads/sites/7/2018/10/Accord-on-Teacher-Education.pdf.

Association of Universities and Colleges of Canada. 2014. *Canada's Universities in the World: AUCC Internationalization Survey, 2014*. https://www.univcan.ca/wp-content/uploads/2015/07/internationalization-survey-2014.pdf.

Babaeff, Robin. 2017. "Going with the Flow: Pre-service Teacher Learning in, About and with Community." In *Narratives of Learning Through International Professional Experience*, edited by Ange Fitzgerald, Graham Parr, and Judy Williams, 63–76. Singapore: Springer. https://doi.org/10.1007/978-981-10-4867-8.

Bernardes, Rogerio P., Glenda Black, James Otieno Jowi, and Kevin Wilcox. 2019. "Teachers' Critical Interculturality Understandings after an International Teaching Practicum." *Critical Studies in Education* 62, no. 4: 502–518. https://doi.org/10.1080/17508487.2019.1620817.

Bhabha, Homi K. 1994. *The Location of Culture*. London: Routledge.

Black, Carol. 2010. "Schooling the World: The White Man's Last Burden." Documentary film. http://carolblack.org/schooling-the-world.

Black, Glenda L., and Roger P. Bernardes. 2014. "Developing Global Educators and Intercultural Competence through an International Teaching Practicum in Kenya." *Canadian and International Education* 43, no. 2: 1–15.

Canadian Bureau for International Education. 2016. *A World of Learning: Canada's Performance and Potential in International Education*. https://cbie.ca/wp-content/uploads/2017/07/A-World-of-Learning-HI-RES-2016.pdf.

Cole, Teju. 2012. "The White-Savior Industrial Complex." *The Atlantic*, March 21, 2012. https://www.theatlantic.com/international/archive/2012/03/the-white-savior-industrial-complex/254843/.

Cushner, Kenneth. 2007. "The Role of Experience in the Making of Internationally-Minded Teachers." *Teacher Education Quarterly* 34, no. 1: 27–39.

Cushner, Kenneth, and Jennifer Mahon. 2009. "Intercultural Competence in Teacher Education." In *The Sage Handbook of Intercultural Competence*, edited by D. K. Deardorff, 304–320. Thousand Oaks, CA: Sage.

Cushner, Kenneth, and Ata U. Karim. 2004. "Study Abroad at the University Level." In Handbook of Intercultural Training, 3rd edn, edited by D. Landis, M. Bennett, and J. Bennett, 289–308. Thousand Oaks, CA: Sage.

Driussi, Laurie. 2019. "Wayfaring: A Phenomenology of International Teacher Education." PhD diss., Simon Fraser University. http://summit.sfu.ca/item/19322.

Fels, Lynn, and George Belliveau. 2008. *First Flight into Performative Inquiry*. Vancouver: Pacific Education Press.

Forum on Education Abroad. April 9, 2013. "Lili Engle, 2013 plenary speaker." YouTube video. https://www.youtube.com/watch?v=N0lDgjQR7i8.

Ingersoll, Marcea, Alan Sears, Mark Hirschkorn, Lamia Kawtharani-Chami, and Jeff Landine. 2019. "What Is It All For?: The Intentions and Priorities for Study Abroad in Canadian Teacher Education." *Global Education Review* 6, no. 3: 30–48.

Jefferess, David. 2012. "The 'Me to We' Social Enterprise: Global Education as Lifestyle Brand." *Critical Literacy* 6, no. 1: 18–30.

Kulkarni, Saili S., and Cheryl Hanley-Maxwell. 2015. "Preservice Teachers' Student Teaching Experiences in East Africa." *Teacher Education Quarterly* 42, no. 4: 59–81.

Kumashiro, Kevin K. 2015. *Against Common Sense: Teaching and Learning Toward Social Justice*. New York: Routledge, Taylor & Francis Group.

Larsen, Marianne A. 2016. "Globalisation and Internationalisation of Teacher Education: A Comparative Case Study of Canada and Greater China." *Teaching Education* 27, no. 4: 396–409. https://doi.org/10.1080/10476210.2016.1163331.

Larsen, Marianne A., and Michelle J. Searle. 2017. "International Service Learning and Critical Global Citizenship: A Cross-Case Study of a Canadian Teacher Education Alternative Practicum." *Teaching and Teacher Education* 63: 196–205. https://doi.org/10.1016/j.tate.2016.12.011.

Malewski, Erik, and JoAnn Phillion. 2009. "International Field Experiences: The Impact of Class, Gender and Race on the Perceptions and Experiences of Preservice Teachers." *Teaching and Teacher Education* 25, no. 1: 52–60. https://doi.org/10.1016/j.tate.2008.06.007.

Maynes, Nancy, John Allison, and Lynn Julien-Schultz. 2012. "International Practica Experiences as Events of Influence in a Teacher Candidates' Development." *McGill Journal of Education* 47, no. 1: 69–91. https://doi.org/10.7202/1011667ar.

Merriam, Sharan B. 2009. *Qualitative Research: A Guide to Design and Implementation*, 2nd edn. San Francisco, CA: Jossey-Bass.

Merryfield, Merry M. 2000. "Why Aren't Teachers Being Prepared to Teach for Diversity, Equity, and Global Interconnectedness? A Study of Lived Experiences in the Making of Multicultural and Global Educators." *Teaching and Teacher Education* 16, no. 4: 429–443.

Miles, Matthew B., A. Michael Huberman, and Johnny Saldaña. 2014. *Qualitative Data Analysis: A Methods Sourcebook*. Thousand Oaks, CA: Sage.

Mwebi, Bosire Monari, and Susan Brigham. 2009. "Preparing North American Preservice Teachers for Global Perspectives: An International Teaching Practicum Experience in Africa." *Alberta Journal of Educational Research* 55, no. 3: 415–428.

Pence, Holly M., and Ian K. Macgillivray. 2008. "The Impact of an International Field Experience on Preservice Teachers." *Teaching and Teacher Education* 24, no. 1: 14–25. https://doi.org/10.1016/j.tate.2007.01.003.

Phillion, JoAnn, Erik L. Malewski, Suniti Sharma, and Yuxiang Wang. 2009. "Reimagining the Curriculum: Future Teachers and Study Abroad." *Frontiers* 18, no. 1: 323–339. https://dx.doi.org/10.36366/frontiers.v18i1.269.

Pinar, William, and Rita L. Irwin. 2005. *Curriculum in a New Key: The Collected Works of Ted T. Aoki*. Mahwah, NJ: Lawrence Erlbaum Associates.

Scholefield, Anne C. 2006. "International Education as Teacher Education: A Curriculum of Contradictions." PhD diss., Faculty of Education, Simon Fraser University. http://summit.sfu.ca/item/2874.

Sensoy, Özlem, and Robyn DiAngelo. 2017. *Is Everyone Really Equal?: An Introduction to Key Concepts in Social Justice Education*, 2nd edn. New York: Teachers College Press.

Sharma, Suniti. 2009. "From the Red-Dot-Indian Woman to Jet-Set-Mangoes and all the Hyphens In-Between: Studying Abroad and Discovering Myself." *Journal of Curriculum Theorizing* 25, no. 3: 119–136.

Smolcic, Elizabeth, and John Katunich. 2017. "Teachers Crossing Borders: A Review of the Research into Cultural Immersion Field Experience for Teachers." *Teaching and Teacher Education* 62: 47–59. https://doi.org/10.1016/j.tate.2016.11.002.

Stake, Robert E. 1995. *The Art of Case Study Research*. Thousand Oaks, CA: Sage.

Stake, Robert E. 2005. "Qualitative Case Studies." In *The Sage Handbook of Qualitative Research*, edited by Norman K. Denzin and Yvonna S. Lincoln, 3rd edn, 443–466. Thousand Oaks, CA: Sage.

Study Group on Global Education. 2017. *Global Education for Canadians Equipping Young Canadians to Succeed at Home & Abroad*. The Centre for International Policy Studies and the Munk School of Global Affairs. https://844ff178-14d6-4587-9f3e-f856abf651b8.filesusr.com/ugd/dd9c01_ca275361406744feb38ec91a5dd6e30d.pdf.

Tarc, Paul. 2013. *International Education in Global Times: Engaging the Pedagogic*. Switzerland: Peter Lang.

Tiessen, Rebecca. 2012. "Motivations for Learn/Volunteer Abroad Programs: Research with Canadian Youth." *The Journal of Global Citizenship and Equity Education* 2, no. 1: 1–21.

Tiessen, Rebecca, and Robert Huish, eds. 2014. *Globetrotting or Global Citizenship?: Perils and Potential of International Experiential Learning*. Toronto, ON: University of Toronto Press.

Trilokekar, Roopa Desai, and Polina Kukar. 2011. "Disorienting Experiences During Study Abroad: Reflections of Pre-Service Teacher Candidates." *Teaching and Teacher Education* 27, no. 7: 1141–1150. https://doi.org/10.1016/j.tate.2011.06.002.

Tripp, L. Octavia, Angela Love, Nancy Barry, Chippewa M. Thomas, and Jared Russell. 2020. "A Qualitative Analysis of Teacher Candidates' Study Abroad Experiences in Malawi." In *Study Abroad for Pre- and In-service Teachers: Transformative Learning on a Global Scale*, edited by Laura Baecher, 129–45. New York: Routledge.

Vande Berg, Michael, Michael R. Paige, and Kris Hemming Lou. 2012. *Student Learning Abroad: What Our Students Are Learning, What They're Not, and What We Can Do about It*. Sterling, VA: Stylus.

Wong, E. David. 2015. "Beyond 'It was Great'? Not so Fast!" *Frontiers* 26, no. 1: 121–135. https://doi.org/10.36366/frontiers.v26i1.362.

Wong, E. David. 2018. "Intercultural Learning may be Impossible in Education Abroad: A Lesson from King Lear." *Frontiers* 30, no. 3: 38–50. https://doi.org/10.36366/frontiers.v30i3.428.

Yin, Robert K. 2014. *Case Study Research: Design and Methods*, 5th edn. Thousand Oaks, CA: Sage.

6

Challenges Faced by Japanese English Teachers Applying Knowledge after Study Abroad

Steve Marshall and Brent Amburgey

Introduction

Following university policies of internationalization, international collaboration, and international engagement, it has become common for education departments and faculties in universities in English-speaking countries to seek out professional development partnerships with universities and school boards across the world in the field of teacher education. In particular, given the dominant position of English as a lingua franca in the world today (Jenkins 2009; Seidlhofer 2011), professional development partnerships designed for pre-service and in-service English language teachers have become a notable area of growth for international partnerships. In this chapter, we analyze data from one such partnership, presenting data from a study of Japanese in-service English language teachers who took a professional development program at a university in Western Canada, a program that had the dual aims of improving English language competence and learning about international trends in education and language teaching.

A major aim of many professional development programs for English language teachers studying abroad is to provide opportunities for practicing teachers to reflect on their own practices and beliefs, the contexts of their teaching, and to reimagine themselves as teachers. Moreover, central to this multilayered process of developing professionally, and key to the effectiveness and sustainability of such programs, is the application of knowledge post-program, which has been the focus of several studies, for example, Barkhuizen (2017), Barkhuizen and Feryok (2006), Garbati and Rothschild (2016), and Marshall and Spracklin (2022). In other words, teachers' willingness and/or ability to consider/apply the knowledge that they have learned during the study abroad period when they return to their schools is a very important factor in programs' long-term success and purpose. That said, it should be noted that applying theory and new pedagogical knowledge to practice is never without complications for in-service teachers. This is especially the case when in-service English language teachers (from countries around the world) study abroad, taking professional development courses in countries where English is the main language, such as Australia, New Zealand, the United States, Canada, the UK, and Ireland, for example. In such cases, differences in languages, cultures, and ideologies—from one country to another—need to be addressed and bridged as part of self-reflection processes and future application of knowledge learned. Moreover, potential constraints related to policies, curriculum, and relations with colleagues may also play important roles in the successful application (or not) of knowledge. It has been suggested that teachers may often lean toward reproducing rather than challenging dominant discourses (Archer 2003; Benwell and Stokoe 2006; Butler 1993; cited in Marshall 2022) post-course instead of challenging them.

Accordingly, we analyze the experiences and challenges that four English language teachers from an urban school board in Japan have faced when it comes to applying new knowledge in their teaching contexts after taking a ten-week professional development program at a Canadian university. In narrative writing during the program, and in interviews taking place a year after completion of the program, participants described a number of challenges that they would face/had faced/were facing when it came to applying knowledge learned in the program in their Japanese junior and senior high schools, schools that are subject to policies set at various levels, including internationalization policies set by the Japanese Ministry of Education, Culture, Sports, Science and Technology.

Internationalization is without doubt a big topic in Japanese education today, in primary, secondary, and tertiary education. While internationalization policies may have broadly stated goals in terms of interculturalism, student development, and future benefits to Japan and its citizens, improving students' competence in English is key to the future success of these policies. In this regard, there are many potential/imagined benefits for students that have been associated with learning English in Japanese schools: English being the world's lingua franca; fluid international borders; and tangible social, economic, and cultural capital that can come with being competent in English (Bouchard 2017). However, the future fluid international borders and cultural capital that can come with English language competence may not be accessible to all—some students may lack the will, resources, or professional contexts to engage internationally through

English in their future careers and lives. Moreover, the dominant position of English as *the* foreign language in schools means that other languages lose out and may not be taught in schools, namely, other community languages in Japan (e.g., Ainu, Portuguese, Chinese, Tagalog, and Vietnamese), and those of other neighboring regions and countries. From a critical perspective, the dominant position of English as *the* foreign language to be learned in the Japanese education system has been analyzed in detail by Kubota (2011), who highlights a number of problematic related issues, including the fact that many students will not need to use English in their future working lives.

Another possible reason for the increase in the number of professional development programs for English language teachers studying abroad is the growing consensus that English language teaching in Japanese schools needs to move on from traditional teaching methods, perceived by many as unsuccessful, such as grammar translation, rote learning, and vocabulary memorization, with classes taught via prescribed curricula and textbooks, and competencies measured in national standardized examinations (Marshall 2022). Moreover, the need for increased professional development has also grown as a result of education policies that encourage Japanese teachers to use English rather than Japanese as the medium of instruction in their English classes in schools (see Takegami 2016 for a study of the impacts of the English through English [ETE] policy in Japan and its impacts on teachers, and Takegami 2020 for an analysis of the "positive disharmonies" that teachers negotiate through ETE policies). Together, these multiple factors would appear to be the major driving force in Japanese school boards' decisions to invest considerable efforts and funding in sending selected English language teachers abroad for professional development in Anglophone countries: to learn more about international trends in English language teaching, improve their own English language competence through immersion, to develop as teachers, and to become future change-makers in the education system.

The Study

We have selected data from a larger study of a group of Japanese English teachers from an urban school board in Japan who attended a ten-week professional development program at a university in Western Canada. During the program, the teacher-students attended a combination of English language classes and classes on international trends in education and TESOL. For the duration of their stay in Canada, the teacher-students stayed with homestay families so as to gain experience of local cultures and to live in an English-speaking environment. During the program, the teacher-students did a range of reflective writing tasks; taught demonstration lessons to peers; sat in on undergraduate lectures in education; and wrote action plans in which they considered their past, present, and future practice (see Marshall 2022 for an in-depth analysis of the content of the teacher-students' reflective narrative writing).

Interviews took place around one year after the completion of the program during the first year of the global COVID-19 pandemic. Although the changes that came about during the COVID-19 pandemic are not a main focus of this chapter, they do provide a partial backdrop to the participants' attempts to apply knowledge in their classes once restrictions were imposed in Japanese schools. After the project received ethics approval to proceed, the former teacher-students were invited by email to take part in online interviews via Zoom and to share samples of their writing from the program for the researchers to analyze. The four teachers whose data we present in this chapter were teachers in junior and senior high schools in Japan and were given the following pseudonyms to guarantee confidentiality: Eiji, Mika, Tamiko, and Toshi. To further guarantee confidentiality, no further information about the participants' backgrounds and schools is provided. In the upcoming presentation and analysis of data, we focus primarily on interview excerpts in which participants discussed (after guided questions from the interviewer and more spontaneously in general conversation) issues related to the challenges that they faced when trying to apply knowledge that they learned during the program in Canada in their classes in Japan. We look for answers to two questions in our analysis:

1. What challenges did the teachers face when attempting to apply knowledge learned in Canada in their classes in Japanese schools?
2. What strategies did the teachers employ to deal with these challenges?

In the "Data Analysis" section, data excerpts are presented without changes to language, with three periods (. . .) indicating that text has been cut from the original excerpt, while two periods (. .) indicate an abrupt stop mid-utterance.

Study Abroad and Applying Knowledge

The study abroad experiences of students, teachers, pre-service and in-service, have been the focus of several important studies in recent years, in a number of contexts. With a specific focus on study abroad students, for example, Amadasi and Holliday (2018) analyzed the experiences of a newly arrived postgraduate study abroad student with a focus on changing cultural trajectories, while Badwan (2017) studied the out-of-class communication of a study abroad student in the UK. And focusing on the experiences of pre-service and in-service teachers studying abroad, Santoro and Major (2012) investigated the study abroad experiences of fifteen pre-service teachers from Australia who took part in study abroad programs in India and Korea, while Bodycott (2015) analyzed intra-group conflict among a group of Bachelor of Education students from Hong Kong while they were studying abroad in Canada. Additionally, Santoro, Fosu, and Fassetta (2016) looked at a group of teachers from Scotland, focusing on their attitudes to studying abroad, and in an earlier study by Rapoport (2008), the author analyzed a number of issues that came up in exchange programs involving educators from Russia and the United States, including impacts on professional practice, professional status, career development, and application of knowledge post-program.

There are also a number of studies that have focused specifically on the study abroad experiences of pre- and in-service teachers of English who take professional development programs in different Anglophone countries. Barkhuizen and Feryok (2006) studied a group of pre-service English teachers from Hong Kong who had taken part in a short study abroad program in New Zealand, focusing on how the host institution and the researchers could build upon the lessons learned through the international collaboration. Later, Barkhuizen (2017) carried out follow-up interviews with one participant from a study abroad program in New Zealand after one year of study and again five years later after returning to Hong Kong, using narrative writing to explore the student's identities and the impacts of the study abroad experience. Reflective narrative writing was also employed by Garbati and Rothschild (2016), along with analysis of email communications, in an analysis of two study abroad student participants, looking at factors related to languages, cultures, identities, and the impacts of the study abroad experience. And finally, Devlin (2014) investigated learners' experiences during study abroad in terms of different contexts of language contact, how learning was affected when it took place in different locations, and how learners developed their linguistic competence over time.

Of specific relevance to this study, a small number of studies have analyzed the experiences of Japanese pre-service and in-service teachers of English who have attended study abroad programs in Canada. In Douglas, Sano, and

Rosvold's (2018) study, the authors looked at the experiences of a group of third-year teacher candidates from Japan who took a program in Canada that focused on the learning of educational content and improving English language competence, using narrative inquiry as a research tool. Focusing on narrative inquiry as a pedagogical research tool, the authors analyzed the "storied experiences" of the participants, highlighting the importance of factors such as meaningful intercultural engagement with the local communities, including local First Nations, varied extracurricular activities, and rich content learning during the program.

Some authors have also considered the issues and constraints that Japanese English teachers faced after their programs in Canada when they attempted to apply new knowledge in their classrooms. For instance, Cook's (2010) study highlighted a number of constraints that impacted the successful incorporation of content learned in Canada on returning to Japan: for example, teachers feeling obliged to conform to colleagues' teaching approaches and the prevalence of grammar or translation-based entrance examinations in Japanese schools. Similarly, Cook and Gulliver (2014) mentioned several constraints faced by Japanese teachers of English after professional development in Canada, namely, the pressures of entrance examinations, lack of time to try new approaches, fixed curricula, and prescribed textbooks. In addition, in a study of a group of in-service teachers of English from urban Japanese junior and senior high schools who took a professional development program in Canada, Marshall (2022) analyzed teacher-students' reflective narrative writing done during the program in which they considered a range of factors around their professional development, including the upcoming constraints that they would have to overcome to make changes in their teaching. Related issues raised were having to work with colleagues from different classes, following colleagues' curriculum and modes of assessment, lack of seniority required to persuade colleagues to change, and previous experiences of working with colleagues who were unwilling to collaborate with innovations.

Sustainability and Knowledge Application

An important goal of the program from which we have collected data for this chapter was to build in sustainability in as many ways as possible. As stated by Ilieva, Beck, and Waterstone (2014), sustainability in internationalization initiatives in higher education is a key factor that all educators involved in international education should consider. In terms of the focus of our study, a key factor in developing a sustainable program was effectively addressing the question of applying knowledge in context post-program, in respectful, appropriate ways. This involved reflective writing activities during the program in which the teacher-students considered the social and institutional contexts of their practices and looked ahead to their future imagined self, as well as possible constraints they may face (Marshall 2022).

In a broader sense, Marshall and Kent Spracklin (2022) put forward a framework for sustainable research and practice with regard to English language teachers studying abroad, basing their work on a group of English language teachers from higher education institutions in four Southeast Asian countries. Participants in the study raised several issues that they faced when applying knowledge learned in a Canadian-led graduate program. First, several participants cited what they considered to be a lack of exposure to a culture of critical thinking among the local students whom they taught in their home countries, making approaches such as inquiry-based learning and critical thinking difficult to employ on return to their institutions. Second, one participant in the study mentioned a lack of a culture of independent learning among students at their home institution, while another mentioned an episode in which students complained to the university management about teachers who were trying out "Western" teaching approaches. Three other factors emerged in the study: a lack of English language competence among teachers and students; a lack of time to innovate due to very busy teaching schedules; and a reluctance among some colleagues to collaborate with teaching methods perceived to be "Western": as stated by one participant's colleagues in the title of Marshall and Kent Spracklin's (2022) work, "We are in our country. Why do we have to resort to Western ways of doing things?" (1). Therefore, in their framework for researching and working in ethical, inclusive, and sustainable ways with English language teachers in international collaborations, the authors stress the need for the following: an understanding of internationalization that is collaborative rather than solely Western-led, program delivery that welcomes collaboration with local educators and knowledge, an understanding of borders (both national and epistemological) as fluid rather than clearly delineated, a focus on teacher identity as fluid and disrupted (Barkhuizen 2022) rather than fixed, and a focus on target learners who use English as a lingua franca rather than aiming for native speaker competence.

In our analysis that follows, we draw on the key themes from this framing of English language teachers studying abroad as well as from the literature reviewed above. Summing up, following the goals of sustainability and intercultural awareness, there was considerable effort during the professional development program to create and maintain learning spaces across zones that promoted dialogue, interaction, tolerance, and critical reflection (Baecher and Chung 2020; Marshall and Spracklin 2022), in which Canadian/Euro-Western approaches to knowledge formation in higher education and language teaching were not presented as being superior to other approaches.

Data Analysis

In this section, our main focus is excerpts from the interviews that took place via Zoom around one year after the program with four of the participants who agreed to take part in the study. Our thematic focus is on issues and themes that are related to applying knowledge post-program and the challenges therein; however, rather than presenting our findings thematically, we have decided to present data excerpts per participant to provide a more holistic view of their perceptions and practices. The data are presented in the following order for each participant: (1) a brief synopsis of any related key issues that the same participants mentioned in narrative writing during the program (e.g., reasons for taking the program and possible future challenges) (see Marshall 2022 for a detailed analysis of the participants' narrative writing); (2) responses to a post-program interview question in which participants were asked their reasons for signing up for the program (we see these reasons as contextualizing, and thus connected to, the application of knowledge post-program); and (3) excerpts from post-program interview questions in which participants reflected on issues that arose as they tried to apply ideas from the program in their local schools in Japan. A brief analysis will be made in each subsection, followed by a more detailed analysis and synthesis in the following "Discussion and Conclusion" section, which will consider the data in terms of the literature and framework reviewed above.

Eiji: Negotiating Ambivalence

During the program, in the different narrative writing tasks, Eiji had described himself as a teacher who wants to hand the learning over to the learners, to let go more, and to give his students more space to develop their ideas. In the post-program interview, Eiji was asked why he had signed up for the program and responded as follows:

Eiji: Well, to be honest, I wasn't doing it voluntary. Actually, I was offered twice, one year and then one year later too . . . Then at the second time, my principal said that I should go there. So, yeah, kind of half-forced, half mandatory. Yes, cause I was interested in . . , to be able to learn abroad, but I was really afraid that I may, I mean, it affects other teachers a lot in Japanese school system to go out of the school system for a while—that means they need to take care of a lot of things for my students. So, worrying about that too.

Eiji expresses considerable ambivalence toward taking the program in the excerpt above, a sense of ambivalence that was also echoed by a number of other teacher-students taking the program. It seems that Eiji is split, somewhere in between, feeling forced to attend the program and wanting to gain the study abroad experience. Added to this sense of ambivalence is Eiji's concern that his absence will create a burden for his colleagues, some of whom will have to cover for him while he is away. Yet, on return to his school, it was not teaching colleagues who Eiji mentioned in terms of affecting his application of knowledge effectively (or not) post-program, but rather the new principal of his school. When asked about the challenges he faced post-program, Eiji answered as follows:

Interviewer: Do you have any resistance in your school to doing things in different ways?

Eiji: Actually, the one who said that I am not controlling the class was my [new] principal.

Interviewer: How did you, how did you respond?

Eiji: I didn't really respond, actually. I didn't fight against those words, but I also worried that I might not be evaluated well. I worried also, the evaluation of my payment too. But, basically, I didn't doubt my way of doing so, I think, I knew that I don't change anything. I was doing the right thing, I think.

The figure of the principal seems to loom large in Eiji's response: as both someone who strongly encouraged, perhaps gently forced, Eiji to take up the chance to study abroad in Canada, and as someone who Eiji perceived as a constraint to applying knowledge post-program. However, Eiji explained that it was a new school principal that took issue with him not controlling his class— not the former principal who encouraged him to take the program. Added to Eiji's pre-program ambivalence about whether to attend the program was a sense of post-program ambivalence of a different nature. In the case of the latter, Eiji had to weigh the concerns about receiving a negative evaluation that could have financial implications against his personal belief in his own way of teaching.

Clearly, institutional hierarchy and power relations in schools are playing a key role: the choices that teachers make in their classes post-program, and their inability to exercise their agency freely in doing so, relate to perceptions of judgment and possible recrimination/sanction from more senior colleagues.

Mika: Inquiry, Collaboration, and Time Constraints

In Mika's narrative writing during the program, she described how she feels that the exam-oriented classes that she teaches stifle students' imaginations; Mika also expressed a desire to be able to encourage students to consider why they are studying English, to encourage learner autonomy in her classes, and to implement inquiry-based learning as an alternative to more teacher-led approaches. In the post-program interview, Mika gave reasons for attending the program that did not show the same ambivalence as Eiji's above:

Interviewer: And why did you take the program?

Mika: Because I . . . my major was English literature when I was a student in the university. So, I really wanted to study TESOL, the teaching methods . .

Interviewer: And what were your goals, before you took the program? What did you want to achieve?

Mika: To get the teaching methods, systematically. To learn one by one is really important for me. And to talk about . . . to talk with other members was also great experience for me.

During the program, Mika wrote about the need to move away from exam-focused learning and to promote learner autonomy and inquiry-based learning. Mika's description of her reasons for taking the program that she shared a year later in an interview showed her to be an ideal candidate for studying abroad with her aim of widening her repertoire of teaching knowledge. Mika has a background in English, wants to study teaching methods systematically, and mentioned that she saw sharing ideas about teaching with other members of the program as something that would be beneficial to her professional development. In other words, Mika linked her learning goals *during* the program to collaboration with colleagues. However, this link between goals and collaboration was more problematic when it came to applying knowledge *after* the program as it depended partly on her relationship with a co-teacher, with whom she had to teach the same materials and follow the same assessment. Mika described what she saw as the main constraint, her colleague's lack of time, when attempting to work together collaboratively:

Mika: It was hard to, he understands what I want to do, every time. But he's very busy to do that work every day. So, we don't have enough time to think about better English class.

Interviewer: Are you too busy?

Mika: I'm not. Maybe the other one is.

Unlike Eiji's description of colleague-related constraints being down to hierarchy and understandings about classroom management, Mika described lack of time as the constraining factor that inhibited her professional development post-program in a collaborative sense through working together with colleagues. Put simply, Mika's colleague did not have as much time as she did to develop professionally. Mika went on to explain how she balances what she described as Japanese and Canadian ways of teaching in her classes:

> Mika: I think Canadian style is very fascinating. But I know the Japanese way and Canadian way is different. So, I didn't mix them up. Japanese is Japanese and Canadian is Canadian. That's it. I just want to copy the good points from Canadians' way. And I can use for Japanese students.

Of interest here is both Mika's flexibility in employing multiple approaches in her classes as well as her stating that she does not mix what she sees as separate approaches. Evidently, for Mika, national and epistemological boundaries are clearly fixed rather than blurred when it comes to applying knowledge post-program.

Tamiko: (Not) Doing Things "the Canadian Way"

In her narrative writing during the program, Tamiko used the metaphor of a lawn mower teacher when describing her previous teacher self: following the textbook, focusing on tests, and not opening up spaces for her students to engage with their own errors and mistakes or to think about issues deeply. Looking ahead to teaching post-program, Tamiko wrote that, despite the fear that colleagues with whom she works may be unwilling to change their ways, she saw her future self as a change-maker, embracing inquiry-based learning.

During the post-course interview, Tamiko described her goals for taking the program as primarily relating to self-improvement as a teacher and more effectively promoting intercultural tolerance and world peace through language learning. Tamiko also described one area where she had tried to apply new knowledge and teaching methods at her school through deeper engagement with students: negotiating the syllabus.

Interviewer: I think, that you'd tried to let your students negotiate the syllabus with you. How did that go?

Tamiko: The only class that I could do it in is only my elective class, English conversational class. Other classes, the classes that I have to teach with other teachers, it's impossible.

The view that colleagues were reticent about trying out new methods learned in Canada was definitely a major theme that came up in the interview with Tamiko. In the following excerpt, Tamiko builds on a discussion with the interviewer about some colleagues' resistance to embracing what she had studied in Canada:

Tamiko: If I say suddenly OK we share the same class, let's do Canadian way. I teach you how, like this like this like that. But then they, they cannot do it. Like some teachers just conduct lessons, mainly in Japanese and then they may feel why do I have to speak English so much? I am not really sure if I'm correct, I make mistakes . . . They think they should not make any mistakes in class when we speak. That makes us a lot of pressure speaking English in class.

It would be safe to describe Tamiko as among the keenest students in the program in terms of wanting to learn and willingness to acquire and apply new knowledge. In her narrative writing and interviews, Tamiko described herself as an idealistic teacher who wants to move away from being a teacher who solely conveys information to being a teacher who wants her students to develop through deep thinking and inquiry. For both Tamiko and Mika above, a major stumbling block to applying new knowledge collaboratively was related to how they were required to work together with colleagues. However, unlike Mika, who cited colleagues' lack of time, Tamiko linked colleagues' reticence to an inability to do things "the Canadian way," highlighting the fear of making English language mistakes in front of students as a key related factor.

When it came to applying new ways of teaching in her school, Tamiko's approach was to tread carefully:

Tamiko: As long as I don't talk about Canada, it's OK (laughing). Like if I just say, "you know, in Canada," they may show me that face and say . . I don't know, when I came back some other teachers, science teacher, young teachers, they came to see my lessons. They are not even English teachers, but they said "okay, I wanna see Canadian way of teaching. Can I visit your class?" And I said "oh, welcome, come, come." But like, English teachers, they don't really come to my class.

From the various data sets, it is evident that Tamiko employs critical self-awareness and self-monitoring when it comes to bringing up what she learned in Canada with her colleagues. Moreover, of interest is Tamiko's statement that while English teachers do not come to watch her classes, teachers of other subjects do. In this sense, it would appear that Tamiko is required to employ a delicate reflexive balancing act of welcoming those who are interested in seeing what she has learned in Canada while not pressuring English teacher colleagues at the same time.

Toshi: From Old to New to Old

A key focus of Toshi's narrative writing during the program was the constraints that come with the textbooks that he uses in his classes. Toshi wrote that he faced the challenge of how to make them interesting and how to engage students while using textbooks. In this regard, Toshi explained that he saw his role as a teacher as a bridge between the textbooks and the students. When Toshi was interviewed a year later, he explained that he felt that he had met his goals for taking the program:

> Toshi: I really achieved my goal during my stay in Canada . . . I had time to think about what is applicable in my own school, and also, what is good point and bad point of my own school. So, in appearance, it didn't, it didn't change so much but in my inside, my thought has drastically changed.

During the interview, Toshi focused on the goals that he had achieved: weighing the pros and cons of his school and practice in Japan, and in doing so, undergoing a drastic change in his views on teaching. That being said, the drastic change in Toshi's teacher identity did not translate itself into sustained change in practice, as he explains in the excerpt below:

Toshi: At first I tried to change my style. Kind of inquiry based or something. And I increased the time students work in groups or something. But it requires my time in preparing the lesson. And also, the students are quite not accustomed to the new style. And I found, I find, myself gradually getting back to the old style.

Interviewer: How would you define the old style?

Toshi: Uh, just following the textbook or . . . in a way that is first read the textbook and teaching vocabulary and then ask questions in the textbook and so on . . . I don't mean I'm satisfied with that way . . . but I think it takes time, but I want to improve my teaching English in the future.

It would appear that a combination of time constraints (the time it would take to develop new approaches) and students' unfamiliarity with inquiry-based approaches led Toshi to move full circle from old self, to new self, then back to old self in his classes (relying on the textbook for teaching skills such as vocabulary and reading comprehension). This shift from a new self back to an old self was despite Toshi's stating that he had undergone a dramatic change of views about his role as a teacher and was tempered by his stated desire to develop in the future—noting that "it takes time."

Discussion and Conclusion

Our study has focused on the issues and challenges that four Japanese English language teachers faced after taking a professional development program at a Canadian university, specifically in terms of applying the knowledge that they had learned during the program in their classes on returning to Japan. We looked for answers to two research questions in our study.

The first question focused on the challenges that teachers faced when attempting to apply knowledge learned in Canada in their classes in Japanese schools. We began our analysis of data by referring to narrative writing that teachers had done during the program as a tool for reflection and engaging with teachers' professional identities and imagined future self (a data gathering tool also employed by Amadasi and Holliday 2018; Barkhuizen 2017; Douglas, Sano, and Rosvold 2018), followed by excerpts from interviews carried out one year after the participants had completed the program. We found that the issues and challenges that were highlighted in other studies on Japanese teachers/students, pre-service and in-service, studying abroad in Canada, also played roles in constraining participants' application of knowledge. Most notable among these issues were teachers needing to conform to colleagues' teaching approaches, the focus on testing, lack of time, and the textbooks that teachers were required to use (Cook 2010; Cook and Gulliver 2014).

Our second question asked what strategies teachers used to deal with the challenges that they faced when attempting to apply knowledge. This is an important question to address because it throws light on how and why ideas developed through involvement in a professional development program in a Canadian university may (or may not) be applied in local Japanese schools. The responses from the four participants provide valuable insights in this regard. Firstly, Eiji's strategy in response to his principal's questioning his teaching was to *not* respond: "I didn't really respond, actually. I didn't fight against those words," but to continue regardless and believe in his way of doing things. Mika's strategy involved recognizing and embracing difference by employing what she saw as both Canadian and Japanese ways in her classes—but not mixing them: "the Japanese way and Canadian way is different. So, I didn't mix them up. Japanese is Japanese and Canadian is Canadian." While not explicitly describing a strategy, Toshi's approach was one of trying things out and returning to his old style of teaching when he found that he lacked time and students were not used to his new ways: "I found, I find, myself gradually getting back to the old style." Finally, Tamiko described both being careful about talking too much with colleagues about what she learned in Canada as well as welcoming colleagues who wanted to see what she referred to as the Canadian way into her classes: "As long as I don't talk about Canada, it's OK. (laughing)" and "they said 'okay, I wanna see Canadian way of teaching. Can I visit your class?' And I said 'oh, welcome, come, come.'" To answer the second question, therefore, the participants described a range of strategies which related to different situations that came up in their post-program practice: strategic resignation and acceptance (Eiji), embracing different approaches separately (Mika), trying out new approaches but not shying away from returning to old ways (Toshi), and both self-monitoring and sharing with colleagues (Tamiko).

As stated above, we consider that understanding and facilitating the critical, successful, and culturally appropriate application of knowledge post-program should be a key goal, perhaps even the key stage, in striving for sustainability in international teacher education partnerships. In terms of the key features of sustainable international education, in terms of practice and research, highlighted by Marshall and Spracklin (2022), the following can be highlighted as coming to the fore in our analysis. The first is the central question raised by a participant in Marshall and Spracklin's study, which we have adapted to the contexts of Japan as follows: Why should teachers in countries such as Japan feel pressured to resort to Western ways of doing things? The data that we presented above give insights into answering this question. For example, it was noted above by Tamiko that when she suggested to some colleagues to do things "the Canadian way," they could, or would, not do it; moreover, colleagues may also question why they should have to speak English so much in their classes. In this case, Western ways also meant teaching through English and exposing oneself to the risk of losing face by having errors picked up by students. For Eiji, doing things the Western way meant letting go and handing over more to the learners in his classes—this faced resistance from his new school principal on the grounds that he was perceived to not be controlling his class. In this case, the so-called Western way perhaps challenged local perceptions about classroom management and the role of a teacher in a teacher-led language class. And for Toshi, the process of negotiating the need to teach in the Western way was described as centering around him as a teacher, not colleagues, and his returning to the old after trying out the new.

In sum, applying knowledge and teaching approaches conceptualized as being Western, Canadian, or not-Japanese is a complex process, involving colleagues, collaboration, a sense of self, ideologies, and practical concerns such as a lack of time and working within the constraints of prescribed textbooks. Returning then to the framework set out by Marshall and Spracklin (2022), our findings highlight the need for international teacher education collaborations to avoid being solely Western-focused and Western-led, and to recognize the fluidity and changes in teachers' identities and ideologies—while setting up programs (before), while teaching them (during), and when doing follow-up research (after).

References

Amadasi, Sara, and Adrian Holliday. 2018. "'I Already Have a Culture.' Negotiating Competing Grand and Personal Narratives in Interview Conversations with New Study Abroad Arrivals." *Language and Intercultural Communication* 18, no. 2: 241–256.

Badwan, Khawla M. 2017. "'Did We Learn English or What?': A Study Abroad Student in the UK Carrying and Crossing Boundaries in Out-of-Class Communication." *Studies in Second Language Learning and Teaching* 7, no. 2: 193–210.

Baecher, Laura, and Samantha Chung. 2020. "Transformative Professional Development for In-Service Teachers Through International Service Learning." *Teacher Development* 24, no. 1: 33–51.

Barkhuizen, Gary. 2017. "Investigating Multilingual Identity in Study Abroad Contexts: A Short Story Analysis Approach." *System* 71: 102–112.

Barkhuizen, Gary. 2022. *Language Teachers Studying Abroad: Identities, Emotions, and Disruptions*. Multilingual Matters.

Barkhuizen, Gary, and Anne Feryok. 2006. "Pre-Service Teachers' Perceptions of a Short-Term International Experience Programme." *Asia-Pacific Journal of Teacher Education* 34: 115–134.

Bodycott, Peter. 2015. "Intragroup Conflict During Study Abroad." *Journal of International Students* 5, no. 3: 244–259.

Bouchard, Jeremie. 2017. *Ideology, Agency, and Intercultural Communicative Competence*. Singapore: Springer.

Cook, Melodie Lorie. 2010. *Outsourcing In-Service Education: The Effects of a Canadian Pedagogical Programme on Japanese Teachers' of English Teaching Practices*. Macquarie University, Sydney.

Cook, Melodie Lorie, and Trevor Gulliver. 2014. "Helping Japanese Teachers of English Overcome Obstacles to Communicative Language Teaching in Overseas Teacher Development Programs." *Asian EFL Journal Professional Teaching Articles* 79: 24–46.

Devlin, Anne Marie. 2014. *The Impact of Study Abroad on the Acquisition of Sociopragmatic Variation Patterns: The Case of Non-Native Speaker English Teachers*. Oxford, UK: Peter Lang.

Douglas, Scott Roy, Fujiko Sano, and Mark Rosvold. 2018. "Short-Term Study Abroad: The Storied Experiences of Teacher Candidates from Japan." *Learning Landscapes* 11, no. 2: 127–140.

Garbati, Jordana F., and Nathalie Rothschild. 2016. "Lasting Impact of Study Abroad Experiences: A Collaborative Autoethnography." *Forum: Qualitative Social Research* 17, no. 2.

Ilieva, Roumiana, Kumari Beck, and Bonnie Waterstone. 2014. "Towards Sustainable Internationalisation of Higher Education." *Higher Education* 68, no. 6: 875–889.

Jenkins, Jennifer. 2009. "English as a lingua franca: Interpretations and Attitudes." *World Englishes* 28, no. 2: 200–207.

Kubota, Ryuko. 2011. "Questioning Linguistic Instrumentalism: English, Neoliberalism, and Language Tests in Japan." *Linguistics and Education* 22, no. 3: 248–260.

Marshall, Steve. 2022. "Japanese English Teachers' Professional Development in a Canadian University: Perceptions of Self and Imagining Practice." In *Language Teachers Studying Abroad: Identities, Emotions and Disruptions*, edited by Gary Barkhuizen, 35–46. Bristol: Multilingual Matters.

Marshall, Steve, and Arlene Kent Spracklin. 2022. "'We Are in Our Country. Why Do We Have to Resort to Western Ways of Doing Things?': An Analytic Framework for Knowledge Application in Language Teachers Studying Abroad." *Educational Linguistics* 1, no. 2: 267–289.

Rapoport, Anatoli. 2008. "Exchange Programs for Educators: American and Russian Perspectives." *Intercultural Education* 19, no. 1: 67–77.

Santoro, Ninetta, and Jae Major. 2012. "Learning to be a Culturally Responsive Teacher Through International Study Trips: Transformation or Tourism?." *Teaching Education* 23, no. 3: 309–322.

Santoro, Ninetta, Edward Sosu, and Giovanna Fassetta. 2016. "'You Have to be a Bit Brave': Barriers to Scottish Student-Teachers' Participation in Study-Abroad Programmes." *Journal of Education for Teaching* 42, no. 1: 17–27.

Seidlhofer, Barbara. 2011. *Understanding English as a lingua franca - Oxford Applied Linguistics*. Oxford: Oxford University Press.

Takegami, Fumi. 2016. "An Exploratory Study on the Impact of the New Teaching English Through English (TETE) Curriculum Policy in Japan: A Case Study of Three Teachers." *International Journal of Social and Cultural Studies* 9: 15–45.

Takegami, Fumi. 2020. "Identifying Existing Positive Disharmonies for Reconstructing Teaching Practice: A Case Study in Japan." *International Journal of Education* 12, no. 2: 46–66.

7

Staff as Third Space Professionals

Chelsey Laird and Kumari Beck

Introduction

For over a decade, I (Chelsey) have worked as a staff member at various higher education institutions (HEIs) in Canada. In my various staff roles, I have observed how the intensification of internationalization at our institutions was impacting the everyday work of staff working at our institutions, as internationalization was becoming more complex, and extended into new domains, most notably, immigration. When I began my doctoral studies, this is the area I became most interested in exploring as there was little I could see in the literature on staff and international higher education (IHE).

Most scholarship on stakeholders' experiences of IHE in Canada has focused on faculty members, senior administrators, and students (Kang and Metcalfe 2019; Trilokekar and El Masri 2019). This may be influenced by the lack of national and institutional data on administrative and support functions in HEIs (Losinger 2016; Stevens 2018). Having a deeper understanding of staff experiences of internationalization is important in creating an inclusive and supportive IHE environment that values and reflects all stakeholders. Stein, Andreotti, and Suša (2019) call for greater engagement in conversations about the complexities and ethical dilemmas in the everyday work of IHE, particularly for staff and faculty members, and this study adds to that conversation.

The purpose of this chapter is to illuminate staff experiences in the face of unprecedented policy change and institutional commitment to internationalization in Canada. Despite the growth in IHE as a career orientation for staff (Bulut-Sahin and Kondakci 2022) and the necessity of staff to operate HEIs (Brown, Bossu, and Denman 2018), the experiences of staff members are not usually sought in the work of internationalization. As integral contributors to the achievement of institutional goals, however, their experience and views are important. As Losinger (2016) notes, staff experiences should be a part of the history of the institution where they work.

The chapter will begin with a summary of higher education staff literature, followed by the conceptual framework of the study. A brief overview of the methodology will be presented next before moving on to a thematic description of staff interview data. A discussion of the data will be integrated with the data, and we conclude with implications for policy and practice and recommendations for future research.

Staff in HEIs

This literature review aims to provide a brief overview of the scholarship on staff in higher education. Staff have typically been defined in binary categories, such as "professional/support staff" (Brown et al. 2018) or identified by their workplace functions (Schneijderberg 2015). They are sometimes defined as what they are not (Losinger 2016; Szekeres 2011), like *non*academic or *non*teaching. In addition, staff are typically seen as secondary support without a role in achieving academic or strategic goals (Losinger 2016). Staff make up a large proportion of the employee population at HEIs depending on the institution, country, and occupation classification and type (Padro 2018). Staff are a key resource to operationalize the activities and actions of HEIs as "[they] hold much of the systemic knowledge, the intellectual capital, required to ensure the functioning of the university" (Graham 2012, 439). In Canada, staff members are employees at institutions and are subject to provincial labor laws (Jones et al. 2012), and there are no formal categorizations of higher education staff members at provincial or federal levels.

Staff roles are diverse and have become increasingly professionalized and specialized because of the complexity and diversification of higher education institutional strategic goals and functions (Brown et al. 2018). Some staff roles are highly professionalized, emphasizing corporate and managerial approaches typically seen in the private sector, and others are increasingly regulated or specialized (Padro 2018). For example, higher education staff members in Canada who work in immigration are required to maintain certification, which is regulated by a federal organization (Brunner 2017).

The evolving roles and responsibilities of staff are reflective of the complexities influencing HEIs. Whitsed et al. (2021) liken the university to a hybrid organizational structure and culture, influenced by global changes and societal demands. These complexities suggest that university operations are in a constant state of change and adaptation, resulting in the need for institutions to balance competing demands and agendas (Whitsed et al. 2021). Hunter, Jones, and de Wit (2018) argue that staff contributions are at times invisible, but staff are nevertheless expected to adapt to changing institutional needs, develop new skills, knowledge, and ways of doing their work, all the while providing the requisite levels of service, with or without appropriate training. As a result of the increased expectations for efficiency, productivity, and adaptation, staff have reported an increase in anxiety, stress, exhaustion, overwork, frustration, and overall decrease in mental health (Brewster et al. 2022; Szekeres 2004, 2006).

Recent studies have emphasized the importance of training and skill development for staff to contribute to the administrative and strategic goals of internationalization (Hunter 2018). The recognition that staff are fundamental to the success of IHE and enabling them to become active and empowered contributors to IHE is seen through investment in large-scale projects focused on training and development for systemic change (Hunter et al. 2018). This approach centralizes the institutional objectives and leaves out staff's lived experience. In this context, staff members' lived experiences of internationalization would be nuanced and complex, and they would vary greatly based on institutional context, individual identities, and personal values.

A recent study by Miao and Yang (2021) explores the lived experience of student affairs staff members at universities in the United States and Canada, finding that the influence of their ethnic and cultural identities, and personal values and experiences can both enrich and bias their everyday work in the higher education environment. Racialized staff, for example, experience many challenges in their work in higher education such as being a token representative on committees to reflect diversity and being often praised for their connection to diaspora ethnic communities (Rizvi 2023). Racialized staff are also seen as the "go-to" for informal mentorship of students, faculty, or other visitors to the institution who share their culture, ethnicity, and/or language. They are assumed to be able to provide more individualized support (Hassouneh et al. 2014; Miao and Yang 2021), often resulting in increased workload, including emotional labor, particularly related to typically gendered roles (Brewster et al. 2022).

In summary, the literature pertaining to staff in higher education underscores the evolving staff roles and responsibilities, necessitating a better understanding of their functions. This warrants a heightened research agenda to understand the complexities of staff members' contributions and experiences in the higher education environment.

Conceptual Framework

We are informed by Celia Whitchurch's (2008, 2009, 2013, 2015, 2018) notion of Third Space Professional (TSP), for the conceptual framework guiding this study. First introduced in the field of cultural studies by postcolonial scholar Homi Bhabha (1990, 1994), "Third Space" refers to a liminal and hybrid zone where cultures intersect, where hybridity allows for the emergence of "something new and unrecognizable," a space "which enables other positions to emerge" (Bhabha 1990, 211). Whitchurch (2013) builds on Bhabha to theorize aspects of higher education function, specifically, the intersection between the academic, professional, and managerial domains affected by the changing nature of HEIs. Whitchurch (2015) points to the neoliberal agenda of HEIs (e.g., increased pressure for revenue generation, achieving high performance indicators through ranking systems) as a factor for the changes to traditional practices and a blurring of practice boundaries for staff. This includes a focus on role relationships and power dynamics in the higher education environment, and the evolving expectations on staff members whom she names a "Third Space Professional." A TSP navigates the higher education work environment in novel ways, specifically utilizing social networks which span beyond traditional or organizational structures and boundaries, making previously unseen connections visible and amplifying new perspectives (Whitchurch and Gordon 2017).

The TSP concept encompasses various dimensions of work in the higher education context, such as the blurring of perceived divisions between academic and nonacademic roles and activities. The concept captures the emergence of new professional identities as a result of the interweaving of personal and professional aspects into higher education work environments. In earlier work on HEIs, Whitchurch (2008, 2009, 2013) identified categories of higher education staff, referring to how and why staff engage or operate in certain functions or activities: bounded, unbounded, cross-boundary, and blended. Bounded professionals are staff members who have clear, specific functions based on their job description; unbounded professionals are staff members who are project based and not connected to the core operations at an institution. Cross-boundary professionals are staff members who strategically use—or negotiate—boundaries to improve their own capacity building, and blended professionals are staff members whose roles and responsibilities span academic, professional, and managerial domains in their everyday work (2013). She concluded that cross-boundary and blended professionals are TSPs, as they tend to work beyond traditional structural boundaries in the HEI and, as a result, work in complex environments and face ambiguities in their roles. Characteristics that TSPs embody to navigate this include adaptability, creativity, ability to improvise, negotiate, and the capacity to problem solve and continuously encounter dilemmas and paradoxes in the work they do (Whitchurch 2013). Whitchurch initially concluded that TSPs tend to work in "bundles of activity" (2013), but she now attributes the development of Third Space environments in higher education as being widespread, suggesting that higher education roles, responsibilities, and functions "are all third space now" (Whitchurch 2018, 16).

Whitchurch, Locke, and Marini (2019) identify several factors that have led to the increase of TSP roles in HEIs. Factors include diversification of the professional experience staff in higher education have, particularly those who have been trained or worked in other sectors; generational disparities among staff, particularly how the younger generation takes a more proactive and interpretative role in defining their role; and a more frequent mismatch between formal understandings of institutional policy and the ways they are enacted or interpreted in practice by staff.

Whitchurch et al. (2019) further enhanced the conceptualization of TSPs by outlining the conditions for TSP roles to emerge, and then identified typical practices that TSP undertake while working in the higher education environment. First, they identified that TSPs operate in spaces marked by ambiguity and plural conditions, where staff rely on personal knowledge and experience due to the absence of established policies or precedents. Second, TSPs tend to generate new forms of institutional knowledge relationally, by bridging those working in academic units, departments, and other internal and external communities, usually guided by their personal and professional experiences. Finally, TSPs tend to engage in relationships characterized by flattened hierarchies, prioritizing partnerships with academic colleagues over traditional service or administrative responsibilities. In summary, TSPs navigate and innovate new functions of HEI by fostering collaborative approaches within traditionally defined roles and operations.

Methodology

This study was part of a larger study on critical internationalization investigating the experiences of students, faculty, and staff related to internationalization activities at a Canadian university. The data shared in this chapter presents staff experiences of internationalization and is a qualitative case study, which is a research method that aims to understand a specific phenomenon within its real-life context (Yin 1994). This method was chosen to provide a rich and holistic description, analysis, and interpretation of staff members' experiences of internationalization in their daily work.

The principal research question for the study was: How do staff members experience internationalization at a HEI? The study was conducted at Simon Fraser University (SFU), which has a long history of international initiatives and commitment to international education in its strategic plans, policies, programs, and projects. Staff and faculty have been involved in SFU's internationalization activities for decades, including exchange and mobility programs, research initiatives, and development projects. Staff are the frontline contacts for all institutional operations related to internationalization and typically serve stakeholders including international students, faculty, and visitors.

A total of thirteen staff members (twelve women and one man) from academic departments and service units participated in the study. The recruitment process involved a combination of snowball sampling and public advertising to ensure a diverse range of perspectives from various units within the university. Semi-structured interviews were the main method of data collection. Interviews were conducted (pre-pandemic) in-person and varied in length between forty-five and ninety minutes. Interviews were audio-recorded with participants' consent, and field notes were taken to capture additional observations and contextual information. Initially, all audio recordings were transcribed verbatim, and pseudonyms were assigned or chosen by participants to ensure confidentiality. Transcripts were member checked and modified. As staff members engaged in internationalization are few in number and easily identifiable, we will not be identifying participants' specific unit to protect their anonymity. The transcripts were then imported into NVivo, a qualitative data analysis software for coding and organization. Codes were derived through an iterative process of open coding, focused coding, and constant comparison. Themes and patterns were identified and refined, and connections between codes and themes were established. Data were analyzed using thematic analysis aimed to capture the diversity of experiences while identifying commonalities across participants (Miles, Huberman, and Saldaña 2014).

To ensure trustworthiness and rigor in this study, several strategies were employed. Participants confirmed the accuracy of data transcripts through member checking. Peer debriefing was utilized, where the research team reviewed the research design, data analysis process, and emerging themes. Researcher reflexivity was maintained throughout the research process, with the researchers continuously reflecting on their own biases and assumptions that may have influenced data collection and analysis. The data are presented below.

Experiences of Working at an Internationalizing Institution

Three prominent themes emerged from staff views and experiences shared in the interviews. They are: (1) the impact of values and personal experiences on their work, (2) the changing nature of work, and (3) improvising in their roles.

Values and Personal Experience

Many participants referred to their own experiences as immigrants and living or studying abroad, highlighting the importance of that transition in their own lives and using their own experience to relate to international students or professional skilled immigrants. Charlie shared that it helped to "shed some light on the situations they [students] are facing." Participants drew on several variations of their own personal experiences as key to developing the skills they needed to successfully implement and operationalize internationalization activities in their jobs.

Charlie shared how she related to both the international students she supports and the employers who hire them. She imagined herself in both positions, as she had personal experience both as an international student and an employer. She reflected on a tense situation where she coached both the student and the employer to come to a solution. Because of her personal experience, she was able to identify the gaps in understanding from each party and individually identify steps forward to rectify the situation. She equated that experience to "part of the education for the employer" while being empathetic to the international student, having to adapt and navigate a new profession and life in Canada. Charlie shared that upon immigrating to Canada, she too had to pivot her career in Canada due to a mismatch in professional accreditation. She reflected:

> I think that what helps me work with international students, helps me be successful working with them, is also my coming from a different country as an immigrant and going through that transition myself and then working with immigrants, professional skilled immigrants. . . . In time, I think I've acquired this big picture and most of the students come to talk to me, my relating to their story where I might have something in the past that I can bring in and just have that, you know, shed some light onto an issue.

The experience of being an immigrant and establishing a new life in Canada was corroborated by other participants as it allowed them to express great empathy for international students and visiting faculty members. These staff experiences also illustrate the importance of relationality as a key element in the role of TSPs, having a shared experience or commonality to build trust and legitimacy between stakeholders (Whitchurch and Gordon 2017).

Linda drew on her understanding as a first-generation Canadian with lived experience of working and being educated "overseas." This is an important part of her identity and personal values, and when she reflected on why she went abroad for work and school, she shares:

> I think [through being educated in a country different than the one you were raised in] you understand your place in the world. I think education is about our next generation understanding their place in the world, and I think the way we [Canadians] decided to craft the world is that we make any part of the world accessible to anybody at any time. So I don't think it's an option for us to tell the students not to understand the rest of the world. . . . So that's why I personally I am a big fan of our students going abroad, because when they do see more of the world, they are practicing a lot more of understanding, reflecting on why they stand for something or why they don't stand for something because they're explaining it to other people, right?

Linda projected her own lived experience, for example, the development of her worldview from living and studying in an international environment, as necessary and "an important tool" for students she serves at work. She highly valued international experiences as "tools" to practice understanding and reflection for identity building, career development, and lifestyle choices, and ultimately, she deems these experiences as the point of higher education. Linda's failure to recognize the privilege inherent in her ability to travel and work abroad is evident as she overlooks the disparities in international student mobility to access higher education, underscoring the privileged nature of her perspective and projects a more simplistic understanding of IHE.

Naomi referred to her experience of studying abroad in an international graduate program with an internationalized curriculum as informing her professional practice. She referred specifically to the fact that there were "a lot of international students, so it [internationalization] was a part of the program." She explained that the curriculum would "be very different, different contexts, different issues to deal with, so having both international students in the class to bring this real-world experience of working in different places really added to our experiences of thinking of how [our approaches] may be applied in different settings." She placed great emphasis on the reflexivity developed through this experience and applies it in her work. For example, Naomi notes a shift in how student support programs have changed to strengths-based approaches. In the past, she noted that programs would be centered around international students being "deficient" linguistically or culturally. The shift to strengths-based approaches in program development recognizes the strengths of all students, regardless of whether they are international or domestic students. She also referred to completing an international internship during her time as a graduate student, and her reflexivity contributed to the enhancement of her intercultural skills. For example, she identified skills such as "openness, flexibility, kindness, respect, [and being] someone that they [international students] can actually talk to and who are not going to, kind of, pigeonhole them or that [someone] can be reflexive and reflective about their own experience" as being key for her work.

Morci, Mina, and Helen also referred to their experience as immigrants, or working and studying abroad as allowing them to build intercultural skills, such as empathy, curiosity, understanding, and tolerance for ambiguity. They noted that having the experience of "living outside of your comfort zone" (Morci) has enhanced their reflexivity. Helen related her international experience to being "very connected to who I am as a person" and shared that living and working abroad has given her the skills to see diverse perspectives. She shares, "I try and see where I'm coming from and where they're coming from [and figure out] how we work together, coming from all of these different places." These examples demonstrate TSP characteristics of utilizing personal agency and relationality to build relationships with those they serve, particularly international students.

Staff who have had personal experiences with international travel, as immigrants, or opportunities to study or work abroad, often possess a heightened sense of empathy and understanding of the challenges faced by international students. These experiences allow them to relate to the unique needs and struggles of international students, enabling them to provide more meaningful and sensitive support (Miao and Yang 2021). However, most participants failed to verbalize or acknowledge the privilege inherent in having access to international mobility, for study or work, which shows the limitations in recognizing privilege and the specific challenges faced by racialized immigrants and newcomers.

To be successful in operationalizing internationalization activities, staff need to possess intercultural fluency, sometimes described as a certain set of skills (Hunter 2018) that enable staff to navigate diverse cultural contexts, communicate effectively across cultural boundaries, and bridge gaps in understanding. Whitchurch (2013) indicated that TSPs seek out continuous opportunities for professional development and possess skills such as adaptability and creativity, perhaps acquired from international experiences, that help staff maintain a culturally sensitive perspective and continuously improve their support strategies. This literacy also needs to include an understanding of power relations in international relations.

Empathy allows staff to put themselves in the shoes of international students, understanding their emotions, challenges, and aspirations. Staff with international experiences often feel they have a deeper connection with international students and serve as a role model and source of inspiration (Miao and Yang 2021). As racialized students are more drawn to seek mentorship with faculty and staff with whom they share identity or background (Dahlvig 2010), staff who are immigrants or are racialized themselves can draw from their own diverse backgrounds and understand cross-cultural interactions to create a more inclusive and supportive campus environment. However, this places additional labor, often invisible, on these staff members to provide these supports to students.

While staff draw on their values and personal experiences to make sense of the pluralistic and complex nature of working in the higher education environment, they also exhibited limitations in fully grasping the intricate power dynamics of racial and cultural difference within the academic space. Many staff members may have inadvertently overlooked or downplayed these aspects. The rarity of participants like Laura acknowledging the inequities associated with the "primacy of the English language" in the university underscores the broader tendency to overlook systemic disparities, highlighting the need for a more comprehensive and critical examination of the web of relations in higher education environments.

Changing Nature of Work

Many of the participants noted that with the increased institutional focus on IHE, they experienced changes in their daily work. Most staff noted that their workload had increased, suggesting they are often "doing work off the side of my desk" (Helen) or taking on more responsibility, like "continuously monitoring any changes [to immigration policy]" (Jessica).

All participants acknowledged that institutional interest in internationalization had impacted their jobs. Some described internationalization as a "buzz word" (Charlie) and yet some participants, like Linda, asked "what does it mean? And how do I do it [internationalization], and what resources are you going to give me?" Helen complained that "there is never enough people, there is never enough time" and "there aren't additional resources to support additional work." With the increase in demand, participants shared how they employed strategies for efficiency, like connecting with other service units and sharing information and expertise to help get the job done (Sara, Helen, Linda). Participants also noted that these tensions were recognized by their leaders or managers who were trying to make additional resources available through hiring more staff or providing more opportunities for training and development, but it was challenging to keep up with the pace and demand (Helen, Naomi, Tori, Nelson, Mina). Whitchurch (2015) accounts for some of these tensions in her conceptualization of TSP being connected to the neoliberal agenda of HEIs. The institutional pressure to generate revenue and to achieve status in the rankings can leave units and departments understaffed due to high international student enrollments and added responsibilities to market and brand the institution internally and externally.

Predominantly, the high number of international students on campus was seen as having the most impact on staff capacity: "there's a lot of talk about increased use of services by international students" (Naomi). Eloise and Charlie described how this has impacted their workday. For example, meetings with international students tend to take longer (than domestic students) because there are many additional factors to consider, including explaining the cultural context of a given process or policies. Sara, Linda, and Laura noted that international students need more complex support, for example, noting language difficulties and personal issues, such as loneliness and isolation in their new cultural environment. Sara and Laura suggest that working with international students is not necessarily more work but is of a different nature, such as implications in it that are difficult to account for in the administrative roles that they hold.

In Laura's experience, she often feels her role "spills into personal counselling" and a lot of the international students she sees are "often struggling personally and academically [. . .] things are not working out as they had envisioned." This not only causes stress and anxiety for the student, but also for Laura because she recognizes "there is a clear line that we are not counselors, but we are responding to a human being." She recognizes the professional boundaries of her role, skills, and training, but she does not let this come in the way of responding to the student's needs. As Whitchurch (2013) argued, TSP's experience paradoxes and dilemmas in their work. Brewster et al. (2022) argued frontline staff who engage with students constantly navigate between attending to the student's mental health needs without addressing their own. Laura shared an example of this paradox by identifying that she has to prioritize between professional and personal boundaries to address her own mental health.

Participants also noted that they were spending more of their time getting work done due to complex admissions processes, grant or research applications, and international student support services. For example, Charlie shared how interactions with international students were more time consuming because students needed more help. She believed:

> What is really important for anyone who works in this environment [with international students] is [to be] open to adapting the policies, the processes and procedures. [. . .] I mean, I'm not talking about breaking policies or anything like that, but being able to listen to the student and being able to understand why that student did not understand that.

Nelson also talked about going beyond the job description, noting that his contract does not say "'you only do this, but you don't do this' [but it is my job to] go and figure out how is the best way to do that" and sees himself as being responsible for taking in multiple perspectives, from leadership, from students, from colleagues, and "kind of play this little triangle in the middle to make sure that we keep most people happy [with our services]." Several participants acknowledged in a variety of ways that "figuring it out" is an important part of their work. While Nelson is an enthusiastic supporter of internationalization and happy to adapt programs to address cultural differences, he acknowledged that for him, there is a limit to how much cultural adaptation should be warranted. He shared:

> There's a part of me that's wondering how far it is gonna go. I mean my fear is that we've become too involved in dealing with international students that we forget about our regular students, I mean I don't want to feel alienated in my own country and I am from an international country, but Canada is my home. [. . .] I am going to give some of the comforts of your home but I want you to experience the comforts of my home—and where's the fine line?

Nelson's dilemma is the "fine line" between adapting services to the cultural differences of the people staff are serving. While he understood his role is to provide services and to "figure things out" he believed he was missing the mark for "regular" or domestic students. Other participants' perspectives (Naomi, Christine) extend beyond this perspective, noting that their units develop programs for all students, appreciating the diverse needs of students not only defined by their status at the university. The tensions in the perception of international students as a deviation from providing services to "regular" students can be problematic in several ways. First, it can lead to the marginalization of international students, making them feel excluded or unwelcome. This exclusionary mind-set can hinder their academic and social integration, ultimately affecting their overall educational experience.

Second, treating international students differently can perpetuate stereotypes and biases, reinforcing notions of "us versus them." Such attitudes can hinder cultural understanding and exacerbate cultural differences. Failure to critically examine the dichotomy of providing services perspective not only perpetuates discrimination and inequality but also undermines the goals of internationalization, like cultural understanding, within universities.

In other circumstances, it was a lack of policy that left staff having to "figure things out." For example, Helen's academic unit does not have a specific internationalization strategy, leaving her feeling lost or isolated when needing to make decisions in her daily duties. She explains that she gets pulled into different aspects of international work (student advising, exchange/mobility, partnerships, projects) and without specific direction or real agency over her work feels "spread really thin across a lot of different areas." She stated that a lot of her work to support students is done off the side of her desk because it is not explicitly stated in a strategy or work plan. Similarly, Sara expressed frustration with a lack of strategy and not understanding the intention for decisions made that impact her work. For example, she referred to an international transfer agreement that brings large numbers of international students to her academic unit, exclaiming "Ugh, it's confusing. Even I don't really know the mechanism behind that."

New demands and expectations on their work leave staff in a tensioned space between policy or strategy and reality, interpreting policy and their own job descriptions and figuring things out along the way. Some participants strive for autonomy and agency and others avoid it, indicating it is "not in [my] job description" (Eloise) or that responsibility for "figuring it out" was someone else's responsibility. These tensions can lead to feelings of frustration and confusion, particularly when institutional objectives lack clarity, leaving staff to deal with the repercussions. Whitchurch's (2013) TSP concept aptly acknowledges this intricate interplay, recognizing that TSPs not only confront these tensions and paradoxes but also possess the capacity to innovate and resolve challenges. However, this agency is not constant, as there are moments when individuals may feel confined by their job descriptions, hindered by the very structures meant to support them. These examples of staff experiences of the changing

Improvisation: Being "Comfortable in the Grey"

Many participants described how they are creative in completing their daily tasks or performing a task spontaneously or without formal preparation. Eloise, Tori, and Nelson recognized that some processes and policies can be disadvantageous or be unfair to certain stakeholders at the institution, such as international students or visiting international faculty members, but they express that decisions to change these policies are "above my paygrade" (Morci) so they collaborate with colleagues and consult with management, which results in a "combination of us figuring out what works" (Nelson). For example, Tori noted that senior leadership in her academic department tried to be more proactive in responding to requests for international partnership agreements by identifying key countries and research strengths that were a priority for the department and allocating resources to support those partnerships first. She suggests the department took this approach so they "can kind of control things" but even with the strategic prioritization for international partnerships, Tori noted it ends up being "a bit ad hoc." She shared an example of "having to host a delegation for political reasons" appreciating that colleagues from across the university "try to pitch in" as much as they can but that she felt like she had to think on her feet a lot, particularly noting cultural differences in hosting. She expressed a desire to have someone on staff to be able to advise on specific traditions for hosting international visitors, as she often thought "what do we give them? how do we welcome them?".

Linda, Christine, Charlie, Helen, and Nelson shared examples of being creative in dealing with the mismatch between institutional policy and operational practices. Linda shared her frustration regarding admissions policies, suggesting that they should be more flexible when looking at international student applicants. She believed that admissions processes are developed with a specific type of student in mind (domestic, high school applicant) and don't account for applicants from a diverse range of countries and walks of life, education systems, multiple languages, or specialized skills. Admissions processes to her department are "very complicated for international applicants" and working with international applicants necessitates a different approach because it "deviates from the norm in a band aid kind of way." She feels that more flexible processes for admissions would create more equitable pathways for international students in particular, and clear instructions for staff. She described how some colleagues were averse to and critiqued "breaking these rules for international students." This view, in turn, "demonizes the international students as the people who cause you [staff] more problems because we [the institution] don't build it [admissions processes, activities, etc.] the right way to account for diversity. We think that the international students are what cause us more work and yet it is the lack of institutional guidelines that are lagging behind the reality." Linda highlights the tension between policy and practice and how some staff improvise in interpreting policy (Whitchurch et al. 2019) and others, characterized as "bounded," stick to the rules, making for an uneven and inequitable admissions process for international students.

Christine shared that her work relates to figuring out how to negotiate between policy and practice, and she stated that her belief is that the role of staff is to serve the strategic interest of the institution while being mindful that policies and decisions being made are impacting human beings' lives. She understood that policies and procedures at the institution serve the best interests of the dominant culture but based her approach on "thinking outside the box." This suggests that improvisation is an essential capacity needed for working in the higher education sector. She continues:

> It [internationalization of higher education] pushes us beyond the black and white to see the grey, to be comfortable in the grey, to figure out "how to operate in the grey." Advocacy is huge because when you're dealing with a special population, whether it's exchange students, or international students, you're not the status quo, you're not the majority. There are changes you're going to be asking some unit to bend the way they do things, think a little different and that's a pain for a lot of people, right?

Christine acknowledged that she relies heavily on negotiation and advocacy, particularly with various stakeholders at the institution. She was comfortable and confident in her skills to do this and asserted that: "we have to use our skills to not only believe in ourselves but help them [other stakeholders] believe that [changing policy; allowing for complexity] is important."

Some participants noted that thinking outside the box is challenging or not possible due to policy constraints, while others accepted improvisation as part of their service role, adapting to the needs of those they are serving. Implementing the goals of internationalization demands the active involvement of higher education staff who improvise in the course of their daily work.

Staff rely on their skills and personal experience to make internationalization "work" by thinking outside of the box and creating solutions for the issues and complications that arise because of blurred professional boundaries and new situations and circumstances that pop up in different environments. Drawing upon Whitchurch's TSP concept, we see that these staff exemplify traits of negotiation and agency, specifically, those who interpret and improvise to generate new forms of institutional knowledge relationally, enacting the social capital they have built with academic colleagues and those across and outside of the institution, usually guided by their personal and professional experiences.

We have also seen examples of how staff have to "figure things out" in their work because of a mismatch or lack of policy or precedent, and therefore, they rely on their relationships, personal agency, and experience to interpret this into practice and service. Whitchurch's TSP concept sheds light on how these staff operate in the gray areas, maneuvering through the complexities and paradoxes of the work encountered in HEIs.

Becoming TSPs

Higher education staff members' experiences of internationalization reflect the complexities of the work environment of HEIs impacted by neoliberalism. The data in this study highlights a diverse spectrum of staff experiences within higher education, representing staff roles that emulate Whitchurch's (2013) professional identity categorizations of bounded, unbounded, cross-boundary, and blended professional roles. Some participants in this study embodied characteristics representative of "bounded" or "unbounded" roles, where they were less likely to deviate from specific functions based on their job description and thus maintain institutional hierarchies or structures. However, most participants shared experiences or characteristics representative of being in "cross-boundary" or "unbounded" roles, where they exercised their personal agency by relying on their personal experience and values for relationship building, navigating the changing nature of work, and actively addressing the mismatch between policy and practice through creative interpretation that serves the stakeholders. These participants are resoundingly representative of Whitchurch's TSPs, and this dynamic range of professional identities in HEIs underscores the ongoing transformation and complex nature of the work environment in the internationalizing HEIs.

The data revealed that staff who have personal experience as immigrants or have significant international experience (as study abroad participants or professionally working abroad) are more likely to be empathetic, curious, understanding, flexible, and reflective in their approach to working with diverse student populations and other aspects of international work. This, however, may result in an extension of "work" for staff members who are culturally diverse or have transnational connectivity, as minoritized students tend to seek out mentorship from faculty or staff with whom they share identity or background and who can provide more individualized and deeper connection and support (Hassouneh et al. 2014; Miao and Yang 2021).

The data also revealed that the ever-changing nature of work in HEIs produces a paradoxical experience for staff who have to find new ways of getting their work done, and in doing so neglect other work or have to do more with less. Staff noted the increase in their workloads and in more invisible work, such as emotional labor. The ability to improvise to carry out their work is reliant on skills and personal experience to think outside of the box and create solutions for the issues and complications that arise. They are living the influences brought on by global change and societal demands, leading to blurred professional roles and gaps in service. They have to face the increasing cultural diversity of students but have to rely on personal capacities, sometimes inadequately, to deal with cultural difference. This is specifically so in terms of racialized students and staff. They are expected to figure out how to accommodate these differences within institutional rules, and while some of them are comfortable "bending the rules," others are averse to it. Staff members navigate these in-between spaces in varying levels of ease, illustrating how they are becoming TSPs.

This study contributes to developing a more comprehensive and nuanced understanding of staff members working in higher education, particularly of staff contributions to internationalization. More research is needed in exploring how staff are motivated to achieve institutional goals, particularly related to internationalization. Hunter et al. (2018) and Hunter (2018) suggest that staff play significant roles in their institution being more active in and committed to internationalization, and further exploration of personal and professional values could improve this understanding. The findings from this study contribute to the literature on staff experiences of internationalization by suggesting *how* staff work and how they are becoming TSPs. Through their work experiences, mostly through interactions with diverse student populations, staff members identify the impact of values and personal experiences on their approach to internationalization, how they navigate the changing nature of work, and improvise to operationalize internationalization. Staff embrace the challenges and rewards that come with encountering cultural difference in their daily work, but most staff did not identify ethical and critical considerations of internationalization. Staff experiences working in cultural difference highlight the importance of intercultural literacy and the need for ongoing support and professional development to effectively navigate an increasingly complex and interconnected world. The sparse data on how staff address race and racialization highlights how these topics and issues need to be addressed through staff professional development.

The stories shared in this chapter highlight the significant role that staff members have in meeting institutional objectives and goals, but also how they cultivate and create the foundation for cultural difference at internationalizing institutions through their relationships with students, stakeholders, and with each other in the internationalizing university. Some of the challenges for staff members include a lack of clarity about what jurisdiction they have over their roles and highlight a significant professional vulnerability, where staff must demonstrate their value to the workplace because much of the work they do is ad hoc, interpreted, and outside of the formalized structures of the institution. This study does not fully delve into the intricacies of these challenges and their potential solutions. For human resources and institutional leaders, understanding the tensions and complexities experienced by staff highlighted in this study is crucial for managing higher education operations, particularly in the context of internationalization. Unanswered questions persist regarding staff experiences in these roles, including how staff "attend to the ethical dilemmas that accompany the intensification of internationalization" (Stein et al. 2019). Engaging in further research about staff and particularly the concept of TSPs can bring more "multi-voiced conversations and critically-informed analyses" (Stein et al. 2019) to better understand the complexity of internationalization in HEIs. Recognizing staff as TSPs makes it possible to see the contributions they make and how best to support them in their everyday work.

Acknowledgment

This research was funded by a grant from the Social Sciences and Humanities Research Council of Canada.

References

Bhabha, Homi K. 1990. "The Third Space: Interview with Homi Bhabha." In *Identity: Community, Culture, Difference*, edited by Jonathan Rutherford, 207–221. London: Lawrence & Wishart.

Bhabha, Homi K. 1994. *The Location of Culture*. London: Routledge.

Brewster, Liz, Emma Jones, Michael Priestley, Susan J. Wilbraham, Leigh Spanner, and Gareth Hughes. 2022. "'Look After the Staff and They Would Look after the Students' Cultures of Wellbeing and Mental Health in the University Setting." *Journal of Further and Higher Education* 46, no. 4: 548–560. https://doi.org/10.1080/0309877X.2021.1986473.

Brown, Natalie, Carina Bossu, and Brian Denman. 2018. "Responding to a Changing Higher Education Sector: The Role of Professional and Support Staff." In *Professional and Staff Support in Higher Education*, University Development and Administration, edited by Carina Bossu and Natalie Brown, 129–38. Singapore: Springer Nature Pte., Ltd.

Brunner, Lisa Ruth. 2017. "Higher Educational Institutions as Emerging Immigrant Selection Actors: A History of British Columbia's Retention of International Graduates, 2001–2016." *Policy Reviews in Higher Education* 1, no. 1: 22–41. http://dx.doi.org/10.1080/23322969.2016.1243016.

Bulut-Sahin, Betul, and Yasar Kondakci. 2022. "Conflicting Perspectives on the Internationalization of Higher Education: Evidence from the Turkish Case." *Journal of Studies in International Education*. https://doi.org/10.1177/10283153221126245.

Dahlvig, Jolyn. 2010. "Mentoring of African American Students at a Predominantly White Institution (PWI)." *Christian Higher Education* 9, no. 5: 369–395. https://doi-org.proxy.lib.sfu.ca/10.1080/15363750903404266.

Graham, Carroll. 2012. "Transforming Spaces and Identities: The Contributions of Professional Staff to Learning Spaces in Higher Education." *Journal of Higher Education Policy & Management* 34 no. 4: 437–452. https://doi-org.proxy.lib.sfu.ca/10.1080/1360080X.2012.696326.

Hunter, Fiona. 2018. "Training Administrative Staff to Become Key Players in the Internationalization of Higher Education." *International Higher Education* 92: 16–17. https://doi.org/10.6017/ihe.2018.92.10280.

Hunter, Fiona, Elspeth Jones, and Hans de Wit. 2018. *The Staff Who Are Overlooked in Internationalisation*. University World News. https://www.universityworldnews.com/post.php?story=20181031081234166.

Hassouneh, Dena, Kristin F. Lutz, Ann K. Beckett, Edward P. Junkins, and LaShawn L. Horton. 2014. "The Experiences of Underrepresented Minority Faculty in Schools of Medicine." *Medical Education Online* 19, no. 1: 1–14. https://doi-org.proxy.lib.sfu.ca/10.3402/meo.v19.24768.

Jones, Glen, Julian Weinrib, Amy Scott Metcalfe, Don Fisher, Kjell Rubensen, and Iain Snee. 2012. "Academic Work in Canada: The Perceptions of Early-Career

Academics." *Higher Education Quarterly* 66, no. 2: 189–206. https://doi.org/10.1111/j.1468-2273.2012.00515.x.

Kang, Jeong-Ja, and Amy Scott Metcalfe. 2019. "Living and Learning Between Canada and Korea: The Academic and Cultural Experiences of Undergraduate International Exchange Students." *Journal of Comparative & International Higher Education* 11, no. Fall: 28–36. https://www.ojed.org/index.php/jcihe/article/view/1074.

Losinger, Isabella. 2016. "The Non-nons: Secretarial and Clerical Staff." In *Solitudes of the Workplace: Women in Universities*, edited by Elvi Whittaker, 156–171. Kingston: McGill-Queen's University Press.

Miao, Sanfeng, and Haishan (Sam) Yang. 2021. "Foreign-Born Student Affairs Professionals' Impacts and Experiences: The Missing Piece of Internationalization." *Journal of Studies in International Education* 27, no. 1: 82–99. https://doi-org.proxy.lib.sfu.ca/10.1177/10283153211052769.

Miles, Matthew B., Michael A. Huberman, and Johnny Saldaña. 2014. *Qualitative Data Analysis: A Methods Sourcebook*. Thousand Oaks: Sage.

Padro, Fernando F. 2018. "Preface." In *Professional and Support Staff in Higher Education*, edited by Carina Bossu and Natalie Brown, v–xxii. Singapore: Springer Nature Pte., Ltd.

Rizvi, Fazal. 2023. "Internationalization of Higher Education and the Advantage of Diaspora." *International Higher Education* 113: 16–17. https://ejournals.bc.edu/index.php/ihe/article/view/16099.

Schneijderberg, Christian. 2015. "Work Jurisdiction of New Higher Education Professionals." In *Forming, Recruiting and Managing the Academic Profession*, edited by Ulrich Teichler and William K. Cummings, 113–144. https://doi.org/10.1007/978-3-319-16080-1_1.

Stein, Sharon, Vanessa Andreotti, and Rene Suša. 2019. "Pluralizing Frameworks for Global Ethics in the Internationalization of Higher Education in Canada." *Canadian Journal of Higher Education* 49, no. 1: 22–46. https://doi.org/10.47678/cjhe.v49i1.188244.

Stevens, Andrew. 2018. "Working for a Living Wage Around the Ivory Tower." *Canadian Journal of Higher Education* 48, no. 1: 22–38. https://doi.org/10.47678/cjhe.v48i1.187992.

Szekeres, Judy. 2004. "The Invisible Workers." *Journal of Higher Education, Policy and Management* 26, no. 1: 7–22. https://doi.org/10.1080/1360080042000182500.

Szekeres, Judy. 2006. "General Staff Experiences in the Corporate University." *Journal of Higher Education Policy and Management* 28, no. 2: 133–145. https://doi.org/10.1080/13600800600750962.

Szekeres, Judy. 2011. "Professional Staff Carve Out a New Space." *Journal of Higher Education Policy and Management* 33, no. 6: 679–691. https://doi.org/10.1080/1360080X.2011.621193.

Trilokekar, Roopa D., and Amira El Masri. 2019. "International Students Are…Golden: Canada's Changing Policy Contexts, Approaches, and National Peculiarities in

Attracting International Students as Future Immigrants." In *Outward and Upward Mobilities: International Students in Canada, Their Families, and Structuring Institutions*, edited by Min-Jung Kwak and Ann H. Kim, 25–55. Toronto: University of Toronto Press.

Whitchurch, Celia. 2008. "Shifting Identities and Blurring Boundaries: The Emergence of Third Space Professionals in UK Higher Education." *Higher Education Quarterly* 62, no. 4: 377–396. https://doi.org/10.1111/j.1468-2273.2008.00387.x.

Whitchurch, Celia. 2009. "The Rise of the Blended Professional in Higher Education: A Comparison Between the United Kingdom, Australia and the United States." *Higher Education* 58, no. 3: 407–418. https://link.springer.com/content/pdf/10.1007/s10734-009-9202-4.pdf?pdf=button.

Whitchurch, Celia. 2013. *Reconstructing Identities in Higher Education: The Rise of 'Third Space' Professionals*. Abingdon: Routledge.

Whitchurch, Celia. 2015. "The Rise of Third Space Professionals: Paradoxes and Dilemmas." In *Forming, Recruiting and Managing the Academic Profession*, edited by Ulrich Teichler and William K. Cummings, 79–99. https://doi.org/10.1007/978-3-319-16080-1_1.

Whitchurch, Celia. 2018. "Being a Higher Education Professional Today: Working in a Third Space." In *Professional and Support Staff in Higher Education*, edited by Carina Bossu and Natalie Brown, 9–20. Singapore: Springer Nature Pte Ltd.

Whitchurch, Celia, and George Gordon. 2017. *Reconstructing Relationships in Higher Education: Challenging Agendas*. New York: Routledge.

Whitchurch, Celia, William Locke, and Gulio Marini. 2019. "A Delicate Balance: Optimising Individual Aspirations and Institutional Missions in Higher Education." CGHE Working Paper No 44.

Whitsed, Craig, Jeanine Gregersen-Hermans, Marina Casals, and Betty Leask. 2021. "Engaging Faculty and Staff in the Internationalization of Higher Education." In *The Handbook of International Higher Education*, edited by Darla K. Deardorff, Hans de Wit, Betty Leask, and Harvey Charles, 325–342. Bloomfield: Taylor & Francis Group.

Yin, Robert K. 1994. *Case Study Research: Design and Methods*, 2nd edn. Beverly Hills: Sage Publishing.

8

The Experiences of Staff Regarding Language in the Internationalizing University

Camila Miranda and Roumiana Ilieva

Introduction

The global landscape of higher education has been characterized over the past several decades by internationalization processes. One of the drivers of internationalization is student mobility, mainly toward countries in the Global North/West (Maringe and Foskett 2012). As a consequence, there has been an increase in the diversity of cultures and languages coexisting in higher education institutions around the world. Language, which is both "globalizing and globalized" (Fairclough 2006, 3), plays a crucial role in the process of internationalization of education. In particular, the English language plays a dominant role (Jenkins 2013). The ideological aspects of the English language (Byrd Clark, Haque, and Lamoureux 2013), and the power relations inherently associated with it (Baker 2016), are important factors that influence people's overall experience at universities.

The larger study from which the data discussed here is drawn analyzes the perceptions and experiences of different actors (students, staff, and faculty) in relation to linguistic diversity at an internationalizing Anglo-dominant institution in Western Canada. It presents qualitative data collected as part of an institution-wide project about internationalization of higher education in which the first author, Camila, worked as a research assistant. This chapter focuses on the experiences of staff, a group of university stakeholders rarely discussed in academic literature, and addresses the following questions:

- How do staff perceive and experience linguistic diversity in the context of a transcultural university?
- How do ideologies and assumptions about language and multilingualism inform and shape staff's ideas and experiences in an internationalizing university?

It is hoped that the research shared here will augment the sparse literature on staff's perceptions and experiences with internationalization of education and expand on recommendations for more inclusive internationalization practices with respect to language issues.

Even though this study was conducted in the context of internationalization of education, we also use the concept of the transcultural university interchangeably with the notion of the internationalized university in reference to Baker's (2016) idea that in today's world universities are complex institutions that need to move beyond nation-based concepts such as home language and culture in favor of multilingualism and multiculturalism.

Theoretical Perspectives and Review of the Literature

According to Beck (2013), we need to understand "how the economic, political and cultural dimensions of globalization influence internationalization" (45). The landscape of higher education has changed and become more complex over the last several decades with internationalization undergoing "fundamental changes itself" (Knight 2013, 84), being "increasingly characterized by competition, commercialization, self-interest, and status building" (89). One of the causes, and at the same time consequences, of internationalization of education is student mobility (Maringe and Foskett 2012), which has consequences for educational institutions; classroom dynamics; and for the identities of students, faculty, and staff who participate in internationalization.

The idea of university as a local institution creates a contradiction in light of internationalizing practices. (Western) institutions see economic advantages in transnational possibilities by promoting an image aligned with a national identity (and the idea that the West is the best). At the same time, they advertise that students will receive qualifications that allow them to compete in the global marketplace (Beck 2013). Globalization and internationalization also affect the skills and competencies one is expected to possess (Beck et al. 2013).

Internationalization is a key aspect of many Canadian postsecondary institutions' strategic plans, with a focus on investment in student, faculty and staff mobility, recruitment of international students, international partnerships, and internationalization of curricula (Larsen 2015). CBIE statistics show that there was a 92 percent increase in international students in Canada between 2008 and 2015 and 65 percent of international students in Canada are pursuing postsecondary education (CBIE 2016). In addition, the

Canadian federal government had the goal of "doubling international student recruitment by 2022" (Garson 2016, 19) to reach 450,000, but this goal has already been surpassed indicating that internationalization in Canada is largely motivated by an economic rationale (Beck 2012; Beck and Ilieva 2019; Byrd Clarke et al. 2013).

Internationalization Ideologies and Articulations

Stier (2004, 2010) investigates three internationalization ideologies that "influence policy-makers and educators in their understanding and approach to internationalization" (93). The first ideology, idealism, understands internationalization as good per se, with the power to raise the awareness of social injustices and promote a sense of global community. However, this position can be criticized because internationalization is usually done from a Western perspective. The second ideology, instrumentalism, is focused on the global market and "instrumentalists consider higher education to be one means to maximize profit" (90). Academia is compared to other markets since education is considered a global commodity and international students bring money into the system. Educationalism, the third ideology, sees the contact with unfamiliar academic and cultural practices as an enriching educational experience. However, educationalism may lead to *academicentrism*, "manifested in a conviction that 'our' methods of teaching, research and degrees are better than those of other countries" (Stier 2004, 93).

Drawing on Stier's (2004) ideologies of internationalization, Ilieva, Beck, and Waterstone (2014) present a sustainability frame of reference to critically analyze internationalization in its complexity. The authors identify two aspects to be considered for a more ethical internationalization: valuing diversity and mutuality/reciprocity. The first focuses on "expanding knowledge of different educational traditions" (885), as well as acknowledging and valuing the multiple experiences of international students. The latter emphasizes collaboration, the need to "respectfully [acknowledge] the other" (887), and to understand "internationalisation as a partnership and not a one-way flow of expertise" (886).

Internationalization, Linguistic and Cultural Diversity, Inequalities, and Language Ideologies

OECD statistics report that 41 percent of international student enrollment in the last decade has been in countries where English is the dominant language

(Baker 2016). The idea of the "transcultural" is explored by Baker (2016) to refer to internationalizing universities, which are no longer delimited by national boundaries due to the increasing flow of international students, staff, and knowledge. The concept of transcultural universities more accurately reflects the complexity and diversity of languages, communities, and cultures present in many higher education institutions today. Therefore, one of the challenges of internationalizing universities is how to adopt an international orientation if they still focus on the idea "of the university as a national institution set within a national context with a corresponding identifiable national language and culture" (Baker 2016, 440). Even though English is the dominant language of instruction in Anglophone institutions, Baker (2016) warns of the linguistic inequalities that emerge when institutions fail to "adequately address the complexity of the linguistic landscape of international universities" (442).

The relationship between linguistic inequality and internationalization in the Canadian context is explored by Byrd Clark et al. (2013) who present a critical analysis of the role of language and linguistic heterogeneity in discourses and processes of internationalization in Canada. The complex environment of internationalized universities in regard to language issues is also explored by Jenkins (2013), who argues that language is frequently ignored or oversimplified in discussions of internationalization and, as a consequence, international students who are not native speakers of English may face linguistic inequality when Anglophone institutions fail to recognize linguistic practices that deviate from "native" English. The linguistic environment of internationalized universities is much more complex than the assumption that native-like English is the dominant form being used (Baker 2016). In addition to linguistic complexities, internationalized universities also display complex cultural landscapes, but Leask and Carroll (2011), and others, refute the idea that having people from different cultural backgrounds in the same physical space is enough to create transnational flows of knowledge and collaboration.

The inequalities experienced by nonnative English speakers in internationalized universities in English-dominant contexts are often the product of language ideologies. According to Fairclough (2001), ideologies are commonsense assumptions implicit in "conventions according to which people interact linguistically, and of which people are generally not consciously aware" (2). Those conventions are embedded in relations of power and entail what meanings, or linguistic and communicative norms, are considered legitimate, correct, or appropriate.

Lippi-Green (2012) explores the ideology, or myth, of standard language and non-accent behind linguistic discrimination in the United States. More specifically, Lippi-Green (2012) explains that even though the so-called Standard American English is considered a myth by linguists, it is a widespread idea around the world, rooted in the commodification of language. The propagation of the standard language myth, embedded within power relations, is a way to (de)legitimize social groups and control access to institutions. According to the standard language ideology view, nonnative English speakers are seen as "deficient" and have their linguistic skills judged in light of "idealized views of language fluency and sophistication" (Ryan and Viete 2009, 304).

Staff and Internationalization

The experiences of administrative staff are still underrepresented in internationalization literature (Brandenburg 2016; Hunter 2018; Szekeres 2004, 2011; Whitchurch 2008). In her 2004 paper, "The Invisible Workers," Szekeres analyzes a variety of texts about universities and concludes that administrative staff are often neglected or erroneously portrayed in the literature as a result of outdated perceptions of the role these professionals perform in the increasingly complex environment of modern universities. In a following article, Szekeres (2011) argues that even though changes have occurred where universities have become more corporate, staff's contributions to the university continue to be "invisible." A fairly recent example confirming staff invisibility in research on internationalization is Arthur's (2017) study, which focuses on three aspects of academic life that influence international students' experience: academic faculty, counselor, and local students, without referring to other administrative or managerial staff who are also important to the overall student experience.

Pitman (2000) reports the results of a survey about staff's perceptions of academics and students as "customers" in an Australian university. The results pointed to "ambivalent feelings towards academics as customers and highlighted interpersonal skills between the two groups as a major challenge in facilitating quality customer service" (Pitman 2000, 165). On the other hand, participants identified a positive relationship with students and most reported going beyond the role of service providers by also acting as mentors for students. This association with students came from the belief that administrative staff "play a vital role in the teaching and learning processes of the University" (Pitman 2000, 173). Pitman's study, as is the case in Szekere's (2004, 2011) research, also reports staff's perceptions that their work was not recognized or valued, despite their belief that their work is crucial to the institution.

The changes in administrative staff's roles resulting from the increasingly complex environment of modern universities are analyzed by Whitchurch (2008) who identified professional staff in contemporary higher education settings in the UK as having roles and identities that are more complex than what their job descriptions state. Whitchurch identifies a *third space* that has emerged from the increasingly blurred boundaries in staff's activities, leading to a combination of professional and academic roles. The author argues that the redefinition of the nature of work in internationalizing universities calls for universities to recognize this trend and the impacts it might have on staff's identities and professional development.

Clearly, there is limited literature around staff's experiences in the internationalized university. Even less has been published on staff's assumptions about and engagement with the language aspects of internationalization. Staff's views on multilingualism in the context of internationalization at a university in Spain were studied by Llurda et al. (2014). A strong connection was made between internationalization and multilingualism, and staff in general hold optimistic views about multilingual universities, even though they do not necessarily see themselves as agents of internationalization. In our search for relevant literature, we have not been able to locate other studies that specifically discuss language matters in the transcultural university through the perspectives of university staff.

The Study

Simon Fraser University (SFU), where this study took place, is well known in the academic community in Canada for its internationalization efforts. The university's mission statement focuses on engagement of students, research, and communities, with internationalization being one of its main underlying principles. At the time of data collection, the international student population comprised 19 percent of the total undergraduate students and 28 percent of the total graduate students (SFU n.d.a). The economic rationale of internationalization in Canada can be found in online promotional materials, which highlight how well positioned the university is in different rankings.

As mentioned, the interview data discussed here is drawn from a research project which aimed to develop an in-depth understanding of the experiences of students, staff, and faculty engaged in the practices of internationalization to better understand the many dimensions of internationalization. Approaches of institutional ethnography (Smith 1987, 2002, 2012) informed the qualitative study conducted at this medium-sized Canadian university.

Central to institutional ethnography is the concept of ruling relations, which "refers to an expansive, historically specific apparatus of management and control that arose with the development of corporate capitalism and supports its operation" (Devault 2006, 295). The work of the researcher is then to identify and map those relations in an attempt to raise awareness of "how [participants'] own lives and work are hooked into the lives and work of others in relations of which most of us are not aware" (Smith 2002, 27). Therefore, the larger research project aimed to look at the social relations expressed in students', staff, and faculty's narratives to illuminate the ruling relations existing in this internationalizing university.

The participants in this project were recruited from across the departments and disciplines at SFU. Twenty-four administrative staff were interviewed by the research team and shared complex and multifaceted understandings and experiences with internationalization. We narrowed down the data shared here to focus on the narratives of eight staff who consistently talked about language when asked questions about the consequences, challenges, and benefits of internationalization of education. When participants problematized language in the context of internationalization, their answers emerged as a response to a process that has been happening at the university and which they are a part of. Therefore, their perceptions on language issues are not only ideas, they are part of their lived experiences.

Data was collected through qualitative interviews (Kvale and Brinkman 2018) and examined through the lens of Foucauldian discourse analysis as we are interested in the relations of power expressed by the participants when they talk about their perceptions of linguistic diversity in the internationalized university as historically and socially situated. Cheek (2008) explains that a Foucauldian approach to discourse does not explore rules governing meaning-making, but rather focuses on the power inherent in language; it seeks to understand how sources of power, instituted historically and socially, construct via language the wider social world. Our goal was to analyze how language, one of the different aspects of the complex institutional relations organizing the university, shapes staff's professional lives and activities. More specifically, we looked at the interplay between assumptions about language proficiency, power, and everyday/everynight (Smith 2002) experiences. From the data it becomes clear that the work (or activities) of other people (either a professor, a colleague, or a student) directly influence each participant's experience. These social relations are mediated by texts: university policies, job descriptions, classroom materials, university mission statements, and advertisements, as well as texts that reinforce an ideological view of language proficiency, such as the mainstream media. It is important to emphasize that participants' accounts are understandings of their experiences rather than descriptions of a set reality (Cheek 2008).

Staff Experiences

Out of twenty-four interviewees, the eight participants who we focus on here were staff in the following units: Faculty of Education, Faculty of Arts and Social Sciences, Faculty of Health Sciences, Student Services, and the International Office. Jane, a staff member who works with student services, identified the gap in literature on internationalization and the experience of staff members: "When we looked at studies of internationalization, no one has asked staff members, but yet (. . .) a lot of international activity from co-ops to other things are actually happening with staff."

"They have to meet the standards of the people who grew up here": Standard Language Ideology and the Hegemony of English

Eloise has worked in one faculty for more than fifteen years and talks about the increase in international student admission during that time. She holds strong opinions about the levels of proficiency of international students and new immigrants, and she thinks the university should not be admitting students who do not have native-like language skills: "When you have international students who want to learn academically in English (. . .) they have to meet the criteria, the levels, the standards of the people who grew up here have." Her statement refers to an idealized form of standard language held by citizens of a nation-state (Lippi-Green 2012). However, she contradicts herself by also criticizing local students for the poor language skills they present after leaving high school. Her indignation with linguistic expressions other than standard English goes beyond the university environment as she openly criticizes well-known Asian neighborhoods in this metropolitan city for having signs written in a language other than English:

> When you go to [this neighbourhood] you see, or even when you go to [this] mall, everything is in . . . foreign language, there are no English signs anywhere.

> And that's just offensive. I'm not being rude to expect that you should read and write in English and I think that a lot of students here are slipping through the cracks.

Her choice of words reflects an awareness that it is not socially accepted to discriminate against Asian people, but the same is not true for linguistic discrimination (Lippi-Green 2012; Woolard 1998). Eloise's narrative seems permeated by raciolinguistic ideology (Flores and Rosa 2015). Exploring the intersections between language ideologies and race, Flores and Rosa argue that standard English should be conceptualized in terms of the racialized ideologies shared by *listening subjects* rather than the empirical linguistic practices of *speaking subjects*. Thus, it is possible to assume that elements other than linguistic accuracy are responsible for what Eloise complains to be a difficulty in communicating with some students because "language is a huge barrier."

It has to be pointed out that Eloise was the only staff member who expressed discomfort and even contempt for nonstandard forms of the English language: "you can see that this person doesn't have good grammar ... it's something that irks me." According to Woolard (1998), "moral indignation over nonstandard forms derives from ideological associations of the standard with the qualities valued within the culture" (21).

In contrast, Nash believes that internationalization is inherently beneficial but there are "perceptions of the negative side of it" such as the feeling that "people in class do not speak the language well enough." Nash's belief that internationalization is inherently beneficial can be associated with an idealist rationale that sees internationalization as good per se and "should eventually enable a sense of global community and solidarity and prevent ethnocentrism, racism, and self-righteousness" (Stier 2004, 89). Nash also demonstrates awareness of the contradiction of the idealistic approach to internationalization: the propagation of Western ideas and values. For her, "being around people who don't speak English very well is a great opportunity for us to learn a different way of thinking, to support somebody in their aspirations to develop that international competence." She believes foreign languages should be given more importance on campus as a way of countering the hegemony of English: "I think we should be able to teach Shakespeare in Mandarin, what's wrong with that? We all have something to learn from the Mandarin interpretation of Shakespeare, right?". This view can be associated with the ideology of educationalism, which implies that being exposed to an unfamiliar setting "may contribute to personal growth and self-actualization" (Stier 2004, 92).

Laura is an undergraduate adviser in one faculty who recognizes the importance of linguistic and cultural diversity on campus but is also aware of the challenges posed by what are perceived to be students' "low levels of English proficiency on their academic and professional careers." Due to her role in the department, she is able to see the different struggles students face. She is aware of the power and capital associated with the English language, and she questions the different expectations of Canadian students who go abroad to study and international students who come to Canada: "We certainly don't expect English as a first language students to pop over in China and be able to study in Mandarin, even if they are doing a double degree." Those different expectations have a pervasive result on many international students who are not valued for having different ways of thinking, expressing themselves, and writing academically. Laura adds: "I don't know how many times in this job students apologize to me for having an accent, for not being totally fluent in English. So, you think of all the initial assumptions that go into that happening." She goes on to say that she does not apologize for not speaking the students' mother tongue and how, in fact, that is not expected from an English-speaking person. On the other hand, she talks about exchanges with graduating students where she had trouble understanding what they were trying to say, which is a real problem for both the student and the institution. Two important issues could be identified in her narrative: first, that the standard language ideology shapes the assumptions students make on how they and others should be performing linguistically, and second, that language proficiency can impact the choices and opportunities students have access to.

"[We have to be] honest about what the real challenges are": Practical Challenges Brought by Internationalization

In general, staff participants were concerned with the practical, day-to-day aspects of internationalization, such as how to support English as an additional language students, how to integrate international and domestic students, and the resources available. These concerns confirm Arthur's (2017) position in the sense that universities' efforts to recruit international students must be done in consideration of the conditions that impact these students' "adjustment, academic preparedness, and access to resources" (888).

Christine highlights the importance of having additional resources to support additional work brought about by engaging with multilingual and multicultural students. According to her, with the increased number of international students coming to SFU every year and the pressure for the internationalization of the curriculum, some adaptations are necessary but require specific resources. Christine uses an example that was a common complaint of some students who participated in the larger research project: that of an international teaching assistant who does not have the level of language proficiency necessary for the job. She argues that this challenging situation is happening in many classrooms and has a negative impact on the TA, the students, and the institution, and therefore must be addressed:

> We're really trying to move away from this sort of deficit model that international students are problems to be solved and really, you know, have the opportunity to celebrate their gifts and allow them to contribute the way they can, but we can't do that without being honest about what the real challenges are.

Laura reports that it is not uncommon for her to see students failing courses or having to change their choice of major or minor because they could not meet the minimum academic requirements to pass the courses due, mostly, to language difficulties. She reflects on how frustrating it is for an international student to have to change their degree of choice because they were not able to follow complex readings or pass written exams.

Jane shares a concern about how to get international students to succeed in the workplace and the challenges related to language that students face when applying for a position. For Jane, the difficulty is in how to manage students' expectations in light of their language issues:

> How do you deal with an international student who has an accent, who also has a slight speech impediment, and wants to work in health promotion and education in a presentation verbal communication style? That is a tough call. . . . And having to help students think about, you know, if you have this barrier, is that going to impede your ability to move into this kind of role?

Jessica believes people should focus on the benefits of having nonnative English speakers on campus, and she is aware that this positive perception does not always emerge by itself and that work needs to be done by the university in order to foster an inclusive environment:

> We have so much diversity, and I think that if everyone would kind of see the benefits and not always see, let's say, deficiencies, if someone's English is not their language, which is actually a good thing, that they have something else to bring to the table. But . . . if you do nothing, nothing will actually happen by itself. You have to kind of integrate people, it's not just gonna happen by having them here.

Guo and Guo's (2017) study of undergraduate students' perceptions of internationalization in a Canadian university suggests "a gap between the rhetoric and the reality" (864). According to the authors, even though internationalization is a fundamental aspect of Canadian universities' strategic plans, "there has been a lack of support to help international students successfully integrate into Canadian academic environments" (864). This gap between rhetoric and reality is also described by staff members in this study, who seem to have an in-depth understanding of the goals of internationalization and yet have to manage challenging situations that emerge due to a lack of institutional support services needed to achieve those goals.

"Diversity by itself might not bring as much benefit": Internationalization = Intercultural Learning?

Some participants demonstrate the awareness that simply having students from different nationalities and cultures is not a benefit in itself, and that strategies need to be implemented to stimulate meaningful cross-cultural interactions. Jessica believes more work needs to be done to highlight to students, faculty, and staff that even though going abroad is a "fantastic opportunity," they can actually take advantage of being surrounded by different cultures, languages, and experiences without leaving their campus:

> I don't think a lot of students realize that you don't really have to go abroad to, specially being at SFU, to be surrounded by so many different cultures and different experiences . . . we need to definitely take more advantage of what we have here in our own campus. . . . Anyone can benefit from diversity, but diversity by itself may not bring as much benefit.

Similarly, Nash believes internationalization has to be done "in a thoughtful way, in an intentional way that actually makes learning happen." Jessica and Nash's views resonate with Leask and Carroll's (2011) assertion that diversity on campus does not guarantee transcultural knowledge, collaboration, nor intercultural learning. The authors argue that universities should focus on "strategic and informed intervention to improve inclusion and engagement" (647) instead of expecting the benefits of cultural diversity on campus to manifest spontaneously.

"He was looking at the job as an opportunity to learn English": Language as a Commodity at University and at the Workplace

A large part of the linguistic repertoires used in academia reflects the linguistic practices of the workplace (Byrd Clark et al. 2013). At university, students learn not only theory and skills that will help them succeed in the job market, but also the linguistic repertoires expected in order to perform specific professional roles, even if these are not explicitly taught. The workplace influences what is taught at university and vice versa, and that includes language. Nash, who works with international development as well as with communities of immigrants and refugees, compares the struggles they face in regard to lack of Canadian credentials and language barriers in the workplace with the struggles international students face in the classroom:

> We don't take enough time to say what are the assets of this person, we don't evaluate those assets, we don't even acknowledge that they exist.... We just assume that if someone doesn't speak my language or look like me or dress like me that they're not conforming to my idea of what University or learning should be and I don't agree with that.

Many times, international students go through the experience of working during their studies and this can increase the challenge of having to perform in a second (or third) language. Charlie touches on language as a commodity when she talks about an episode where she acted as a mediator between a co-op international student and his supervisor. The student got fired from a job due to language performance issues, and Charlie reached the conclusion that "he was looking at the job as an opportunity to learn English. But he never communicated, and the environment did not actually give the student that opportunity." The student was learning more than English in his job: he was also learning the culture of the workplace, but he was doing so in an informal way, without being explicitly taught, and his boss did not realize what was happening nor was he equipped to deal with the situation. Charlie points out that "they [employer and faculty] will perhaps expect students to learn java or c++, but the student is learning in the environment more on the work in the country, soft skills and all that, and the transition from a culture to another." She was able to explain the situation to the student's supervisor, who agreed to give him another chance at the job.

English is also a commodity for students who are going abroad to non-Anglophone countries. Nash problematized the practice of teaching English as a way of perpetuating colonialism. She was advising a student who wanted to go to Cambodia to teach English in a small community, and she questioned the student's reasons for doing so:

> If they're living in a small community that only speaks Khmer and they have no intention of ever leaving why do they need to know English? It's just perpetuating this, which is a power thing. I think language is really important, language is a

way to teach culture and ways of thinking and knowing, right? So, when you're teaching someone English is not just a practical thing, you're teaching them ways of knowing which is a little bit like colonialism.

The two stories above show two different and complementary ways in which staff's understandings of linguistic and intercultural skills influence their dealings with students. Charlie's understandings allow her to explain to the employer, and sometimes faculty members, that international students are learning specific language needed for the workplace at the same time as learning the culture of the country. Nash's views allow her to question the power of the English language, both at SFU and outside Canada.

"Kind of like an informal partnership, in a way": Staff Going the Extra Mile and the Blurring of Professional Roles

Some staff enact Whitchurch's (2008) category of *unbounded professionals* for their ability to assist students with their individual needs by focusing on a larger institutional strategy goal and, often, working around and beyond their job descriptions to help students with various challenges in their academic lives deriving mainly from linguistic and cultural (mis)interpretations. Barbara identifies a series of issues students might have:

> Immigration is one thing they always find confusing and I don't blame them 'cause the instructions are not very clear at all. The second would probably be language I would say. But language have a lot of side effects. So, how to integrate to the communities, and also impact a significant way on their academic success, we're talking about academic honesty, dishonesty, misconduct, probation, all that, how to work on team settings, how to communicate, how to look for jobs you know, all those kind of go back and tie back with language challenges some of our students have. But the other thing, from my own experience . . . another challenge is how to make friends with Canadian students.

Some participants described interactions with students where they ended up acting as counselors in an attempt to help students facing a problematic situation, even though that is not their specific job. Charlie goes beyond the rules and standard procedures of her role as co-op coordinator and takes the time to "understand why students from a certain culture behave the way they do, or say things they do, do things they do" in order to "foresee some of the problems and be proactive in solving them." For her, it is not enough to, for example, inform a student they missed a deadline. She thinks it is important to investigate why the student missed the deadline and explain to them why meeting deadlines is so important in Canada. Such instances are evident as well in Pitman's (2000) survey of staff's perceptions about students and academics in an Australian university, which suggests that administrative staff see themselves as crucial to the educational process and usually go beyond their job description by incorporating the role of mentor when dealing with students. Charlie's narrative can be seen as another example of a professional who is moving away from fixed roles and structures (Whitchurch 2008).

Jane summarizes what she thinks is one of the biggest barriers between staff and students: "I think too many of us in administrative roles or educator roles it is like the privacy of a person, we are afraid to step on boundaries, we are afraid of cultural barriers, what is appropriate, what is not appropriate." For her, a simple enough strategy in order to connect to students on a more personal level to assist them is "Not being afraid to ask [about students' countries and cultures]."

Overall, staff's narratives provided invaluable insights on themes such as linguistic and cultural discrimination from the perspective of people whose work crosses over the student, the academic, and the institutional realms of the university. Thus, their critiques to, for example, low levels of English proficiency did not focus on the student as a problem or even on internationalization strategies of attracting international students. Instead, they focused on internationalization as an everyday reality they have to experience and talked about what they do to minimize linguistic and cultural discrimination, and on what the institution can do to foster a more inclusive environment. Overall, the complexity of administrative staff's roles in the internationalized university was salient in the narratives of staff who participated in this study.

Discussion and Implications

For Smith (2012), the lives and work of people are directly connected and influenced by the lives and work of others around them. This chapter exemplifies how the lives and work of students, staff, and faculty are intertwined on campus and how their actions in relation to linguistic diversity shape the experiences of others. Even though neither students nor faculty, who were part of the larger study, referred to staff in their narratives, staff's work is directly interconnected to both groups. At the same time, the way participants experience linguistic diversity on campus is influenced by their assumptions and ideologies about language.

Two ideological views about language proficiency can be inferred from staff's narratives. First, the ideology that nonnative English speakers can and should master an assumingly standard variety of "native" English seems to pervade the institution as staff repeatedly spoke about how this ideology should be countered. As stated, according to Lippi-Green (2012), standard language is a myth constructed to ascertain power over people who speak different varieties and have different accents. The second ideological assumption about language refers to "native" English as the academic lingua franca. Since English is one of the official languages in Canada, it is understandable that participants make the connection between the language of the institution and that of the country. However, the process of internationalization transforms universities in transcultural institutions where English is one of the many coexisting languages (Baker 2016). Some staff, like Nash, question the hegemony of native English in academic practices.

In general, staff's perspectives differed from those of most students and faculty members who participated in the larger study in the sense that most of them do not see international students as linguistically deficient or as a problem to be fixed. With the exception of one participant, staff emphasized the benefits of having international students on campus and transferred the blame for linguistic challenges from the individual to the institution. Nash and Laura would like the institution to actually recognize different linguistic practices brought by students in terms of having other languages being officially used for some purpose on campus. The key issue is that the linguistic and cultural complexity inherent to the process of internationalization should not be disregarded in favor of fixed academic practices (Baker 2016) in Anglo-dominant contexts.

Multilingualism and multiculturalism are two important characteristics of transcultural universities (Baker 2016). The issue of expectations for international students to assimilate to Canadian cultural and linguistic norms was present in staff narratives. However, with the exception of one participant who made negative comments about students from other cultures, staff mostly talked about multiculturalism on campus in relation to helping international students navigate the Canadian culture, which most of the time is not part of their job description and illustrates the blurred boundaries in staff's roles discussed by Whitchurch (2008).

One of the key principles in SFU's International Engagement Strategy's guiding principles is to "foster global citizenship and encourage the development of international and intercultural competencies" (SFU website). Mentions of language are found in the document in respect to language support systems and English proficiency requirements for admission. However, no mention of supporting or valuing linguistic diversity was found, which confirms Byrd Clark et al.'s (2013) stance that "[d]espite immigration, increased mobility, and the emergence of trans-global identities, official education policies and curriculum have not expanded to include the explicit development of multilingual repertoires or societal multilingualism in classrooms" (5).

The institution's mission of fostering global citizenship and intercultural knowledge seems to lack an important aspect: valuing linguistic diversity, which has been identified and its absence criticized by many staff participants. Jessica, a staff member understanding that "diversity by itself does not bring as much benefit," agrees with Leask and Carroll's (2011) idea that cultural diversity does not automatically mean intercultural learning. Staff in general were critical of the institution's rhetoric of internationalization and the hegemony of English on campus. They suggested that structural changes in the way the university supports students and faculty should be made to better address everyone's needs. Most staff participants highlighted the importance of recognizing and supporting linguistic and cultural diversity on campus as a key aspect for the success of internationalization.

Staff's holistic views provide invaluable insights into the functioning of the university as a whole and its ruling relations. By looking at their narratives through the lens of Foucauldian discourse analysis, it is possible to identify and challenge ways of thinking that have come to be viewed as natural and are taken for granted (Cheek 2008). In addition, this lens stresses one of Smith's (2002) institutional ethnography aims, which is to uncover the ways in which people's "own lives and work are hooked into the lives and work of others in relations of which most of us are not aware" (27).

Suggestions for a More Inclusive Internationalization

Linguistic practices are an important aspect of internationalization. Despite the importance of English as a global lingua franca, and the economic and cultural capital associated with it, the current landscape of internationalization requires a reconsideration of established Western academic practices. This study can be used as a reference for fostering more linguistically inclusive practices. An ethical and inclusive process of internationalization should consider the important role of linguistic diversity on campus. Drawing on the experiences shared by staff, we envision that internationalization at SFU needs to go beyond policies and classroom practices and also involve other groups on campus. Since the university has a strong internationalization orientation as part of its strategic plan, the implementation of campus-wide initiatives should be achieved through collaboration between administration and other groups.

For Hébert and Abdi (2013), internationalization should foster practices that lead to "more equitable social and learning relationships" (23) together with inclusive learning practices. As mentioned, a detailed frame of reference for more equitable and sustainable practices of internationalization of education is found in Ilieva et al. (2014). One theme refers to "valuing the resources international students bring and opening up to diversity while negotiating curriculum with more attention to global/local interactions" (884), as well as "expanding knowledge of different educational traditions" (885). Valuing diversity was pointed out by staff participants in this study as a way of creating a more inclusive campus environment.

Our suggestions for a more inclusive internationalization include flexibility in communicative practices (Baker 2016), more linguistically inclusive pedagogical practices (Anderson 2015; Ilieva, Beck, and Waterstone 2014; Pennycook 2005), and professional development focused on cross-cultural competencies (Leask and Carroll 2011) not only for faculty, but for staff as well. Based on the interconnections in student, staff, and faculty's experiences unveiled in staff's narratives, we argue that the implementation of internationalization initiatives has more chances of being successful when they target the academic community as a whole. This study demonstrates that the experiences of different actors influence to a large extent the experiences of others in the institution. Therefore, initiatives that focus on improving student experience cannot disregard staff (and faculty's) perspectives.

Acknowledgment

This research was funded by a grant from the Social Sciences and Humanities Research Council of Canada.

References

Anderson, Tim. 2015. "Seeking Internationalization: The State of Canadian Higher Education." *Canadian Journal of Higher Education* 45, no. 4: 166–187.
Arthur, Nancy. 2017. "Supporting International Students Through Strengthening Their Social Resources." *Studies in Higher Education* 42, no. 5: 887–894. https://doi.org/10.1080/03075079.2017.1293876.

Baker, Will. 2016. "English as an Academic Lingua Franca and Intercultural Awareness: Student Mobility in the Transcultural University." *Language and Intercultural Communication* 16, no. 3: 437–451. https://www.tandfonline.com/doi/abs/10.1080 /14708477.2016.1168053.

Beck, Kumari. 2012. "Globalization/s: Reproduction and Resistance in the Internationalization of Higher Education." *Canadian Journal of Education* 35, no. 3: 133–148.

Beck, Kumari. 2013. "Making Sense of Internationalization: A Critical Analysis." In *Critical Perspectives on International Education*, edited by Yvonne Hébert and Ali A. Abdi, 43–60. Rotterdam: Sense Publishers.

Beck, Kumari, and Roumiana Ilieva. 2019. "'Doing' Internationalization: Principles to Practice." *SFU Educational Review Journal*. Special Issue on Internationalization of Higher Education. https://doi.org/10.21810/sfuer.v12i3.1031.

Beck, Kumari, Roumiana Ilieva, Ashley Pullman, and Zhihua Zhang. 2013. "New Work, Old Power: Inequities Within the Labor of Internationalization." *On the Horizon* 21, no. 2: 84–95. https://doi.org/10.1108/10748121311322987.

Brandenburg, Uwe. 2016. "The Value of Administrative Staff for Internationalization." *International Higher Education* 85: 15–17.

Byrd Clark, Julie, Eve Haque, and Sylvie Lamoureux. 2013. "The Role of Language in Processes of Internationalization: Considering Linguistic Heterogeneity and Voices from Within and Out in Two Diverse Contexts in Ontario." *Comparative and International Education (Ottawa, Ont.)* 41, no. 3. https://doi.org/10.5206/cie-eci .v41i3.9212.

CBIE. 2016. "A World of Learning: Canada's Performance and Potential in International Education 2016." http://cbie.ca/media/facts-and-figures/.

Cheek, Julianne. 2008. "Foucauldian Discourse Analysis." In *The SAGE Encyclopedia of Qualitative Research Methods*, edited by Lisa M. Given, 356–357. Thousand Oaks: SAGE Publications.

Devault, Marjorie L. 2006. "What Is Institutional Ethnography?" *Social Problems* 53, no. 3: 294–298. https://academic.oup.com/socpro/article-abstract/53/3/294 /1613057.

Fairclough, Norman. 2001. *Language and Power*. London and New York: Routledge.

Fairclough, Norman. 2006. *Language and Globalization*. London and New York: Routledge.

Flores, Nelson, and Jonathan Rosa. 2015. "Undoing Appropriateness: Raciolinguistic Ideologies and Language Diversity in Education." *Harvard Education Review* 85, no. 2: 149–171.

Garson, Kyra. 2016. "Reframing Internationalization." *Canadian Journal of Higher Education* 46, no. 2: 19–39.

Guo, Yan, and Shibao Guo. 2017. "Internationalization of Canadian Higher Education: Discrepancies Between Policies and International Student Experiences." *Studies in Higher Education* 42, no. 5: 851–868. https://doi.org/10.1080/03075079.2017 .1293874.

Hébert, Yvonne, and Ali A. Abdi. 2013. "Critical Perspectives on International Education: Redefinitions, Knowledge-making, Mobilities and Changing the World." In *Critical Perspectives on International Education*, edited by Yvonne Hébert and Ali A. Abdi, 1–42. Rotterdam: Sense Publishers.

Hunter, Fiona. 2018. "Training Administrative Staff to Become Key Players in the Internationalization of Higher Education." *International Higher Education* 92: 16–17. http://dx.doi.org/10.6017/ihe.2018.92.10217.

Ilieva, Roumiana, Kumari Beck, and Bonnie Waterstone. 2014. "Towards Sustainable Internationalization of Higher Education." *Higher Education* 68: 875–889. https://doi.org/10.1007/s10734-014-9749-6.

Jenkins, Jennifer. 2013. *English as a Lingua Franca in the International University: The Politics of Academic English Language Policy*. Oxon: Routledge.

Knight, Jane. 2013. "The Changing Landscape of Higher Education Internationalization – For Better or Worse?" *Perspectives: Policy and Practice in Higher Education* 17, no. 3: 84–90. http://dx.doi.org/10.1080/13603108.2012.753957.

Kvale, Steinar, and Svend Brinkmann. 2018. *Doing Interviews*. London: SAGE Publications. https://doi.org/10.4135/9781529716665.

Larsen, Marianne. 2015. "Internationalization in Canadian Higher Education: A Case Study of the Gap Between Official Discourses and On-the-Ground Realities." *Canadian Journal of Higher Education* 45, no. 4: 101–122. https://doi.org/10.47678/cjhe.v45i4.184907.

Leask, Betty, and Jude Carroll. 2011. "Moving Beyond 'Wishing and Hoping': Internationalisation and Student Experiences of Inclusion and Engagement." *Higher Education Research & Development* 30, no. 5: 647–659. https://doi.org/10.1080/07294360.2011.598454.

Lippi-Green, Rosina. 2012. *English with an Accent: Language, Ideology, and Discrimination in the United States*. London and New York: Routledge.

Llurda, Enric, Josep-Maria Cots, and Lurdes Armengol. 2014. "Views on Multilingualism and Internationalisation in Higher Education: Administrative Staff in the Spotlight." *Journal of Multilingual and Multicultural Development* 35, no. 4: 376–391. https://doi.org/10.1080/01434632.2013.874435.

Maringe, Felix, and Nick Foskett. 2012. "Introduction: Globalization and Universities." In *Globalization and Internationalisation in Higher Education*, edited by Felix Maringe and Nick Foskett, 1–15. London: Continuum International Publishing Group.

Pennycook, Alastair. 2005. "Teaching with the Flow: Fixity and Fluidity in Education." *Asia Pacific Journal of Education* 25, no. 1: 29–43. https://doi.org/10.1080/02188790500032491.

Pitman, Tim. 2000. "Perceptions of Academics and Students as Customers: A Survey of Administrative Staff in Higher Education." *Journal of Higher Education Policy and Management* 22, no. 2: 165–175. https://doi.org/10.1080/713678138.

Ryan, Janette, and Rosemary Viete. 2009. "Respectful Interactions: Learning with International Students in the English-speaking Academy." *Teaching in Higher Education* 14, no. 3: 303–314. https://doi.org/10.1080/13562510902898866.

Smith, Dorothy E. 1987. *The Everyday World As Problematic: A Feminist Sociology*. Boston: Northeastern University Press.

Smith, Dorothy E. 2002. "Institutional Ethnography." In *Qualitative Research in Action: An International Guide to Issues in Practice*, edited by Tim May, 17–52. London: SAGE Publications.

Smith, Dorothy E. 2012. "Institutional Ethnography." In *The SAGE Encyclopedia of Qualitative Research Methods*, edited by Lisa M. Given, 434–436. Thousand Oaks: SAGE Publications.

Stier, Jonas. 2004. "Taking a Critical Stance Toward Internationalization Ideologies in Higher Education: Idealism, Instrumentalism and Educationalism." *Globalisation, Societies and Education* 2, no. 1: 83–97. https://doi.org/10.1080/1476772042000177069.

Stier, Jonas. 2010. "International Education: Trends, Ideologies and Alternative Pedagogical Approaches." *Globalisation, Societies and Education* 8, no. 3: 339–349. https://doi.org/10.1080/14767724.2010.505095.

Szekeres, Judy. 2004. "The Invisible Workers." *Journal of Higher Education Policy and Management* 26, no. 1: 7–22. https://doi.org/10.1080/1360080042000182500.

Szekeres, Judy. 2011. "Professional Staff Carve Out a New Space." *Journal of Higher Education Policy and Management* 33, no. 6: 679–691. https://doi.org/10.1080/1360080X.2011.621193.

Whitchurch, Celia. 2008. "Shifting Identities and Blurring Boundaries: The Emergence of *Third Space* Professionals in UK Higher Education." *Higher Education Quarterly* 62, no. 4: 377–396. https://doi.org/10.1111/j.1468-2273.2008.00387.x.

Woolard, Kathryn A. 1998. "Language Ideology as a Field of Inquiry." In *Language Ideologies, Practice and Theory*, edited by Kathryn A. Woolard, Bambi B. Schieffelin, and Paul V. Kroskrity, 20–85. New York; Oxford: Oxford University Press.

9

Implementing a Post-entry Language Assessment in a First-Year Engineering Course to Center Academic Language and Literacy in an Internationalizing University

Amanda Wallace and Michael Sjoerdsma

Introduction

The Faculty of Applied Sciences (FAS) at SFU has embraced internationalization and the institution's mantra of "engaging the world," leading to a richness in linguistic and cultural diversity within the faculty. The ratio of international students across the four schools (Engineering Science, Computing Science, Mechatronic Systems Engineering, and Sustainable Energy Engineering) in FAS is significantly high at approximately 29 percent. That is, 1,250 out of 4,281 students enrolled in the 2020–21 academic year were on student visas (Institutional Research and Planning 2021). A more granular examination of these statistics reveals that students from China account for 48 percent of all international students in the faculty, followed by India (26 percent), Vietnam (8 percent), and the Republic of Korea (8 percent) (Institutional Research and Planning 2021). These numbers, however, do not accurately depict the linguistic and cultural diversity of FAS students.

The term international student is often used as a proxy for students who speak English as an additional language (EAL); however, it fails to accurately capture the linguistic diversity of FAS's entire student cohort. Along with international students, a significant number of FAS's domestic students have EAL backgrounds (i.e., speak a language other than English as their first language). Data suggest that FAS has the highest percentage of EAL students across all of SFU's eight faculties at 38 percent (Institutional Research and Planning 2020). These statistics reflect the faculty's diverse linguistic landscape and warrant a closer examination of the implications for teaching and learning. This chapter details the design, implementation, and analysis of a post-entry language assessment[1] (PELA) in a required first-year engineering science course and discusses the affordances and challenges encountered in the project. However, we begin with a discussion about the impetus for this intervention and highlight the unique context of SFU's School of Engineering Science (ENSC).

ENSC, Accreditation Boards, and Internationalization

SFU's ENSC is an accredited engineering program. In Canada, although provinces regulate professions (Andrews, Shaw, and McPhee 2018), provincial engineering associations rely on the Canadian Engineering Accreditation Board (CEAB) to evaluate and certify programs (Engineers Canada 2021). The accreditation process requires schools to demonstrate that students meet hourly requirements in several categories, including natural sciences, complementary studies, engineering science, and engineering design. This input-based model of accreditation was supplemented around 2010 with learning outcomes, called graduate attributes. The intention of incorporating course-based assessments to reveal program-level attributes closes the loop to improve student learning (Banta and Blaich 2010). Engineering schools must demonstrate that their curricula meet twelve mandated graduate attributes, one of which is communication skills with the following description:

> An ability to communicate complex engineering concepts within the profession and with society at large. *Such ability includes reading, writing, speaking and listening*, and the ability to comprehend and write effective reports and design documentation, and to give and effectively respond to clear instructions. (Canadian Engineering Accreditation Board 2015, 21; italics our own)

SFU's ENSC program is somewhat unique because it integrates communication courses throughout its curriculum to teach so-called soft skills, which are often defined as interpersonal and communication skills (Bancino and Zevalkink 2007; Matteson, Anderson, and Boyden 2016). ENSC was at the forefront of such integration, which Reave (2014) advocates as the best way of teaching engineering students these skills. Although first-year students often need to be persuaded that communication skills are just as critical as math and physics, industry and academics have recognized the importance of the former. English is a tool of engineering (Kynell 1995), and the ability to communicate effectively using appropriate terms forms a discourse community (Winsor 2013) for engineers. Danilova and Pudlowski (2007) discuss the communication skills needed for engineering from a linguistics viewpoint, drawing on research showing its importance in engineering practice. In their book, *A Whole New Engineer*, Goldberg and Somerville (2014) put forward six minds necessary for engineers, one of which is the linguistics mind, highlighting the importance of natural language in the engineering process and speech acts. Engineers have reported that communication is an activity that they spend at least half their time on (Hailey 2000; Hertzum and Pejtersen 2000; Vest, Long, and Anderson 1996).

The graduate attribute description for communication skills does not explicitly reference English; however, from our experience, it is operationalized with English in mind. As Marshall (2020) observes, as the number of plurilingual students increases, there is a tension between learning processes that incorporate (or encourage) students to use languages other than English and the products that are monolingual and submitted in English. Marshall's (2020) study identified that faculty members have their own beliefs on incorporating plurilingualism in the classroom. While each class may vary, reporting out to CEAB at the program level propagates English as the only language. Accreditation does not preclude plurilingualism, but accreditation also does not encourage it. Faculty in engineering schools (and beyond) are not applied linguists and may have the opinion that language issues are not their responsibility (Airey 2012), so it is unreasonable to expect them to grapple with these issues. Moreover, there may also be hesitation because of how accreditation is (negatively) viewed (Uziak et al. 2014).

CEAB's move to graduate attributes followed similar changes in ABET (an American organization that accredits engineering and technology programs), which was in response to accreditation being viewed as impeding the development of innovative programs (Prados, Peterson, and Lattuca 2005). The introduction of graduate attributes has allowed a point of reflection for ENSC to consider its curriculum. In ENSC's case, the program already had an established, integrated communications program. Indicators associated with the communications attribute are distributed throughout ENSC's program with two first-year courses focusing on communication: ENSC 100 (Engineering, Science, and Society) and ENSC 105W (Process, Form, and Convention in Professional Genres). Together, these courses provide students with an opportunity to practice communication skills. Through written assignments and a semester-long design project, students have several opportunities to communicate through writing and oral presentations. CEAB's attribute for communication skills showed that, although ENSC was covering writing and speaking, the program was not capturing reading and listening. ENSC was focusing on the outputs and neglecting the inputs.

Teaching ENSC

I (Michael) was hired as a continuing lecturer in ENSC in May 2005 after being a sessional instructor for several semesters as a graduate student. Because I completed my undergraduate degree in ENSC, I was well versed in the content, but as a graduate student in North America, I was not trained to teach the material I had learned (Boyer 1990). This deficit was addressed by a mentor, Steve Whitmore, who provided guidance, and by SFU's Teaching and Learning Centre (TLC),[2] where I became part of a community of practice (Wenger 1998) and connected with other faculty members and educational consultants who were passionate about teaching and learning.

A salient moment that changed my view of students in ENSC occurred about four years into my appointment as a lecturer. I met with a student to review her paper, and during our conversation, I learned that this was the first paper she had ever written. She was an international student, and where she was educated, papers and essays were not part of the curriculum. I knew many students in ENSC used EAL, but, for the most part, my teaching was based on assuming all students had the same proficiency, resulting in my efforts to improve my teaching while ignoring the needs of many of my students. That conversation with the student began my learning journey, where I completed a Teaching English to Speakers of Other Languages (TESOL) certificate. While this training has been valuable and has affected my pedagogy, it also showed me the resources and expertise needed to support students adequately. With it came the realization that I lack both in my current course.

These observations also informed my role as ENSC's accreditation officer. In this capacity, I was responsible for ensuring that ENSC met CEAB's requirements for graduate attributes. As detailed above, the graduate attributes related to reading and listening were not being captured, which led me to collaborate with the Centre for English Language Learning, Teaching and Research (CELLTR).

EAL Support across SFU

CELLTR was established in 2014 in response to the university's increasing linguistic diversity and concerns from faculty members that "inadequate language skills are hampering the academic success of some multilingual and EAL students" (Simon Fraser University 2011, 1). CELLTR's mandate was to provide a comprehensive range of EAL supports and services to the university community to better support multilingual students with their academic and discipline-specific academic language and literacy needs. The center embraced a content and language integrated learning approach. Specifically, the center sought to "employ 'adjunct strong' (e.g. workshops supporting language development within a time-tabled course; collaborative design of curriculum incorporating language and content goals) or embedded models (e.g. team teaching) in their collaborations" (Wallace, Spiliotopoulos, and Ilieva 2020, 130). Lecturers, both limited-term and continuing positions, with expertise in applied linguistics/EAL were hired to liaise with a specific faculty within the university.

Supporting EAL Initiatives in FAS

I (Amanda) came to SFU's Faculty of Education in September 2016 as both a limited-term lecturer (two-year term) teaching a foundational course in EAL and as a doctoral student in the Languages, Cultures and Literacies program. In the first year of my PhD program, I was hired as a Research Assistant on a project examining the work of CELLTR's liaisons coled by my supervisor and the director of CELLTR. Over the next two years, my work with CELLTR expanded to include other research projects, such as TA development and being the interim liaison to the Faculty of Arts and Social Sciences for one semester. I first met Michael in September 2018, when CELLTR hired me in a part-time capacity as the faculty liaison to FAS. I was tasked with supporting key faculty-facing and student-facing projects.

In our initial conversations, we discussed the lack of student uptake in the drop-in support sessions offered by CELLTR for students in ENSC 105W. We investigated ways to identify students who would benefit from this one-on-one, discipline-specific support and ways to encourage them to use it. With my understanding of PELAs from the literature and how other institutions have used them, we thought it could help students in ENSC while also providing data for accreditation purposes.

The Case for PELAs

As higher education institutions (HEIs) embrace internationalization, faculty and university leadership have become increasingly concerned about students' proficiency levels in English and whether they (both international and domestic) can meet the academic language and literacy demands of their courses (Birrell 2006; Briguglio 2014; Murray 2013, 2016). As O'Loughlin and Arkoudis (2009) note, the challenge is how institutions will address this issue to ensure that all students can satisfy curricular demands. In the context of SFU, such concerns were first brought to the forefront in 2011 by faculty members who observed that "inadequate language skills [were] hampering the academic success of some multilingual and EAL students" (Simon Fraser University 2011, 1). An extra layer of complexity is added for degree programs with explicit accreditation requirements related to communication skills (i.e., reading, writing, listening, and speaking), such as ENSC. Students who fail to achieve these communication skills may face employment difficulties postgraduation (Arkoudis et al. 2009); for others, they may fail to graduate from their degree program (Gautam et. al. 2016).

In response to the challenges above, several HEIs, in particular those in New Zealand and Australia, have implemented a PELA to identify students who may benefit from further English language development through their university studies (Barrett-Lennard, Dunworth, and Harris 2011) and/or identify academic language needs (Read 2013). PELAs can be designed and operationalized in different ways. For example, they can be generic in design and administered across a student cohort regardless of program of study (e.g., the University of Melbourne, the University of Auckland). Conversely, they can be discipline specific (e.g., the University of Sydney). PELAs designed within a specific course or degree program can be integral in developing disciplinary (rather than generic) support for multilingual students. Identifying students in need of support and directing them to tailored support services can assist their academic language development within their chosen field of study and set them up to be successful. English language proficiency exams like the International English Language Testing System and the Test of English as a Foreign Language provide insight into students' general communicative competence in English; however, they do not assess a student's proficiency in and understanding of the disciplinary discourses and conventions of their chosen field of study (Murray 2013).

PELAs are generally operationalized in two stages: a screening phase and a diagnostic phase administered face-to-face or online. The initial screening phase entails a vocabulary exercise and a timed reading task or cloze-elide procedure. The vocabulary exercise requires students to correctly define isolated words from the Academic Word List (Coxhead 2000), followed by a timed reading task where students identify redundant words added to the text. If students score high on both of these tasks, the assumption is that they have sufficient competency in academic language literacies to be successful in their coursework (Read 2016). Students who fail to reach the minimum threshold on these tasks must complete the diagnostic phase of the PELA. This phase, depending on how it is designed, requires students to complete listening, reading, and writing tasks with the goal of using the results to design tailored academic support(s) for the students.

Within the Canadian context, some engineering schools have embraced a disciplinary-specific PELA (rather than generic) in first-year undergraduate courses. Engineering-specific PELAs are akin to current math proficiency tests commonly used in undergraduate programs. The two assessments differ in that math skills are generally "more discreet and easier to isolate, identify and then instruct towards improvement, than learning to use a language to learn new content" (Kinnear et al. 2016, 4). Like ENSC at SFU, the engineering faculties at the University of Toronto, Queen's University, and Carleton University have, in recent years, experienced an uptick in students with EAL backgrounds who struggle to meet the demands of the curriculum due to linguistic issues. In response to this issue, the three institutions designed and implemented a PELA to identify students at risk and to create a learning profile detailing tailored academic support(s) for such students (Fox, Haggerty, and Artemeva 2016; Kinnear et al. 2016). The work of these peer institutions informed the collaborative research project discussed here between an applied linguist (Amanda) and an engineering faculty member (Michael) to design and implement a discipline-specific PELA in a first-year engineering course to better understand if students' reading proficiency or lack thereof is affecting their performance in the written assignments and to bridge the gaps in the accreditation data. Moreover, in the dynamic landscape of an internationalized university, characterized by a student body with diverse linguistic and cultural backgrounds, our work offers valuable insights for educators in similar settings facing parallel challenges. Collaborations between content faculty and applied linguists, as illustrated by our project, are one approach to address the linguistic challenges encountered in such a diverse academic environment.

SFU's ISTLD-MLC Grant Program

Serendipitously, as we began discussing possible interventions, SFU's Institute for the Study of Teaching and Learning in the Disciplines (ISTLD) and CELLTR launched a joint grant program, *Inquiring into Your Multilingual Classroom:*

An Integrated Seminar Series and Grants Program (ISTLD-MLC), in Fall 2018. This program provided faculty members with a one-time grant of up to $6,000 to "gain background knowledge related to working with . . . [multilingual] . . . students while at the same time crafting an inquiry project to support related changes to teaching and learning in their classrooms" (SFU-ISTLD 2021). The grant encouraged faculty members to explore a teaching and learning issue related to multilingual students.

As mentioned, we intended to design a PELA to assess students' reading proficiency to identify those who may be at risk, with the hope that having an assessment would help them realize they needed support. We surmised that by providing students with this detailed information in their first year, they would subscribe to the various academic supports and resources, if any, throughout their degree program. We also hoped students would appreciate that academic language and literacy skills are tied to a specific discipline and develop over time (Lea and Street 2006; Lin 2016). In broader terms, we sought to shift the deficit perspectives pervasive in many postsecondary institutions that characterize multilingual students as needing remediation (Marshall 2009) to an asset-based perspective that values the diversity of languages. Given these considerations, the purpose of designing and implementing a PELA in ENSC was fivefold:

1. to identify students who may be "at risk" of not completing course assignments at a satisfactory level and thus in need of supplemental language and literacy support throughout the course (e.g., creating a reading support plan);
2. to inform the services offered through the CELLTR @ FAS program;
3. to adapt the curriculum of future iterations of the course to better serve the needs of the students;
4. to assist in assessing literacy-based (i.e., reading) components of graduate attributes; and
5. to help students better understand the strengths and weaknesses of their academic language and literacy skills, specifically reading.

The PELA Design and Findings

The development of our PELA was an iterative process based on current examples with modifications to reflect ENSC's program, and it is briefly discussed below. Those readers interested in the process details can consult our final internal ISTLD-MLC grant report (Sjoerdsma and Wallace 2021).

We conducted two pilot studies to hone the instrument. The two primary constraints imposed on the development of the instrument were the resources available for marking and the fifty minutes allocated for each lecture of ENSC 105W. We designed the PELA with twenty minutes in mind to account for the time needed in class to provide instructions, distribute, and collect the PELAs. Question types were limited to multiple-choice (MC), true/false, and fill-in-the-blanks (FIB).

Identifying relevant articles was challenging. From a topic perspective, many articles were suitable but were either too long for the given time or too sparse in terms of content to allow for questions to assess reading comprehension. We considered using abridged versions of longer articles; however, these modified versions lacked overall context and resulted in text that would be difficult to understand. Eventually, we decided to pilot two articles, Article A (Climate Change 2015) and Article B (Strickland and Zorpette 2019), during the summer term of 2019, recruiting four students from the previous fall's offering of ENSC 105W. While no longer representative of first-year students, we reasoned that these recruited students were ideally suited to critique whether the articles were like the course readings. If these students were to have difficulty with our PELA, then the instrument would not be appropriate for first-year students.

The results from the first pilot demonstrated that the articles we selected and the questions used to assess students' reading comprehension were appropriate. Although students noted that the articles used for the PELA were easier to understand than the articles they had read in ENSC 105W, no student received a perfect score. Student performance on the PELA revealed no differences between the articles, with some students performing better on Article A and others performing better on Article B. No student completed Article A within twenty minutes. In a follow-up interview, students commented that Article B was easier to interpret because it was shorter and more straightforward. In general, the students said that the instructions for completing the PELA were clearly articulated and easily interpreted. This pilot showed that the two articles and questions we developed were appropriate. The only recommendation for change was increasing the allocated time for the assessment from twenty to twenty-five minutes.

The second pilot was administered in two courses at Fraser International College (FIC) during the second month of the summer 2019 semester. FIC serves as a pathway program to SFU for students who fall below SFU's English language proficiency requirements. At FIC, students fulfill course requirements for SFU degrees that often have smaller enrollments and have embedded language support. These students were selected because they were the only representative sample of ENSC 105W students associated with SFU during the developmental phase of the PELA. We analyzed students' performance on both articles, and we could not make any statistical claim that one was better than the other. Therefore, our selection was based on student feedback via the survey and interviews, where students commented that Article B was more appropriate, corroborating the feedback from the first pilot. Based on student performance and comments regarding Article B, we modified and added some questions, including removing all FIB questions because they are too time consuming to mark and there are no resources to hire additional markers. MC questions allow for automated marking.

After revising the PELA based on the information gleaned from the two pilots, students ($N=100$) enrolled in ENSC 105W were given the PELA at the end of September 2019. We decided it was best to implement the assessment once they were familiar with the course assignments and had completed one preliminary assignment related to their persuasive paper. In total, one hundred students completed the PELA with their performance ranked into three bands: *proficient, developing*, and *emerging*. Students in the first category are considered competent and for them no other support is necessary. Those in the second category are considered moderately at risk. Students identified as being in these two categories are informed of their results via an email that outlines appropriate resources they may consult. Students in the high-risk category are offered one-on-one support by CELLTR personnel. Fifteen of the one hundred students were identified as *emerging* and in need of support.

Unfortunately, the timing of the PELA coincided with an institutional restructuring of service units that brought together CELLTR, the TLC, and the Centre for Online and Distance Education to form CEE. This meant the embedded CELLTR support in ENSC 105W was no longer available. Because of the lack of clarity around institutional support for students who speak EAL, we did not have the means to offer additional support to students in the lower performance bands, nor could we investigate whether the PELA was reliable in accurately identifying students in need of academic language and literacy support. We were unable to do the latter because follow-up support for students identified as "at risk" was unavailable, and we could not cross-check students' performance on the PELA with their course assignments and final grade. In the next section, we discuss how these changes to institutional policy and structures affected the development and implementation of the PELA and examine the implications for key stakeholders from across the university and, more broadly, internationalizing HEIs.

Reflections from the Margins: Collaborative Relations, Implications, and Recommendations

Before reflecting upon institutional policy and structures and exploring implications, we first discuss what we both consider to be a key factor in facilitating such a project: positive collaborative relations. Interdisciplinary collaborations between applied linguists (i.e., Amanda) and content faculty (i.e., Michael) occur in a "trading zone" where power relations (e.g., rank) and institutional structures and policies can have various, constraining or sustaining, effects (Wallace, Spiliotopoulos, and Ilieva 2020). Our collaboration was very sustaining despite our different positions within the university (limited-term lecturer vs senior [tenured] lecturer). It was characterized by a positive and equal partnership grounded in a common goal—supporting student success— and, coupled with Amanda's job to work collaboratively with key stakeholders from across the university to support faculty members in their teaching of multilingual students, our collaboration was quite successful despite some of the constraints and challenges we faced. Our experience mirrors the findings in the work of both Jacobs (2010) and Zappa-Hollman (2018) who both found that successful collaborations are built on the positive interactions of the two collaborators. These positive interactions were reflected in both our willingness to defer to each other's areas of expertise and the open and respectful exchange of ideas (e.g., choosing an appropriate article, length of PELA, type of questions). At no time did either of us become territorial in terms of content ownership. In some partnerships, the understanding of who owns course content can become an impediment to successful collaborations where such knowledge is often understood as belonging to the content faculty member (i.e., Michael) (Davison 2006; Siskin 2013). For faculty members considering entering a collaboration such as ours, we encourage them to first reflect upon the "requisite personal characteristics for the collaborations to be successful" (Zappa-Holman 2018, 596), including commitment, interpersonal skills, patience and perseverance, attitude, genuine curiosity, and interest in improving student learning, among others.

Notwithstanding a positive and respectful collaborative relationship, instructors wanting to design a similar intervention should first consider the purpose of a PELA. Clearly articulating the reasons for identifying students who may be at risk of not successfully completing the course will help facilitate support and buy-in from both the students and administrators. Equally important is investigating the type of provisions for support available, if any, across department/faculty/university-wide levels as this has implications for the sustainability of the project.

In terms of the design of the PELA, instructors would benefit from collaborating with a language and/or assessment specialist from within the university to help ensure the reliability and validity of the instrument. The effectiveness of a diagnostic reading assessment is, after all, only as good as its design. Ideally, multiple iterations of the PELA (a minimum of two) would be piloted before integrating it into a course. Instructors would be wise to make the PELA a part of the formal class schedule, and if possible, devote a minimum of fifty minutes to it. Instructors will also have to consider how to balance the need for an effective assessment design with grading considerations (e.g., short-answer questions, large class size, TA capacity). If the PELA is a formal part of the curriculum/assignments of the course, it would mitigate such issues.

The challenges we encountered at the institutional level during various phases in the design and implementation of the PELA are not uncommon. Fox and Haggerty (2014) liken the development of a PELA to a "balancing act" wrought with "issues and tensions" (as cited in Fox, Haggerty, and Artemeva 2016, 50). The pedagogical barriers originate in part from institutional structures and policies that do not necessarily align with the daily realities of faculty and staff who support students and are, more often than not, driven by financial reasoning. Under-resourcing forces faculty and staff to deal with issues that should be institutional responsibilities, thus increasing workloads. Certainly, in the course of employment, faculty members completing professional development activities is an appropriate expectation; however, the expertise required to support multilingual students is fundamentally different. Supporting students who speak EAL requires specialized skills, training, and education, and institutions cannot expect faculty to acquire these attributes as a normal part of their development.

SFU senior administration acknowledged that recruitment of international students "has brought financial benefits to the university" and the "need to ensure that [they] are well supported in their programs, and that instructors have opportunities to educate themselves about working with international students" (Driver 2016, 4). In recognition of these very facts, CELLTR was created to provide some training for faculty and to raise awareness. The real innovation, however, was the embedded model that paired faculty (as content experts) with applied linguists to develop collaborative partnerships to support multilingual students. This model did not assume faculty members had to become applied linguists or, vice versa, that applied linguists had to become content experts. Rather, it promoted a partnership that creates "discursive spaces for the collaboration" among applied linguists and content faculty, "to facilitate the embedding of [academic language and literacy skills] into disciplines of study" (Jacobs 2005, 475). Without the disciplinary expertise we both brought to the collaboration, the PELA would never have been developed. We acknowledge that many content faculty members are disinclined to see themselves as teachers of English as "it is seen (by them) to be outside their domain" (Goldsmith and Willey 2016, 121) and are resistant to these types of collaboration. However, for us, the collaborative model is not asking content faculty to be English teachers. It is about experts in their respective disciplines working together to make the tacit (i.e., disciplinary discourses and conventions) explicit (Jacobs 2007). We suggest that universities establish embedded applied linguists in each faculty or department to foster sustained collaborative approaches that can support initiatives in individual courses and across the curriculum.

The process of developing the PELA also served as a reminder of institutional shortcomings. The ISTLD-MLC funds were useful, but they only covered hiring an RA to assist with some of the work. We both provided many hours above and beyond our normal duties. Additionally, this was one-time funding, and no ongoing funding or other resources were provided. Once again, supporting students becomes an initiative from the bottom, using unpaid labor to manage circumstances the institution created. The impetus to create the PELA was a result of a situation which stemmed from institutional decisions and underresourcing. The university needs to properly fund these initiatives as well as determine whether a combination of top-down and bottom-up approaches would be more appropriate (Murray and Nallaya 2016). As demonstrated by our experiences, without explicit university-wide policies and practices that address language development, these programs may not be sustainable (Arkoudis and Harris 2019).

The Australian context provides an example of what could happen should SFU and other HEIs fail to center language issues and support them appropriately. In 2009, Australia's Department of Education, Employment and Workplace Relations (DEEWR) published the *Good Practice Principles* (DEEWR 2009) for HEIs in order to improve the English language proficiency of international students. These principles, along with the creation of the Tertiary Educational Quality and Standards Agency, "indicate that a shift is taking place in the way in which [HEIs] are regulated, monitored and evaluated" (DEEWR 2011 as cited in Arkoudis, Baik, and Richardson 2012, 9). This government mandate behooves institutions to be proactive lest they run the risk of losing autonomy in crafting language policies and initiatives that best serve the unique needs of their faculty, staff, and students.

As internationalization has taken hold in HEIs, scholars have argued for university-wide strategies to address issues of language (Arkoudis and Harris 2019; Fenton-Smith et al. 2017; Murray and Nallaya 2016). However, centering language issues within HEIs is difficult due to institutional structures, policies, and discourses that reflect a neoliberal stance wherein universities are "becoming more consumer- and market-oriented" (Beck 2012, 137). As a result, Anderson (2015) writes:

> [this]can pose challenges for universities regarding the need to balance fiscal pressures with their social and educational responsibilities to students. The extent to which universities have or have not been able to adapt to and accommodate the shifting student demographics in this era of hyper-internationalization remains an area of concern, particularly for some culturally and linguistically diverse students who speak English as a second . . . or additional language . . . and has created an ethical tension between the various benefits of larger numbers of foreign students versus the potential challenges and accommodations of adapting to increasingly diverse university populations. (169)

There is no easy way to provide language support across a university, and there is clearly no one-size-fits-all model. However, as long as HEIs continue to recruit increasing numbers of international students, they have an ethical obligation, a duty of care, to properly support these students by allocating appropriate resources to faculty and staff (CAUT 2017). We also believe this is an opportunity for HEIs to center language at the institutional and disciplinary core by embracing a fundamental shift in how we value the rich linguistic diversity of students. Can we take up Preece and Marshall's (2020) call that the time has come "for the Anglophone higher educational sector to develop policies and practices that are informed by 'language-as-resource'" (117) ethos? Given the international nature of engineering work, it is time to update the view of English as an engineering tool to plurilingualism as an engineering tool.

Concluding Thoughts

With increasing linguistic diversity in HEIs worldwide, language issues will continue to be of concern (Murray 2014). Institutional stakeholders, policies and structures, and outside factors, like accreditation bodies, add further complications due to contrasting priorities. This chapter illustrates some of the complexities of designing and implementing a PELA in a first-year engineering course. Collaborative partnerships between content faculty and applied linguists are critical to the development of PELAs, as are time (on top of teaching, service, and research responsibilities), funding, and support from the university's leadership. Unfortunately, the timing of our PELA in ENSC 105W coincided with a reorganization of key units that support teaching and learning across SFU's faculties. The embedded support available to students in ENSC 105W through faculty liaisons at CELLTR was discontinued, and, as such, the PELA is no longer viable without institutional support. Our experience demonstrates the precarious nature of language-centered initiatives like CELLTR and PELAs, thus highlighting the importance of institutional champions who advocate for the necessary provisions to sustain them.

Although it remains to be seen what types of support the new CEE and its EAL Initiatives Team can provide, we believe the PELA to be a worthwhile exercise in future iterations of ENSC 105W because of the importance of discipline-specific language and literacy skills for both scholarly and professional success, the increasing linguistic diversity within ENSC, and the school's accreditation responsibilities. Coupled with SFU's commitment to internationalization and "engaging the world," a PELA can be an integral pedagogical instrument for faculties seeking to identify students early in their program of study who may be at risk and in need of extra support. We call upon senior leadership at SFU to heed the points raised in this chapter as they contemplate ways to best support SFU's growing cohort of multilingual students and the teaching and learning community needed to support these students.

Acknowledgments

Support for this research project is gratefully acknowledged through SFU's Transforming Inquiry into Learning and Teaching (TILT, formerly known as the ISTLD) and the CELLTR program *Inquiring into Your Multilingual Classroom* (grant number G0306).

Notes

1. Also referred to in the literature as post-enrollment language assessment and/or a post-admission language assessment.
2. Now known as the Centre for Educational Excellence (CEE).

References

Airey, John. 2012. "'I Don't Teach Language.' The Linguistic Attitudes of Physics Lecturers in Sweden." *AILA Review* 25, no. 25 (January): 64–79. https://doi.org/10.1075/aila.25.05air.

Anderson, Tim. 2015. "Seeking Internationalization: The State of Canadian Higher Education." *Canadian Journal of Higher Education* 45, no. 4: 166–187. https://doi.org/10.47678/cjhe.v45i4.184690.

Andrews, Gordon C., Patricia Shaw, and John McPhee. 2018. *Canadian Professional Engineering and Geoscience: Practice and Ethics*, 6th edn. Toronto: Canada: Nelson Education.

Arkoudis, Sophie, Chi Baik, and Sarah Richardson. 2012. *English Language Standards in Higher Education: From Entry to Exit*. Camberwell: Acer Press.

Arkoudis, Sophie, and Anne Harris. 2019. "EALD Students at University Level: Strengthening the Evidence Base for Programmatic Initiatives." In *Second Handbook of English Language Teaching*, edited by Xuesong Gao, 317–336. Switzerland: Springer.

Arkoudis, Sophie, Lesleyanne Hawthorne, Chi Baik, Graeme Hawthorne, Kieran O'Loughlin, Dan Leach, and Emmaline Bexley. 2009. "The Impact of English Language Proficiency and Workplace Readiness on the Employment Outcomes of Tertiary International Students." Full Report, 1–157. Melbourne: Centre for the Study of Higher Education, University of Melbourne.

Bancino, Randy, and Claire Zevalkink. 2007. "Soft Skills: The New Curriculum for Hard-Core Technical Professionals." *Techniques: Connecting Education and Careers (J1)* 82, no. 5: 20–22.

Banta, Trudy W., and Charles Blaich. 2010. "Closing the Assessment Loop." *Change: The Magazine of Higher Learning* 43, no. 1: 22–27. https://doi.org/10.1080/00091383.2011.538642.

Barrett-Lennard, Siri, Katie Dunworth, and Anne J. Harris. 2011. "The Good Practice Principles: Silver Bullet or Starter Gun?" *Journal of Academic Language and Learning* 5, no. 2: A99–A106. https://ro.ecu.edu.au/cgi/viewcontent.cgi?article=1172&context=ecuworks2011.

Beck, Kumari. 2012. "Globalization/s: Reproduction and Resistance in the Internationalization of Higher Education." *Canadian Journal of Education* 35, no. 3: 133–148.

Birrell, Bob. 2006. "Implications of Low English Standards Among Overseas Students at Australian Universities." *People and Place* 14, no. 4: 53–64.

Boyer, Ernest L. 1990. *Scholarship Reconsidered: Priorities of the Professoriate*. Lawrenceville, NJ: Princeton University Press.

Briguglio, Carmela. 2014. *Working in the Third Space: Promoting Interdisciplinary Collaboration to Embed English Language Development into the Disciplines*. Sydney: Office for Learning and Teaching.

Canadian Engineering Accreditation Board. 2015. "A Guide to Outcomes-based Criteria from Visiting Team-chairs and Program Visitors Ver 1.25." March 1, 2015. https://engineerscanada.ca/sites/default/files/draft_program_visitor_guide_v1.25.pdf.

Canadian Association of University Teachers. 2017. "International Students: CAUT Policy Statement." Retrieved April 26, 2021, from https://www.caut.ca/about-us/caut-policy/lists/caut-policy-statements/policy-statement-on-international-students.

Climate Change. 2015. "Time for Strong Global Plan and Climate Action Commitments." *The Globe and Mail*, December 1, 2015. https://search-proquest-com.proxy.lib.sfu.ca/hnpglobeandmail/docview/2122296622/9150F1A3C7D24DD8PQ/1?accountid=13800.

Coxhead, Averil. 2000. "A New Academic Word List." *TESOL Quarterly* 34, no. 2: 213. https://doi.org/10.2307/3587951.

Danilova, Elena A., and Zenon J. Pudlowski 2007. "Important Considerations in Improving the Acquisition of Communication Skills by Engineers." *Global Journal of Engineering Education* 11, no. 2: 153–162.

Davison, Chris. 2006 "Collaboration Between ESL and Content Teachers: How Do We Know When We Are Doing It Right?" *International Journal of Bilingual Education and Bilingualism* 9, no. 4: 454–475. https://doi.org/10.2167/beb339.0.

Department of Education, Employment and Workplace Relations (DEEWR) 2009. "Good Practice Principles for English Language Proficiency for International Students in Australian Universities: Final Report." Canberra, Australian Capital Territory. http://hdl.voced.edu.au/10707/208559.

Driver, J. 2016. "Consolidated 2013–2018 Academic Plan Progress Report. Academic Plan Progress Report." (June). Simon Fraser University. https://docushare.sfu.ca/dsweb/Get/Document-1133733/S.16-89.pdf

Engineers Canada. 2021. "About Accreditation." Retrieved April 29, 2021, from https://engineerscanada.ca/accreditation/about-accreditation.

Fenton-Smith, Ben, Pamela Humphreys, Ian Walkinshaw, Rowan Michael, and Ana Lobo. 2017. "Implementing a University-wide Credit-bearing English Language Enhancement Programme: Issues Emerging from Practice." *Studies in Higher Education* 42, no. 3: 463–479. https://doi.org/10.1080/03075079.2015.1052736.

Fox, Janna, John Haggerty, and Natasha Artemeva. 2016. "Mitigating Risk: The Impact of a Diagnostic Assessment Procedure on the First-Year Experience in Engineering." In *Post-admission Language Assessment of University Students*, edited by John Read, 43–65. Switzerland: Springer. https://doi.org/10.1007/978-3-319-39192-2.

Gautam, Chetanath, Charles L. Lowery, Chance Mays, and Dayan Durant. 2016. "Challenges for Global Learners: A Qualitative Study of the Concerns and Difficulties of International Students." *Journal of International Students* 6, no. 2: 501–526. https://doi.org/10.32674/jis.v6i2.368.

Goldberg, David E., and Mark Somerville. 2014. "A Whole New Engineer." *The Coming Revolution in Engineering Education*. Douglas: Threejoy. https://doi.org/10.4271/0986080004.

Goldsmith, Rosalie, and Keith Willey. 2016. "'It's Not My Job to Teach Writing': Activity Theory Analysis of [Invisible] Writing Practices in the Engineering Curriculum Practices in the Engineering Curriculum." *Journal of Academic Language and Learning* 10, no. 1: A118–A129.

Hailey, Jeffrey C. "Effective Communication for EMC Engineers." In *IEEE International Symposium on Electromagnetic Compatibility. Symposium Record (Cat. No. 00CH37016)*, Vol. 1: 265–268. https://doi.org/10.1109/isemc.2000.875575.

Hertzum, Morten, and Annelise Mark Pejtersen. 2000. "The Information-Seeking Practices of Engineers: Searching for Documents as Well as for People." *Information Processing & Management* 36, no. 5: 761–778. https://doi.org/10.1016/s0306-4573(00)00011-x.

Institutional Research and Planning. 2020. "Undergraduate Students: EAL Status by Student-Faculty." Simon Fraser University. Retrieved April 15, 2020, from https://irp.its.sfu.ca/ibi_apps/bip/portal/enrolment.

Institutional Research and Planning. 2021. "Undergraduate Headcount by Faculty and Visa. Enrolment Portal." Simon Fraser University. Retrieved April 29, 2021, from https://irp.its.sfu.ca/ibi_apps/bip/portal/enrolment.

Jacobs, Cecilia. 2005. "On Being an Insider on the Outside: New Spaces for Integrating Academic Literacies." *Teaching in Higher Education* 10, no. 4: 475–487. https://doi.org/10.1080/13562510500239091.

Jacobs, Cecilia. 2007. "Towards a Critical Understanding of the Teaching of Discipline-Specific Academic Literacies: Making the Tacit Explicit." *Journal of Education* 41, no. 1: 59–81.

Jacobs, Cecilia. 2010 "Collaboration as Pedagogy: Consequences and Implications for Partnerships Between Communication and Disciplinary Specialists." *Southern African Linguistics and Applied Language Studies* 28, no. 3: 227–237. https://doi.org/10.2989/16073614.2010.545025.

Kinnear, Penny, Micah Stickel, Brian Frank, and James Kaupp. 2016. "Early English Language Assessment to Improve First-Year Student Success." *2016 ASEE Annual Conference & Exposition Proceedings*. https://doi.org.10.18260/p.26876.

Kynell, Teresa. "English as an Engineering Tool: Samuel Chandler Earle and the Tufts Experiment." *Journal of Technical Writing and Communication* 25, no. 1: 85–92. https://doi.org/10.2190/7l28-aqt3-pvu7-tyc5.

Lea, Mary R., and Brian V. Street. 2006. "The 'Academic Literacies' Model: Theory and Applications." *Theory into Practice* 45, no. 4: 368–377. https://doi.org/10.1207/s15430421tip4504_11.

Lin, Angel M. Y. 2016. "How Language Varies: Everyday Registers and Academic Registers." In *Language Across the Curriculum & CLIL in English as an Additional Language (EAL) Contexts*, 11–27. https://doi.org/10.1007/978-981-10-1802-2_2.

Marshall, Steve. 2009. "Re-Becoming ESL: Multilingual University Students and a Deficit Identity." *Language and Education* 24, no. 1: 41–56. https://doi.org/10.1080/09500780903194044.

Marshall, Steve. 2020. "Understanding Plurilingualism and Developing Pedagogy: Teaching in Linguistically Diverse Classes Across the Disciplines at a Canadian University." *Language, Culture and Curriculum* 33, no. 2: 142–156. https://doi.org/10.1080/07908318.2019.1676768.

Matteson, Miriam L., Lorien Anderson, and Cynthia Boyden. 2016. "'Soft Skills': A Phrase in Search of Meaning." *Portal: Libraries and the Academy* 16, no. 1: 71–88. https://doi.org/10.1353/pla.2016.0009.

Murray, Neil. 2013. "Widening Participation and English Language Proficiency: A Convergence with Implications for Assessment Practices in Higher Education." *Studies in Higher Education* 38, no. 2: 299–311. https://doil.org/10.1080/03075079.2011.580838.

Murray, Neil. 2014. "Reflections on the Implementation of Post-Enrolment English Language Assessment." *Language Assessment Quarterly* 11, no. 3: 325–337. https://doi.org.10.1080/15434303.2013.824975.

Murray, Neil. 2016. *Standards of English in Higher Education*. Cambridge University Press. https://doi.org/10.1017/cbo9781139507189.012.

Murray, Neil, and Shashi Nallaya. 2016. "Embedding Academic Literacies in University Programme Curricula: A Case Study." *Studies in Higher Education* 41, no. 7: 1296–1312. https://doi.org/10.1080/03075079.2014.981150.

O'Loughlin, Kieran, and Sophie Arkoudis. 2009. "Investigating IELTS Exit Score Gains in Higher Education." *International English Language Testing System (IELTS) Research Reports 2009*, Vol. 10: 1. Canberra: IELTS Australia and British Council.

Prados, John W., George D. Peterson, and Lisa R. Lattuca. 2005. "Quality Assurance of Engineering Education Through Accreditation: The Impact of Engineering Criteria 2000 and its Global Influence." *Journal of Engineering Education* 94, no. 1: 165–184.

Preece, Siân, and Steve Marshall. 2020. "Plurilingualism, Teaching and Learning, and Anglophone Higher Education: An Introduction Anglophone Universities and Linguistic Diversity." *Language, Culture and Curriculum* 33, no. 2: 117–125.

Read, John. 2013. "Issues in Post-Entry Language Assessment in English-Medium Universities." *Language Teaching* 48, no. 2: 217–234. https://doi.org.10.1017/s0261444813000190.

Read, John, ed. 2016. *Post-admission Language Assessment of University Students*. Switzerland: Springer. https://doi.org/10.1007/978-3-319-39192-2.

Reave, Laura. 2014. "Technical Communication Instruction in Engineering Schools." *Journal of Business and Technical Communication* 18, no. 4: 452–490. https://doi.org.10.1177/1050651904267068.

SFU-ISTLD. "Inquiring into Your Multilingual Classroom: An Integrated Seminar Series and Grants Program." Retrieved April 29, 2021, from https://www.sfu.ca/istld/faculty/grant-programs/mlc.html.

Simon Fraser University. 2011. "English as an Additional Language Supports and Services at SFU: Review and Recommendations." Retrieved March 11, 2021, from https://docushare.sfu.ca/dsweb/GetRendition/Document-479510/html.

Siskin, Leslie Santee. 2014. *Realms of Knowledge: Academic Departments in Secondary Schools.* New York, NY: Routledge Falmer Taylor and Francis Group.

Sjoerdsma, Michael, and Amanda Wallace. 2021. "Designing a Post Entry Language Assessment (PELA) in a 1st Year Engineering Course at a Canadian University." *Simon Fraser University: Institute for the Study of Teaching and Learning in the Disciplines.* https://www.sfu.ca/istld/faculty/programs/projects/MLC/G0306.html.

Strickland, Eliza, and Glenn Zorpette. 2019. "The Coming Moon Rush: Technology, Billionaires, and Geopolitics Will All Help Get Us Back to the Moon, but They Won't Be Enough to Let Us Live There Indefinitely." *IEEE Spectrum* 56, no. 7: 22–25.

Uziak, Jacek, M. Tunde Oladiran, Magdalena Walczak, and Marian Gizejowski. 2014. "Is Accreditation an Opportunity for Positive Change or a Mirage?" *Journal of Professional Issues in Engineering Education and Practice* 140, no. 1: 02513001. https://doi.org/10.1061/(ASCE)EI.1943-5541.0000172.

Vest, David, Marilee Long, and Thad Anderson. 1996. "Electrical Engineers' Perceptions of Communication Training and Their Recommendations for Curricular Change: Results of a National Survey." *IEEE Transactions on Professional Communication* 39, no. 1: 38–42. https://doi.org/10.1109/47.486046.

Wallace, Amanda, Valia Spiliotopoulos, and Roumiana Ilieva. 2020. "CLIL Collaborations in Higher Education: A Critical Perspective." *English Teaching & Learning* 44, no. 2: 127–148. https://doi.org/10.1007/s42321-020-00052-4.

Wenger, E. 1998. "Communities of Practice: Learning as a Social System." *Systems Thinker* 9, no. 5: 1–10.

Winsor, Dorothy A. 2013. *Writing Like an Engineer.* New York: Routledge. https://doi.org/10.4324/9780203811269.

Zappa-Hollman, Sandra. 2018 "Collaborations Between Language and Content University Instructors: Factors and Indicators of Positive Partnerships." *International Journal of Bilingual Education and Bilingualism* 21, no. 5: 591–606. https://doi.org/10.1080/13670050.2018.1491946.

10

Critical Perspectives Toward Assessing Impact and Outcomes in Language Development within Business Education

Valia Spiliotopoulos

Introduction and Context

In the North American context, critical perspectives in education have become increasingly prevalent and have been strongly influenced by the writings of Paulo Freire in the 1960s and 1970s, as well as bell hooks (1994) and Michael Apple (Apple, Wayne, and Gandin 2009). Within the field of applied linguistics, critical theory and ideology are more recent and present in scholarship from the Anglophone world (Canada, the United States, UK, and Australia) (Benesch 2000, 2012; Canagarajah 2006; Janks 2010; Pennycook 2021) as marked by critiques of the linguistic imperialism of the English language (Phillipson 2009), and the multilingual turn in the field of applied linguistics (Lantolf 2000). This critical turn involved the questioning of a language standard and how this standard can serve to exclude and colonize students learning in Anglophone institutions.

Given globalization, internationalization, and immigration trends, the current context is such that the majority of recognized postsecondary institutions in the world and in North America have English as the institutional language or offer programs where English is the medium of instruction. Furthermore, employment into positions in the knowledge economy relies on a high level of competence in English, to the detriment of other languages (Murray 2016).

Alongside this dominance of English in higher education around the world, there is an emerging discourse related to increasing accountability in higher education, and focusing on evidence of impact, uptake, and outcomes of programs, initiatives, and student learning (McKay and Brindley 2007). The accountability discourse in Anglo-dominant contexts is coinciding with equally vocal and determined critical discourse perspectives, including antiracist, equity, diversity, and inclusion initiatives, especially in the higher education context. Given these trends, the challenge most institutions face involves maintaining a fine balance between advancing a critical agenda within a culture of increased accountability in an internationalized university.

This chapter reports on a case study that was undertaken to share and explain strategies for implementing inclusive, multilingual approaches with university-level English language learners, while at the same time aiming to meet institutional processes for accountability and data-driven measures expected in the Anglophone, North American university context. The hypothesis is that there are strategies for supporting inclusion and meeting multilingual students' needs such that they are able to access and engage in the content curriculum, while at the same time participating in expected assessment processes that support diagnostic, impact, and outcomes assessment for institutional accountability. The study took place in a business program in Canada's westernmost province with over seven hundred students a year—approximately 30 percent of whom have English as an additional language (international students, recent immigrant students, exchange students). Given this student diversity, this case study recounts the process of conducting diagnostic assessments to developing impactful curricular interventions that aim to support linguistically diverse students in an inclusive way.

Literature Review

In the Canadian context, most universities are engaging in the internationalization of higher education, and students who have English as an additional language can constitute up to 40–60 percent of the student body (Anderson 2015). An equity, diversity, and inclusion agenda is now part of most institutional and university program mandates, and addressing issues of languages and cultures plays an important role in fulfilling equity goals. Both immigrant and international students' cultural and linguistic resources and narratives are placed at the forefront, encouraging the inclusion of their home languages in the classroom and enacting critical literacies and pedagogies in mainstream courses (Van Viegan and Zappa-Hollman 2020).

Although the diversity present in Canadian education is part of immigration and internationalization trends, there is also a neoliberal discourse that is responsible for the increased internationalization of education through a pay-for-service model (wherein international students may pay up to four times the tuition fees) and a concurrent decrease in funding by the government for university programs (Anderson 2015). Neoliberal discourse is also part of an emergent culture of quality assurance/outcomes assessment that we have witnessed since the US K-12 No Child Left Behind initiative in 2001 and in the postsecondary context (CHEA 1996) in the United States and Canada (i.e., in the Ontario Universities Council on Quality Assurance (2010) and BC Quality Assurance Framework (2013). Furthermore, there is emerging research on the importance of taking measures to assure student preparedness for employability upon graduation (Arkoudis, Baik, and Richardson 2012), and the assessment of academic literacy and professional communication skills (Murray 2016), particularly in the UK, the United States, and Australian contexts. Although resistant to these neoliberal trends for accountability common in the United States and other Anglophone contexts, Canadian higher education has had to contend with these trends, either at the institutional level or within programs in order to stay competitive in university rankings (Stack 2016). The neoliberal approach is designed to improve efficiency and raise standards in a globally competitive environment where institutions are judged according to results (Gottlieb 2006). As such, there is an expectation to report on outcomes of standards or benchmarks that help to monitor and evaluate the performance of students, faculty, and institutions, and to collect baseline comparative data, in both language education and mainstream education across the disciplines (Gottlieb 2006).

Business programs, in particular, have been subjected to the accountability movement for accreditation and have seen the highest levels of enrollment—including international student enrollment—compared with other postsecondary programs in the last ten years (Colby et al. 2011). Business schools in Canada often engage in accreditation processes by European (EQUIS and PRME) and US (AACSB) external accreditors every five years. These processes are often independent or integrated with institutional self-study or government-imposed quality assurance processes. Quality assurance often involves the gathering of data on a number of cross-curricular skills, including student communication skills—both written and oral—in the dominant language of business—English.

This case study focuses on strategies used to gather diagnostic, post-entry language assessment data so as to meet English as an additional language for students' needs (Dunworth 2009; Read 2015, 2016). The study also focuses on the process of using this data to design an inclusive intervention to meet students' needs and to evaluate its effectiveness through an impact assessment.

Methods

Data Collection and Analysis

This case analysis took place over the course of three years within a business program at a comprehensive, research university in Western Canada. A case study (Creswell 2013) is described as an exploration of a "bounded system" or a case over time through detailed, in-depth data collection. This case gathered multiple sources of data, including

- Aggregate diagnostic writing assessment data over the course of three years, which served to analyze student needs and identify trends and patterns, as well as a baseline measure of students' writing performance upon entering the program
- Participant-researcher reflections and observations of the intervention developed to address students' needs
- Student impact assessment data, which served to gather students' input and feedback on the intervention designed to meet students' writing and business communication needs.

The key research questions that were addressed in this study were as follows:

- How can EAL students' linguistic needs be met so that they don't feel marginalized or excluded once they are accepted into a business program?
- What are students' perceptions of institutional efforts to address context-specific linguistic needs within mainstream courses?
- How can institutional demands be addressed, while at the same time reframing the narrative of language support such that it is asset-oriented?

Key Activities in This Case

Initial Diagnostic Assessment

The diagnostic assessment tool to evaluate students' writing involved a course-embedded twenty-minute written response to questions initially related to students' co/extra-curricular interests and career aspirations. The course in which the diagnostic assessment took place was a first-year, multi-section, required foundation course for all first- or second-year business students. The main topic of the course focused on collaborative work environments. Over time—and in keeping with a more content-based approach to writing and language development

(Cammarata 2016; Smit and Dafouz 2012)—a more contextualized writing assessment tool that directly related to the course content was implemented. To that end, the writing topic was changed to focus on the definition of leadership and processes of developing team-building and collaboration strategies when assuming various organizational roles. The redesign of this assessment instrument was a collaboration between both business faculty and language specialists, where language specialists were able to encourage more inclusive and developmental perspectives toward the process (Wallace, Spiliotopoulos, and Ilieva 2020). Students' in-class writing was assessed by language specialists using a co-constructed rubric in the areas of content, organization, language accuracy (grammar), and vocabulary (including spelling); this rubric met the language assessors' expectations for language proficiency, as well as business content faculty expectations in meeting business communications skills standards.

To avoid any perceptions of exclusion or separating out students who did not have English as their first language or mother tongue, all students (approximately 700/year) were expected to participate in this low-stakes writing assessment within a foundations course. To scaffold and address the language demands of writing in the area of collaboration in work environments, students were provided with a reading and lecture on the topic. Language experts then marked the writing samples, and the samples were returned to the students with feedback provided on the sample and the rubric. Those students who were not "meeting expectations" were encouraged to reach out for additional support through a "drop-in" model, but as shown in recent research by Fox, Hagerty, and Artemeva (2016), there is minimal uptake (less than 5 percent) of drop-in support by students. Given that there were at least half of the students—both domestic and EAL students—who were either not meeting expectations or could benefit from additional writing support, language experts and business faculty collaborated to create a writing-intensive course in business that all students would be required to take.

Curricular Intervention

In examining the results of the post-entry diagnostic assessment through faculty-level curriculum meetings, language faculty and content faculty collaborated to create a new course that addressed areas that could be improved upon by all students—namely in the areas of grammar, sentence structure, and vocabulary. A new writing-intensive course was proposed and approved by Senate by making the case that it was designed to scaffold students' writing and critical thinking development early on in the program (students' first or second year). Before this new course was proposed, it had been observed that most of the courses in writing or communication skills development were not offered until the third or fourth year of the program, in which case it may have been too late to offer support in time for graduation and to transition for employment purposes.

This writing-intensive course did not only focus on writing skills, but on using writing skills to express critical thinking in business contexts. As such, the course included problem-solving and case analysis activities from various business perspectives (i.e., marketing, accounting). The course was writing-intensive as students were expected to submit three written assignments over the course of the term, as well as weekly written contributions in an online discussion forum, and participate in a group presentation based on a script or slides. There were at least fifteen sections of the course per year, and approximately forty students in each section of the course. The student body was a mixture of domestic students, international students, recent immigrant students or Generation 1.5 students, and exchange students. The large majority of the students were enrolled in the business program and were required to take the course as a prerequisite for a required communication course offered later in the program, and as a graduation requirement.

Although the course was taught in English and all assignments had to be submitted in English, students were not discouraged from speaking a common home language in group work (both in and outside of class), as long as other students in the class were not feeling excluded, and as long as the use of the home language was purposeful in helping them express a concept or complete a task in English.

Impact Assessment

To understand the impact of the curricular intervention, student self-perceptions of impact were gathered through a post-pre assessment questionnaire where students rated their level of knowledge, skills, and confidence/optimism about business writing, language, communication, and critical thinking on a scale from 0 (not adequate) to 4 (very adequate). They were asked to retrospectively indicate where their level was before taking the course and then after taking the course, thereby expressing the impact it had on various aspects of their learning, including the affective domain. An analysis of the data was conducted by examining the degree of differences between the pre-scores and the post-scores. All students were asked to fill out the questionnaire; however, for the purposes of this chapter, the results focused on the responses of the English as an additional language students.

Results and Key Findings

Diagnostic Assessment to Meet Students' Needs

The global perspective and commitment to equitable access to high-quality business education through the values of equity, diversity, and inclusion that this and other accredited business education institutions support is represented in the linguistic and cultural diversity in the business classroom (AACSB 2021). Students in the current business program can speak multiple languages, and since the school has met accreditation standards, students have demonstrated strong analytical and quantitative skills necessary for pursuing studies in a business degree program. The complexities involved in addressing the needs of such a diverse group of capable students involve recognizing their diversity as an asset and resource, as well as acknowledging the inequity of imposing native-speaking norms in English required to access the curriculum.

That said, due to quality assurance for accreditation processes at the faculty and institutional level, the business program in this institution still has a responsibility to continue to demonstrate that their students can communicate effectively in English, both orally and in writing, to complete work in the various business sectors or disciplines. These students have been hesitant to take decontextualized language courses that do not directly provide them with the lexical, grammatical, and rhetorical strategies relevant to their degree program. Because of a perceived deficit discourse toward EAL students, some EAL students avoid seeking language support and need to be "nudged" into furthering their language development—ideally, alongside domestic students in mainstream content courses (Evans et al. 2009).

As such, a diagnostic language assessment was designed and implemented to identify student needs, as well as support retention, persistence, and academic success of *all students*, including multilingual/EAL learners. Implementing a diagnostic assessment to design and deliver a curriculum intervention that would meet all students' needs was an important step in strengthening business communication skills in English in ways that were inclusive and asset-oriented. The low-stakes initial diagnostic assessment results involved gathering results on key dimensions or criteria in writing and identification of students based on admission pathway and fee status (i.e., internal/external transfer, international/domestic). However, the follow-up course designed to meet those students' needs was required by all students; EAL students received this support in a mainstream business course alongside Canadian Anglophone students.

As can be seen in Figure 10.1, there were more or less consistent results in the first three years demonstrating that about 15 percent of students were not yet "meeting expectations"—essentially according to native English-speaker standards of business communication. It was believed that if these students were identified and notified early on in the program, they would benefit from ongoing developmental language support. It is important to note that students' anonymity was maintained

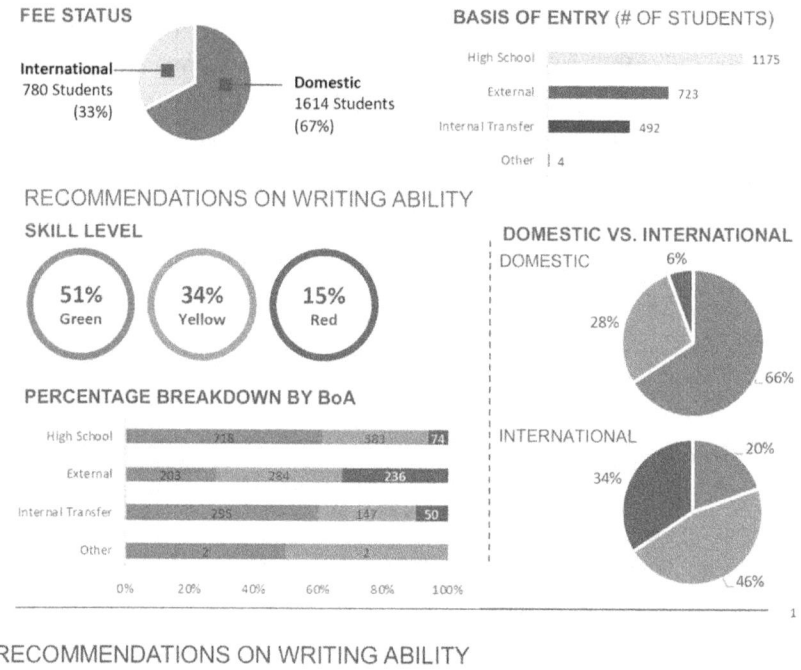

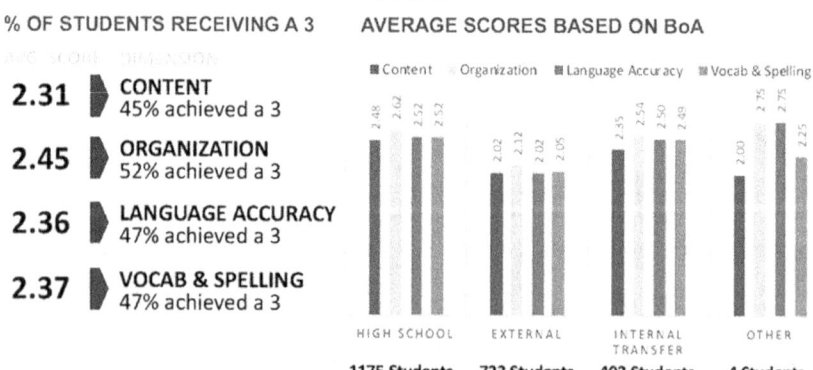

Figure 10.1 Student profile and diagnostic information (SFU 2018, 52–53).

in the reporting of this institutional data, but the data was aggregated, categorized, and analyzed based on students' pathways to admission. The data shows that international transfer students could use ongoing support in their English ability since they have likely had limited exposure to the English language and academic literacy in high school within their home country. Unfortunately, the presentation of this data where these students are represented "in the red" serves to reinforce the deficit discourse in English-medium institutions and does not explain the limited context in which their English learning has occurred.

Although the data suggests that just over one-third of the newly arrived international students[1] were in need of ongoing writing development, it is important to also see that only two-thirds of the "domestic" students were scoring a 3 or above, even after having spent a comparatively extensive period of time—over eighteen years—in English schooling and in an Anglophone environment. Although just over 5 percent of the domestic students were identified as being "in the red," there were still about a third in the "yellow," meaning that they could benefit from ongoing writing support.

Putting aside the connotations that the colors "red," "yellow," and "green" may hold for representing the diversity of the student population in institutional programs, the writing assessment did provide an important snapshot of English language writing ability once EAL students had been accepted into a mainstream business program, and it enabled the school to have some baseline data from which to measure any future assessments. In looking at the various criteria or dimensions for evaluating the written sample, it is interesting to note that the lowest average was in the "content" dimension. This could perhaps speak to the fact that in contextualized, content-based language assessment, all students, including both domestic and international, have not yet developed a full repertoire of conceptual vocabulary in their discipline and may not have been able to write much about the main topic related to the content area of the course, despite some efforts at scaffolding. Including content as a dimension in the writing assessment also raises ongoing issues and questions around construct validity, as it becomes unclear at what point we are assessing language and where we are assessing content. Of course, the challenge, particularly with international students, is that they may have the vocabulary for key concepts in a disciplinary area but may not yet know how to express them. This is also the case for new international high school students, who "sometimes have only to learn new labels for already known concepts" (Garnett 2008, 17) since they may have already developed literacy skills and content knowledge in their mother tongue. A key question faculty and institutions may consider in postsecondary and secondary language assessment practices with recently arrived multilingual/EAL international students is how we might recognize students' content knowledge and literacy skills in their L1? In fact, many of these students may have deeper content area knowledge from attending high school in their home countries, yet need more time and targeted language instruction from a lexical, grammatical, and genre-based perspective.

After numerous attempts to encourage those students who needed ongoing language support to reach out to a variety of campus resources, both language faculty and business faculty agreed that it would be more effective and inclusive to offer a required writing course in the first or second year of the program. This would serve as a clear message to all students that writing, language, and communication skills were important and that students would be honing these skills throughout their degree program. This newly required course at the beginning of the program would also serve as evidence of the school's innovation in program-level design, thereby potentially improving positive outcomes not only in content knowledge but in skills development.

In sum, in response to the first research question, a curricular intervention was designed to meet EAL students' linguistic and social–emotional needs after an initial, baseline writing assessment by not separating out students in need of ongoing support into a separate section or adjunct language course (Fenton-Smith and Humphreys 2015), but by including them into a mainstream course so that they wouldn't feel marginalized or excluded once they were accepted into a business program. However, rather than using a "submersion" (Lin 2016) approach to learning about business writing, teaching and learning activities were designed to teach the language of business discourse (Bargiela-Chiappini, Nickerson and Planken 2013). Although it should be noted that providing content-based language support to EAL students through separate sections and adjunct language courses may be highly effective in bilingual universities (Knoerr, Weinberg, and Buchanan 2018) or in EMI university contexts where the majority language (other than English) is often the language of instruction, doing so does not necessarily carry the same "remedial" label or deficit connotation that we see in most Anglo-dominant institutions in the Western, English-speaking world.

Participant-Researcher Observations and Reflections

Once there was agreement about the design and delivery of a writing-intensive course early on in the program, language specialists began to collaborate on the various course activities and assessments in support of language, writing, and communication skills development. Although there was a significant focus on scaffolding language and writing, business faculty made it clear that this was not to be "an ESL course," thereby reinforcing the divide between language and content, and distancing themselves from any institutional perceptions of this new course being a "remedial" course.

As mentioned, the delivery of a required writing-intensive course for both mainstream and EAL students through collaborative teaching or "embedded" support (Brooman-Jones et al. 2011; Evans et al. 2009; Spiliotopoulos, Wallace, and Ilieva 2022) could be perceived as inclusive practice as EAL students are not separated out into adjunct English courses; placed into separate sections in their discipline course; or forced to take decontextualized, generic academic English language and literacy courses that continue to be perceived by Anglophone institutions as "remedial" support. However, if language issues are not addressed explicitly in this model, learners' needs will not be met. Thus, each session in the course included specific language objectives (alongside content objectives) that were integrated into learning outcomes and that did not only address vocabulary, but also grammar and genre. Extensive feedback was provided to students on all these aspects of language. This more language-embedded, inclusive method of support reinforced that "business discourse" is in fact everyone's second language, and that contextualized writing assignments and assessments did not only improve students' language development and communication skills, but their critical thinking skills. Since most assignments and assessments placed a dual focus on both language and content (where up to 30 percent of a mark focused on language and communication skills), students were able to recognize the strong connection between language and thought and were more aware of how language and writing development could strengthen their critical thinking skills in the content area.

Additional inclusive strategies were used in curriculum, instruction, and assessment design and delivery. Given the significant cultural and linguistic diversity in this course, the instructors focused on the internationalization of the curriculum by encouraging written assignments and reflection on content and cases in the global business context (China, India, Middle East in the news, as opposed to US and Canadian business case studies only). There was discussion and awareness of critical thinking in business from diverse cultural perspectives, rather than just Western conceptualization of critical thinking. Furthermore, assignments focused on intercultural communication that celebrated linguistic and cultural diversity in the classroom and business contexts. These assignments explicitly taught all students cross-cultural considerations of business discourse through oral interaction and through written documentation.

As previously mentioned, the course design had very clear language-related objectives, as well as business content-related objectives, representing a highly contextualized content and language integrated approach (Spiliotopoulos 2018). In terms of course delivery, the pilot sections involved co-teaching by a content instructor and a language instructor through regular collaboration (Zappa-Hollman 2018); however, future sections were able to offer both a language and content TA to support assessment activities and ensure that both content and language objectives were being met. A "language TA" was present and available in class and outside of class hours to support with small group assignments and feedback; some of these TAs were multilingual and could also translanguage (Lin 2016) with students in helping them understand some of the more linguistically and cognitively demanding key concepts in the course with the view to facilitate expression in English. In fact, highly qualified co-instructors and language TAs were hired for the express purpose of representing the diversity in the instructional team. Additionally, plurilingual interaction was encouraged in and outside of the classroom between students for small group work and assignments in strategic ways (Van Viegen and Zappa-Hollman 2020).

The impact of these contextualized and inclusive practices in support of language and writing skills development in English was assessed through a student questionnaire at the end of the course. As part of a course-embedded outcomes assessment model for accreditation, faculty continued to gather "objective" assessment data using classroom-based assessment artifacts (case analyses, business proposals) in order to assess overall trends or improvements at various touchpoints over the course of the degree. The researcher was not able to report out on the results of that outcomes assessment data because this information currently belongs to the faculty; however, impact assessment data on students' perceptions on their writing and critical thinking skills development were gathered and are shared in Figure 10.2 further down.

The following section will report on EAL students' perceptions of how this key intervention helped to meet their linguistic needs. The participant-researcher's observations and perceptions demonstrate the various efforts that were made to meet EAL students' needs—namely, contextualized language support integrated within mainstream content courses using co-teaching or language TAs, as well as encouraging multilingual practice, and the internationalization of the curriculum.

Impact Assessment Results

Student perceptions of the impact of these various inclusive interventions were gathered at the end of the first and subsequent iterations of the new writing intensive course, which all students had to take at the beginning of the business

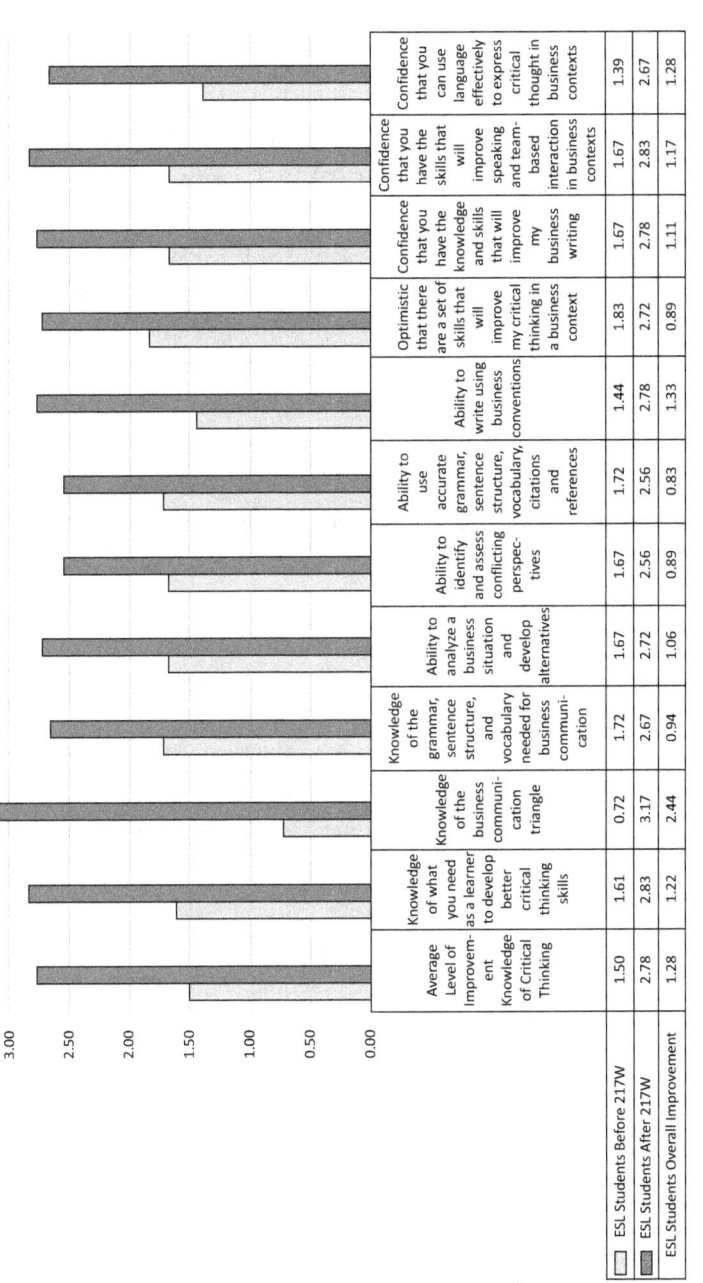

Figure 10.2 Impact assessment results—student perceptions of improvement before and after writing course (SFU 2018, 50).

program—a course that supported the language development of both domestic and EAL learners. As mentioned, the course design involved numerous writing assessments within the various business genres (proposal or business pitch, case analysis, etc.), and contextualized explicit teaching of business discourse (content-based vocabulary, grammar, and genre awareness) and business writing to solve business problems and critically analyze business cases.

Impact assessment data was gathered over a two-year period, with up to fifteen different sections of this course offered every year. However, this chapter reports on a snapshot of two course sections in the spring semester of 2018 (see Figure 10.2). As can be seen in this pre- and post-assessment, students rated their overall level of knowledge, skills, and attitudes in the course as higher after taking this course. The impact assessment questionnaire asked them to reflect on their perceived level before the course in comparison to after the course on a scale of 4 (0—Not adequate to 4—Very Adequate). The students evaluated themselves as having improved along all twelve criteria, with a rating differential ranging between a 0.83 increase to a 2.4 increase as compared to the beginning of the course, particularly in the areas of business communications, language, and writing development.

Although outcomes assessment measures that use actual samples of student work against validated rubrics can further inform whether or not there was improvement over time in students' business writing and communication skills development, a more critical lens also values students' voices and perceptions of their own knowledge, skills, and levels of confidence regarding language (Sun et al. 2022). As such, in any accountability or assessment process, it would be highly encouraged to also invite the students' voices and perceptions of development; however, many of the current assessment processes in institutional and government settings tend to prioritize more "objective" measures of students' knowledge and abilities by faculty and potential employers (Murray 2016).

To that end, in response to the third research question, institutions can reframe the narrative of "language support" by not only gathering baseline writing assessment data or outcomes assessment data that might reinforce a deficit discourse, but also by contextualizing this data based on students' previous experience and exposure to English, as well as by approaching this data as a way to meet students' needs, rather than as a way to measure standards that are based on English norms. Finally, institutions can provide opportunities for EAL students' voices to be heard through survey data or questionnaires that share their judgments about if or how these needs may or may not have been met. These opportunities imply that the institution views these students as an asset and cares about their experience. Reframing a narrative of language support as one that is needs-based and asset-oriented would bring institutions a step closer to the goals of equity, diversity, and inclusion in increasingly internationalizing universities.

Discussion and Conclusions

The current chapter describes a case study of more inclusive approaches to language assessment and course development by investigating the impact they had in a business education context in one Canadian university. This study calls for more inclusive and context-relevant approaches to assessment and teaching that address students' writing, as well as affective needs. It demonstrates that there are strategies that can support multilingual/EAL students to successfully access and engage in a program's curriculum while working within a context that is influenced by accreditation and outcomes assessment processes, common in many professional university programs. In this case, it is important to note that EAL students were not separated through a diagnostic writing assessment activity. Although students were identified, contacted, and encouraged to seek additional language and literacy support, we know from the literature that few students choose self-directed drop-in support (Fox, Hagerty, and Artemeva 2016). To that end, a key inclusive "intervention" was to offer all students—not only EAL learners—a foundational writing-intensive course that supported the language and business discourse development of all incoming students within the first two years of the program.[2] Furthermore, although institutional outcomes assessment data on students' business writing and critical thinking skills were gathered, students' perceptions on the impact of the various interventions—not only in terms of knowledge and abilities but also on affective dimensions such as attitude and confidence—were collected. This approach is different in that it foregrounds EAL student voices and takes into consideration the affective domain of students' learning. Although an outcomes assessment model of learning may share information on EAL students' knowledge and skills areas, there is limited research on how these processes impact students' social–emotional state, including their level of confidence, sense of belonging, or positive outlook. There is emerging research that examines these specific issues of inclusion and sense of belonging (Popadiuk and Marshall 2011), but it has only recently been receiving attention from institutions as an opportunity to demonstrate that they have engaged in equity, diversity, and inclusion initiatives at the university from a social–emotional perspective.

It is important to note that despite the faculty's best efforts to create an inclusive, contextualized, and engaging learning environment for all students, there were still instances where some visible minority EAL students were marginalized and did not initially feel included in group activities, especially at the beginning of the course (Sohn and Spiliotopoulos 2019). This points to the importance of developing intercultural literacy among all learners, especially upon entry into the program. It was encouraging to see that the institution has been developing orientation sessions to support the development of these skills among all students in recent years.

Finally, as indicated by Murray (2016), the professional development of faculty will become increasingly important as the student body becomes more diverse and internationalized, not only in Anglophone universities, but in universities around the world. This professional development can also include intercultural literacy, as well as curricular and instructional strategies for engaging multilingual students in university courses in inclusive ways (Hafernik and Wiant 2012).

In order to pay more than lip service to equity, diversity, and inclusion with multilingual recent immigrant and international students, university policies and resources should be dedicated to these goals. Grants and professional development in this area should become incentivized, strongly encouraged, if not mandated. Faculty efforts at creating linguistically and culturally responsive instruction (Haan and Gallagher 2022) should be rewarded and recognized, not only in teaching, but also in research areas across the disciplines. In addition to enacting educational change at the course and program levels in curriculum, instruction, and assessment, faculty across the disciplines can be encouraged to reexamine pedagogical theories and epistemologies in their field from a theoretical lens that reframes disciplinary ways of knowing and being by drawing on theories and discourses on decolonization and social justice in education. Increased awareness and knowledge of these theoretical lenses will help to change faculty attitudes, roles, and practices (Ilieva, Wallace, and Spiliotopoulos 2019).

Future research in the area of more inclusive language development in disciplinary settings at the university level would involve comparing students' self-perceptions of their development at the beginning of the program and at the end, as well as determining any correlations between their self-perceptions and outcomes assessment data. If there is a mismatch or low levels of confidence despite reaching acceptable performance levels through more objective measures, then this would be an indicator to further refine efforts at inclusive practice. An additional area of research would involve faculty across the disciplines by inquiring into linguistically and culturally responsive pedagogy in their own unique teaching contexts. Recent research in this area has been conducted (Gallagher and Haan 2018; Haan and Gallagher 2022), and should be encouraged in a variety of national and international contexts with a broad range of diverse students and faculty across different disciplinary fields, or linguistic and cultural backgrounds.

This chapter has reported on data that represented an attempt at engaging in routinized assessment and outcomes processes integral to the operation of business programs from a critical, more inclusive perspective. It suggests that there are ways of addressing and meeting students' holistic needs by strategically critiquing, but also working collaboratively within more positivistic disciplinary processes and structures in university contexts from a critical-pragmatic perspective (Benesch 2000). Although more critical and deconstructive approaches would be worth pursuing in our efforts at ethical internationalization (Ilieva, Beck, and Waterstone 2014), diversity, and inclusion, higher education will need some time to make the significant changes in theory, policies, and practice needed to reach a sociopolitical ideal. In the meantime, faculty can continue to move forward and try to enact more inclusive measures within their own fields of influence, and aim to meet social justice goals one course and one student at a time.

Notes

1 In most cases, international students were recent arrivals who may have been in Canada anywhere from two to six months, or recent college transfer international students who may have spent up to two years in Canada before entering the university program.
2 Students entered their first year either as direct entry students from high school, or as second-year transfer students entering from another college or university after having completed a year of general or business studies.

References

AACSB. 2021. "Our Commitment to Equity, Diversity, Inclusion, and Belonging." AACSB. https://www.aacsb.edu/-/media/publications/research-reports/deib _positioning_paper.pdf?rev=1876431c9287467f9395358b2810dfbf.

Anderson, Tim. 2015. "Seeking Internationalization: The State of Canadian Higher Education." *Canadian Journal of Higher Education* 45, no. 4: 166–187. https://doi.org/10.47678/cjhe.v45i4.184690.

Apple, Michael W., Wayne Au, and Luis Armando Gandin. 2009. *The Routledge International Handbook of Critical Education*. New York: Routledge.

Arkoudis, Sophie, Chi Baik, and Sarah Richardson. 2012. *English Language Standards in Higher Education: From Entry to Exit*. Camberwell: Australian Council for Educational Research Press.

Bargiela-Chiappini, Francesca, Catherine Nickerson, and Brigitte Planken. 2013. *Business Discourse*, 2nd edn. New York: Palgrave Macmillan.

Benesch, Sarah. 2000. "Critical Pragmatism: A Politics of L2 Composition." In *On Second Language Writing*, edited by Tony Silva and Paul Kei Matsuda, 161–172. Mahwah: Erlbaum.

Benesch, Sarah. 2012. "Critical English for Academic Purposes." In *The Encyclopedia of Applied Linguistics*, edited by Carol A. Chapelle. Wylie Online Library. http://onlinelibrary.wiley.com/doi/10.1002/9781405198431.wbeal0278/abstract.

Brooman-Jones, Susan, Greg Cunningham, Laura Hanna, and David Nigel Wilson. 2011. "Embedding Academic Literacy – A Case Study in Business at UTS." *Journal of Academic Language & Learning* 5, no. 2: A1–A13.

Cammarata, Laurent. 2016. *Content-based Foreign Language Teaching: Curriculum and Pedagogy for Developing Advanced Thinking and Literacy Skills*. New York: Routledge.

Canagarajah, Athelstan Suresh. 2006. "Understanding Critical Writing." In *Second Language Writing in the Composition Classroom*, edited by Paul Kei Matsuda, Michelle Cox, Jay Jordan, and Christina Ortmeier-Hooper, 210–224. Boston: Bedford St. Martin's.

Colby, Anne, Thomas Ehrlich, William M. Sullivan, and Jonathan R. Dolle. 2011. *Rethinking Undergraduate Business Education: Liberal Learning for the Profession*. San Francisco: Jossey-Bass.

Creswell, John W. 2013. *Qualitative Inquiry and Research Design: Choosing Among Five Approaches*, 3rd edn. Los Angeles: SAGE Publications.

Dunworth, Katie. 2009. "An Investigation into Post-entry English Language Assessment in Australian Universities." *Journal of Academic Language & Learning* 3, no. 1: A1–A13.

Evans, Elaine, Jen Tindale, Dawn Cable, and Suzanne Hamil Mead. 2009. "Collaborative Teaching in a Linguistically and Culturally Diverse Higher Education Setting: A Case Study of a Postgraduate Accounting Program." *Higher Education Research & Development* 28, no. 6: 597–613. https://doi.org/10.1080/07294360903226403.

Garnett, Bruce William. 2008. *A Critical Examination of the Academic Trajectories of ESL Youth*. Vancouver: University of British Columbia. https://open.library.ubc.ca/collections/ubctheses/24/items/1.0055511.

Fenton-Smith, Ben, and Pamela Humphreys. 2015. "Language Specialists' Views on Academic Language and Learning Support Mechanisms for EAL Postgraduate

Coursework Students: The Case for Adjunct Tutorials." *Journal of English for Academic Purposes* 20, no. December: 40–55. https://doi.org/10.1016/j.jeap.2015.05.001.

Fox, Janna, John Hagerty, and Natasha Artemeva. 2016. "Mitigating Risk: The Impact of a Diagnostic Assessment Procedure on the First-year Experience in Engineering." In *Post Admission Language Assessment of University Students*, edited by Daniel J. Read, 43–65. Switzerland: Springer.

Gallagher, Colleen E., and Jennifer E. Haan. 2018. "University Faculty Beliefs About Emergent Multilinguals and Linguistically Responsive Instruction." *TESOL Quarterly* 52, no. 2: 304–330. https://doi.org/10.1002/tesq.399.

Gottlieb, Margo H. 2006. *Assessing English Language Learners: Bridges from Language Proficiency to Academic Achievement*. Thousand Oaks: Corwin Press.

Hafernik, Johnnie Johnson, and Fredel M. Wiant. 2012. *Integrating Multilingual Students into College Classrooms: Practical Advice for Faculty*. Bristol: Multilingual Matters.

Haan, Jennifer, and Colleen Gallagher. 2022. "Situating Linguistically Responsive Instruction in Higher Education Contexts: Foundations for Pedagogical, Curricular, and Institutional Support." *TESOL Quarterly* 56, no. 1: 5–18. https://doi.org/10.1002/tesq.3087.

hooks, bell. 1994. *Teaching to Transgress: Education as the Practice of Freedom*. New York: Routledge.

Ilieva, Roumiana, Kumari Beck, and Bonnie Waterstone. 2014. "Towards Sustainable Internationalisation of Higher Education." *Higher Education* 68: 875–889. https://doi.org/10.1007/s10734-014-9749-6.

Ilieva, Roumiana, Amanda Wallace, and Valia Spiliotopoulos. 2019. "Institutional Roles and Identity Construction of Applied Linguistics Faculty Involved in Interdisciplinary Collaborations for Multilingual Student Success." *TESL Canada Journal* 36, no. 1: 71–96.

Janks, Hilary. 2010. "Language, Power and Pedagogies." In *Sociolinguistics and Language Education*, edited by Nancy H. Hornberger and Sandra Lee McKay, 40–61. Clevedon: Multilingual Matters.

Knoerr, Hélène, Alysse Weinberg, and Catherine Elena Buchanan. 2018. *Current Issues in University Immersion*. Ottawa: University of Ottawa Press.

Lantolf, James P. 2000. *Sociocultural Theory and Second Language Learning*. Oxford: Oxford University Press.

Lin, Angel M. Y. 2016. *Language Across the Curriculum & CLIL in English as an Additional Language (EAL) Contexts: Theory and Practice*. Singapore: Springer Singapore.

McKay, Penny, and Geoff Brindley. 2007. "Educational Reform and ESL Assessment in Australia: New Roles and New Tensions." *Language Assessment Quarterly* 4, no. 1: 69–84. https://doi.org/10.1080/15434300701348383.

Murray, Neil. 2016. *Standards of English in Higher Education: Issues, Challenges, and Strategies*. Cambridge: Cambridge University Press.

Pennycook, Alastair. 2021. *Critical Applied Linguistics: A Critical Re-Introduction / Alastair Pennycook*, 2nd edn. New York: Routledge.

Phillipson, Robert. 2009. *Linguistic Imperialism Continued / Robert Phillipson*. Hyderabad, India: New York: Routledge.

Popadiuk, Natalee E., and Steve Marshall. 2011. "East Asian International Student Experiences as Learners of English as an Additional Language: Implications for School Counsellors." *Canadian Journal of Counselling and Psychotherapy* 45, no. 3: 220–239.

Read, John. 2015. *Assessing English Proficiency for University Study*. London: Palgrave Macmillan.

Read, John. 2016. *Post Admission Language Assessment of University Students*. Switzerland: Springer.

Simon Fraser University. 2018. *CELLTR (Centre for English Language Learning Teaching and Research) Annual Report 2017–2018*. Burnaby: Simon Fraser University.

Smit, Ute, and Emma Dafouz. 2012. "Integrating Content and Language in Higher Education: An Introduction Into English-Medium Policies, Conceptual Issues and Research Practices Across Europe." *AILA Review* 25, no. 1. Amsterdam, the Netherlands: John Benjamins.

Sohn, Bong-gi, and Valia Spiliotopoulos. 2021. "Scaffolding Peer Interaction Within a Language and Content-Integrated Business Curriculum: A Case-study in a Western Canadian University." In *Meaningful Teaching Interaction at the Internationalised University: Moving from Research to Impact*, edited by Doris Dippold and Marion Heron, 80–96. London: Taylor and Francis.

Spiliotopoulos, Valia. 2018. "Lessons Learned from Immersion in Western Canada's Multilingual and Multicultural Post-secondary Context across the Disciplines." *OLBI Journal* 9, no. June: 1–25. https://doi.org/10.18192/olbiwp.v9i0.2340.

Spiliotopoulos, Valia, Amanda Wallace, and Roumiana Ilieva. 2022. "Diffusing Innovation to Support Faculty Engagement in the Integration of Language and Content Across the Disciplines in an Internationalized Canadian University." *Higher Education Research & Development*. https://doi.org/10.1080/07294360.2022.2052813.

Stack, M. (2016). *Global University Rankings and the Mediatization of Higher Education*. Basingstoke: Palgrave Studies in Global Higher Education.

Sun, Shuting (Alice), Xuesong (Andy) Gao, Bita Dwi Rahmani, Priyanka Bose, and Chris Davison. 2022. "Student Voice in Assessment and Feedback (2011–2022): A Systematic Review." *Assessment & Evaluation in Higher Education*. https://doi.org/10.1080/02602938.2022.2156478.

Van Viegen, Saskia, and Sandra Zappa-Hollman. 2020. "Plurilingual Pedagogies at the Post-secondary Level: Possibilities for Intentional Engagement with Students' Diverse Linguistic Repertoires." *Language, Culture and Curriculum* 33, no. 2: 172–187.

Wallace, Amanda, Valia Spiliotopoulos, and Roumiana Ilieva. 2020. "CLIL Collaborations in Higher Education: A Critical Perspective." *English Teaching & Learning* 44: 127–148.

Zappa-Hollman, Sandra. 2018. "Collaborations Between Language and Content University Instructors: Factors and Indicators of Positive Partnerships." *International Journal of Bilingual Education and Bilingualism* 21, no. 5: 591–606. https://doi.org/10.1080/13670050.2018.1491946.

The Development and Impact of a Linguistically Responsive Classroom Series to Address Linguistic Diversity in Higher Education

Amanda Wallace, Eilidh Singh, and Fiona Shaw

Introduction

Like most North American universities, trends in internationalization, massification, and diversification of the student population have led to increasing numbers of multilingual students, both domestic and international (Anderson 2015; Murray 2016). Lacking pedagogical knowledge and expertise for teaching students using English as an additional language (EAL), faculty members face challenges in effectively instructing these students, whom they perceive as not fully prepared for the intensive academic demands of undergraduate studies (Bettinger and Long 2009; Tavares 2021). In light of these challenges, SFU's senior leadership recognized the necessity to establish an EAL Initiatives Team (of which we are the three members) to be uniquely embedded alongside more traditional educational developer roles within the institute's Teaching and Learning Centre, reflecting a targeted approach to address language-related teaching challenges.

Created in 2018, the Centre for Educational Excellence (CEE) collaborates with faculty members and instructors to foster innovative, inclusive, and reflective teaching methods to enhance student engagement in learning. The center champions research-informed teaching and diverse pedagogical approaches and promotes interactive, cross-disciplinary collaboration among instructors. Guided by SFU's Academic Plan, CEE's strategic goals include tailored professional development teaching opportunities, promoting inclusive teaching, supporting SFU's blended and online learning strategy, and expanding faculty development opportunities across all SFU campuses.

Our team's mandate is to operationalize CEE's objectives of fostering the development of inclusive teaching approaches that support diverse learners and pedagogies. In doing so, we aim to empower instructors to effectively facilitate the learning of students who use EAL. Assembled in January 2020, our small team comprises seasoned experts in postsecondary English language teaching, program management, curriculum development, and teacher training. Fiona, serving as the associate director of Inclusive Teaching, and Eilidh and Amanda, both EAL consultants, each bring a unique range of expertise. We are committed to our responsibility of creating EAL initiatives for faculty and the development of multilingual teaching assistants (TAs), in addition to supporting inclusive teaching programs generally. Drawn from classroom practice teaching multilingual students and supporting instructors in postsecondary Canadian and international contexts, our combined experience places an emphasis on prioritizing and supporting the success of multilingual speakers in disciplinary courses. We apply our collective knowledge in second language acquisition, linguistically responsive pedagogy (LRP), and educational development to collaborate with faculty university-wide, driving EAL support and refining linguistically responsive curricula and teaching strategies.

In this chapter, we describe how we approached the challenge of responding to the linguistic complexity at our internationalizing university by directly supporting instructors' teaching development. We begin the discussion by introducing our team and situating our initiative within the relevant literature. After a brief description of LRP, we outline the approach adopted by our team for the development of the Linguistically Responsive Classrooms: Instructor Series (LRCIS). This is framed around how faculty could apply LRP or linguistic responsiveness in their own contexts. We discuss the importance of employing an innovative, contextualized, and motivational design to build faculty buy-in before describing our thematic analysis of the program's material (which included coursework, discussion board posts, reflections, teaching artifacts, and course feedback), and then discussing the promising patterns that emerge which speak to the possible impact of the series. We then examine if, how, and why this program might have met the dual challenge of both motivating instructors to reframe their thinking around their multilingual students and creating a linguistically responsive, contextualized pedagogical artifact in their courses. Finally, we conclude by highlighting the implications that this type of program may have on our ongoing practice as educational developers, particularly in the context of internationalized institutions like ours. We also identify remaining questions for further exploration to deepen our understanding of how best to support faculty in this context.

Situating Ourselves—Contextual Insights

Occupying a unique space at the intersection of applied linguistics, educational development, and teaching experience, our team collaborates with the learning and teaching community to inspire and support innovative, inclusive, reflective, and evidence-based teaching approaches that create engaging learning experiences and support the academic success of SFU's multilingual students. Our emphasis on asset-based EAL strategies plays a crucial role in countering the lingering negative perceptions that some instructors have regarding EAL students in mainstream disciplinary classes (Marshall 2009). By engaging with individual instructors and at the program level, we address pedagogical, linguistic, and assessment challenges through evidence-based practices. Ultimately, our goal is to cater more effectively to the needs of multilingual students, thereby facilitating the growth of all students as they evolve into accomplished emerging academic scholars. Through our specialized expertise, we are committed to making a meaningful impact on both the instructors and the diverse student population they serve, fulfilling the goals of CEE.

Our work is, however, not without challenges that arise from both external and internal factors. In 2020, the COVID-19 pandemic diverted the focus of the team as CEE was called on to support faculty broadly with the rapid transition to emergency remote instruction. While this situation provided our team with the opportunity to demonstrate our awareness of and proficiency in sound pedagogical practices, it also led to a temporary shift away from focusing exclusively on strategies for instructors teaching multilingual students, as this was not deemed a priority in the early stages of delivering just-in-time instructor support across the university. Instead, the team found nimble and flexible ways to highlight this particular group of students, for example, when discussing accessibility, inclusive teaching strategies, and frameworks such as Universal Design for Learning (UDL), an approach that appeared to have more traction than talking about academic language and literacy skills and EAL support directly. At the same time, SFU's focus on Equity, Diversity, and Inclusion (EDI) highlighted the significance of these inclusive strategies. Recognizing that EDI is an established institutional priority (Johnson 2020) that instructors would be more familiar with, our team strategically linked LRP to this mandate. By explicitly connecting it with more widely recognized principles of EDI, including UDL, we aimed to foster faculty buy-in for supporting EAL students and creating linguistically responsive classrooms.

Literature Review

Academic language and literacy skills and EAL support have long been seen as a challenge from both an applied linguistics and an educational development lens (Andrade 2010; Haan, Gallagher, and Varandani 2017; Ryan 2005). As noted earlier, aligning our team's work with the institution's EDI policies and frameworks such as UDL was a necessary approach due in part to an entrenched belief among some faculty members that language support does not fall within their scope of responsibility, and so they often consider themselves ill-equipped to address it (Airey 2012). The responsibility for it is viewed as belonging to others, usually those in English language support roles who are invariably seen to be engaged in remedial work "that is somehow peripheral to the main 'stuff' of the discipline" (Murray 2022, 3). Discipline-specific instructors perhaps wish to distance themselves from the responsibility of it being their work because academic language support is sometimes equated with the "dumbing down" of content and therefore the lowering of curricular standards (Haan, Gallagher, and Varandani 2017). These views are related to concerns about both international and domestic EAL students matriculating into their degree programs with insufficient proficiency in English to meet the linguistic demands of their courses (Briguglio 2014; Murray 2016), reinforcing a deficit mind-set around how multilingual students are viewed in the internationalized university.

Building on the notion that instructors perceive language support as outside of their domain, Andrade's (2010) findings do, to an extent, explain the minimal interest among faculty in learning how to enhance students' English skills and/or understanding of the methodologies that might be useful in teaching multilingual students. However, Murray (2022) argues that this delineation of responsibility for teaching content and academic language and literacy skills might be seen as a historical oddity, given the mutual dependency of knowledge of subject matter and the manner in which that knowledge is articulated in that discipline (e.g., conventions related to language and discourse). He and other scholars believe those need to be taught concurrently to ensure all students benefit and that no students are disadvantaged (Meyer et al. 2015;

Wingate 2018 as cited in Murray 2022). Despite evidence that embedding academic language and literacy skills within disciplinary courses impacts student learning positively (Arkoudis and Doughney 2014; Wingate 2015), and knowing that all students, regardless of first language, apprentice to the language of their discipline (Gee 2003), it is difficult to convince disciplinary faculty to take responsibility for language (Airey 2012; Goldsmith and Willey 2016).

Shifting our lens from the applied linguistics literature, it is also insightful to examine the educational development perspective, particularly in view of our team's unique positioning at the intersection of applied linguistics and educational development. There are long-standing assumptions in higher education that academics are not adequately prepared for their teaching role in general, have unsophisticated conceptions of teaching and learning, and have little knowledge of effective teaching practices, both in general and in their own specific discipline (Evers and Hall 2009). Similarly, Cilliers and Herman (2010) highlight a critical challenge faced by educational developers, stating that "academics may be expected to teach, often having neither much teaching experience, nor a teaching qualification" (254). This lack of knowledge or experience in teaching, coupled with a prevailing deficit mind-set regarding multilingual students (Ryan and Viete 2009), might incline some faculty toward reluctance in viewing the teaching of academic language and literacy skills as part of their responsibilities, perhaps attributable to uncertainty over how to do this, frustration with what is perceived to be inadequate language skills on the part of multilingual students, or a lack of preparation in, and/or reconsideration of, pedagogical practices (Jin and Schneider 2019). This tension may also, at least in part, be attributed to faculty beliefs around internationalization; valuing it in theory on the one hand, while on the other hand resisting the notion that support for multilingual students lies within the scope of instructors and not elsewhere (Haan, Gallagher, and Varandani 2017), outside the classroom in student support units like SFU's Student Learning Commons (SLC). Against this tension of prevailing views, our work is guided by the question of how our team, uniquely embedded in SFU's teaching and learning center, can effectively support disciplinary faculty and TAs while foregrounding the disciplinary language and literacy skills of multilingual students, thus ensuring faculty are best prepared to support and serve the students in an internationalized university.

We now shift our attention to an overview of LRP, followed by a focus on the development and implementation of the LRCIS.

LRP

As discussed earlier in this chapter, the challenge we face as applied linguists uniquely embedded in a teaching and learning center is how to support disciplinary faculty in teaching and course design effectively, while foregrounding the development of disciplinary language and literacy skills of multilingual students. To address this challenge, we turned to the literature on LRP.

Despite its widespread adoption in US K-12 contexts in the early development of culturally responsive pedagogy during the 1990s and early 2000s (Ladson-Billings 1995; Gay 2002), and more recently, culturally sustaining pedagogy (Paris and Alim 2017), LRP, or linguistically responsive instruction (LRI) has only now begun to attract attention in postsecondary settings (Haan and Gallagher 2021). Higher education's delayed engagement with this approach is perhaps unsurprising, considering that language-related issues often do not occupy a central position in institutional discourse and policy development (Murray 2016). However, due to the increased internationalization of universities in English-dominant contexts (Bothwell 2017; Knight 2013; Zappa-Hollman and Fox 2021), institutions like SFU have had to reassess their effectiveness in teaching the growing number of linguistically and culturally diverse students (Wallace, Spiliotopoulos, and Ilieva 2020). This demographic shift poses new challenges for faculty members as they grapple with the complexities of teaching a student body that includes an increasing number of multilingual students.

Haan, Gallagher, and Varandani (2017) illustrate the tension faculty members encounter when it comes to reconciling their theoretical appreciation for an internationalized student body with the practical challenges of teaching linguistically diverse classes. Their research reveals that faculty members do value the enriching aspects of an internationalized campus, such as the "exposure to other cultures" and the creation of a "global learning environment," which they recognize as providing local students with "a wonderful chance to grow and learn from others" (42). However, alongside this appreciation, the same instructors also had "reservations about their own roles in working with a changing student population" (46). This "theory-reality split in beliefs about internationalization and techniques for teaching" (37) is, perhaps, one of the reasons why internationalized postsecondary institutions are only now beginning to explore the efficacy of LRP as a pedagogical tool to support the academic success of multilingual students within disciplinary classes.

LRP is, as defined by Haan and Gallagher (2021), "an intentional content-language-integrated pedagogical approach taken up by faculty in what have been traditionally monolingual settings with the aims of providing well-supported teaching and learning and equitable outcomes from multilingual learners" (3). It is informed by pedagogical approaches such as content-based instruction (Brinton, Wesche, and Snow 2003), and content-language integrated learning (Lin 2016), which emphasize the role of both language and content in teaching and learning. LRP incorporates instructional strategies like scaffolding, culturally relevant content, multilingual approaches (e.g., translanguaging), collaborative learning, and reducing linguistic complexity on assessments. In higher education contexts, LRP has been found to "boost the rigor of classes and better support students, leading to more positive outcomes for all" (Haan and Gallagher 2021, 6). The importance of faculty's active involvement in this, however, cannot be overstated; without it, the overarching goal of internationalization may not realize the targeted benefits of learning, discovery, and engagement that postsecondary institutions strive for (Stohl 2007). With all of this in mind, we drew upon Burke, Haan, and Gallagher's work (2020) to create our linguistically responsive classrooms series, detailed in the section below.

LRCIS

Driven by our team's mandate within CEE and informed by our team's commitment to fostering inclusive teaching approaches and supporting multilingual student success, the LRCIS was shaped not only by the insights provided in the literature discussed above but also by the Coordination Committee for Services and Supports for EAL Students' 2021 report titled *An Update on the Supports and Challenges Facing SFU Students for whom English is an Additional Language*. This report reaffirmed the institution's commitment to inclusive education for all students, stating "SFU is re-committing to support student success inclusive of all language abilities" (Simon Fraser University 2021, 1). In line with these insights, the self-reported data from SFU's Fall 2022 Undergraduate Student Survey revealed that 46 percent of students indicated that they speak at least one non-English language at home, while approximately 11 percent reported speaking no English at home. These statistics underscored the need to address the linguistic complexity within SFU's classrooms, leading to the development of LRCIS. By equipping instructors with the necessary tools and strategies, LRCIS aimed to empower them to create linguistically responsive classrooms and better support the diverse linguistic needs of SFU's students, ultimately enhancing multilingual student success.

The LRCIS comprises six sessions in a blended modality (Sessions 1 and 6 are in-person while Sessions 3–5 are online), one individual consultation, and a capstone project that results in a course artifact. The participants receive a grant of $1,000 to support the development of their course artifact (e.g., they could hire a TA to help support its development). The series design was carefully constructed to ensure optimal participant engagement. It required participants to self-reflect on their curriculum design and instructional choices and to reimagine alternatives. This reflection aimed to foster continuous improvement and a deeper understanding of student needs. We were committed to meeting participants "where they are at," and this is why we conducted individual consultations with each participant. We aspired to create a relevant learning environment and make the sessions directly applicable to their specific classroom context (e.g., size, level, and teaching challenges). Furthermore, we strategically designed the lessons in "bite-sized" pieces and provided a scaffolded approach to reduce feelings of being overwhelmed. This strategy was implemented to improve accessibility and ensure participants felt capable and empowered. With this strong, participant-centered foundation, we developed these specific goals that the series aims to achieve:

1. Improve instructors' confidence in revising and reimagining the language of assignments, assessments, and syllabi to be more linguistically accessible.
2. Enhance instructors' confidence in their pedagogical efficacy within the classroom community, ensuring they reach and teach every student.
3. Raise instructors' awareness of their role as disciplinary language teachers and facilitate the co-creation of a community of practice among participants.
4. Enable instructors to produce a peer-reviewed artifact for their teaching portfolio/dossier.

By focusing on these goals, the LRCIS seeks to address the linguistic diversity of SFU's campuses and provide faculty with the necessary tools and strategies to work toward creating linguistically responsive classrooms that support the academic success of multilingual students.

Our Approach

To better understand faculty members' experiences in the series, we adopted a case study approach. According to Duff and Anderson (2016), a case study "constitutes a qualitative, interpretive approach to understanding the experiences, features, behaviors, and processes of one bounded unit . . . which permits researchers and readers to gain grounded new understandings of issues" (1). Specifically, our aim is to gain new insights regarding a specific issue: the extent to which the LRCIS succeeded in empowering faculty to adapt their pedagogy (through the development of an artifact designed with an LRP lens) to accommodate their linguistically diverse classrooms, thereby better understanding whether the series effectively addressed the pedagogical challenges that linguistic diversity can pose for faculty. If the evaluation of the series suggests that the LRCIS was instrumental in assisting faculty to optimally engage with multilingual students, we will attempt to identify the components and strategies that contributed to its success. Conversely, if emerging themes do not appear to meet these challenges efficiently, we will seek to identify and understand better the reason(s) behind the limitations, which will help us revise the series for better outcomes in future iterations. In other words, we seek to answer this question: *Did this case (i.e., the LRCIS) meet the challenge (issue) of how faculty might positively and pedagogically respond to their linguistically diverse classes? If so, how? If not, why not?*

To this end, our "one-bounded unit" is the first cohort of LRCIS, which was developed and taught by the three of us during the spring term in 2022 as a part of our mandate at CEE. The inaugural cohort comprised twelve participants representing six of the eight faculties at SFU and one student support unit. The participants were faculty members from various disciplines, including Biology, Environmental Science and Geography, Sociology and Anthropology, English, Engineering, and other fields. From the fourteen applications we received, this diverse group was chosen in an effort to capture a wide range of experiences and perspectives from instructors across various disciplines. At the request of CEE's senior leadership, we prioritized the applications of continuing faculty members.

With the diverse inaugural cohort serving as our focal point, and to address the guiding question mentioned earlier, we draw insights from various sources of information, including:

- The Series Curriculum: This includes session materials, lesson plans, participant artifacts, and other pertinent documents that were part of the series.
- Summative and Informal Feedback: Participants completed summative feedback after each session, incorporating anecdotal information and reflections.
- Formative Series Evaluation: Participants completed an anonymous evaluation at the conclusion of the series, offering insights into their cumulative experiences and the perceived efficacy of the LRCIS.

- Discussion Board Postings: Throughout the series, participants actively participated in online discussions, exchanging thoughts, experiences, and concerns pertinent to the series.

With the cohort and our sources of information detailed above, we now shift our focus to the participants' pedagogical and attitudinal responses. By pedagogical response, we refer to the creation of a linguistically responsive artifact, which we will elaborate on below. Following this, we examine their experiences, perspectives, and the overall impact of the LRCIS.

The Artifact: Spotlighting Linguistically Responsive Instructional Practices

The creation of the artifacts necessitated reflection on the part of each participant, not only on their own unique contexts, but also on their ongoing work as disciplinary instructors tasked with building EDI into their instructional practices. Participants were invited to use this reflection to select an existing artifact such as an assignment, syllabus, reading guide, and revise/ reimagine it with a linguistically responsive lens. It was suggested that this could then be included in a teaching portfolio and also shared with peers as a professional development opportunity. Here we highlight several artifacts that were created anew or reworked with all of this in mind.

The first example highlights how one Science instructor in a writing intensive, third-year lab course was considering how best to support their linguistically diverse students in a high-stakes assignment which students found very challenging in terms of both analysis and writing. Over the years, the instructor had provided guidance with clear expectations, extra resources, and examples, but student performance did not improve. The instructor simplified the task by splitting the analysis/writing task into four smaller, more easily achieved pieces. In step one, students were given examples of good analysis and writing one piece at a time. The instructor modeled expectations for students, who were then asked to practice analyzing and writing by doing some asynchronous exercises on Canvas, the learning management system used at our institution. Next, students were asked to share one paragraph and one critical point from their writing and to comment on two other students' work. They were then asked to share a draft outline of the assignment with a peer, who used a simplified rubric to give some initial feedback. In the final step, students submitted the final version of their critical review for grading. By scaffolding this assignment in a staged approach, the instructor was able to guide students through each step, providing opportunities for group, pair, and individual work to strengthen students' understanding of the assignment. In the reworked version, the instructor was more explicit about expectations, modeled the process, and had several lower-stakes tasks instead of one big one.

The second example comes from an English instructor who is herself multilingual. With an interest in giving students agency to discover and share how cultural contexts shape epistemology, leading to diverse conceptualizations of disciplinary discourse, she modified an assignment. The assignment originally focused on analyzing the organization of information in research articles (published in English academic journals), but now she included an option for students to include articles written in languages other than English. The instructor met with each student at the beginning of the semester to clarify expectations and to ensure that students who chose the bilingual option understood that they had to submit sample translated sentences from the non-English articles they chose. This approach embraced an asset- rather than a deficit-oriented approach to multilingual students, which in turn allows for "inclusive opportunities for 'deep learning' that build confidence, and raise awareness of global language and culture diversity" (WIDA n.d.).

An instructor from Applied Science recognized that it was challenging for students, especially multilingual students, to be well prepared for being assessed on their conceptual understanding of fundamental topics in the discipline. To address this, a lesson was created focusing explicitly on the importance of being well prepared, starting with an emphasis on why mastery of relevant topics is a crucial and transferable problem-solving skill, then giving students example problems, modeling good and inadequate responses, followed by guided group practice, review, and feedback. The instructor focused on using clear, simple language in the examples so that they would be comprehensible to all students, allowing them to focus on the content and the development of skills.

Another instructor teaching law wanted to support her students in learning the specialized vocabulary in her discipline. She adapted a popular word guessing game with a bank of specialized and complex vocabulary necessary for students in the field to know and use. The instructions were easy to follow, and the game could be played in pairs or small groups. By giving students a small but regular amount of time to play this game, the instructor provided students with the opportunity to master these terms over time, therefore increasing the likelihood of both longer-term retention and active usage.

Although we are not sure of the impact of these changes (yet), we know that these pedagogical responses demonstrate instructor intentionality to reduce anxiety and to support learning for multilingual students, removing barriers and creating opportunities for students to enrich their classrooms with the diversity of experiences and perspectives they bring. At the very least, we do know that participants left the series with an increased sense of confidence in their ability to (re)create assignments, assessments, and syllabi to be more linguistically accessible. The results of the course evaluation administered at the end of the series indicate a strong majority of 80 percent who agreed or strongly agreed with the statement: "This instructor series increased my confidence in my ability to (re)create assignments, assessments, and syllabi to be more linguistically accessible." Specifically, 20 percent of participants agreed and 50 percent strongly agreed that LRCIS boosted their confidence in their ability to design linguistically responsive course materials. This suggests a high level of perceived effectiveness of the LRCIS in enhancing instructors' confidence in this area. While some of the changes in the reimagining of these course artifacts may seem small, these adjustments not only acknowledge the linguistic diversity of today's student body, but they also reflect instructor disposition toward equity and asset-oriented framing of multilingual students (González-Howard and Suárez 2021), which is ongoing and important work.

Evolving Perspectives: Exploring Participants' Experiences in the Series

To identify common threads, we utilized Braun and Clarke's (2006) thematic analysis approach—a method for detecting, scrutinizing, characterizing, and conveying themes found within documented sources. The initial insights we gathered, which are detailed below, illustrate and reinforce some of the challenges described in the literature and that we face in our ongoing work.

As we explored in depth the insights gathered, three main themes emerged that shed light on the experiences and perspectives of the faculty members who participated in LRCIS. The first theme revolves around the tension between instructor and institutional responsibility and the perceived workload associated with LRI. The second theme, which we have termed "linguistic overwhelm," captures the sense of burden and hesitation some instructors feel when considering the implementation of a linguistically responsive approach. The third and final theme explores the shift in instructor identity and mind-set, particularly in relation to their role in addressing language barriers and fostering an asset-oriented approach toward multilingual students. We will now examine each of these themes more closely.

Theme 1: Instructor and Institutional Responsibility

In exploring the first theme of instructor and institutional responsibility, we identify tension between some participants and the institution at large. This tension is captured by a faculty member from Sociology and Anthropology, who expresses a sense of frustrated resentment at the expectation to take on yet more work; work that they feel is larger than their individual capacity and beyond their area of expertise. "I find myself thinking that the solution is, in the end, framed as yet another thing that faculty are supposed to do to solve problems that are bigger than they are, that is outside of the scope of their area [of] knowledge" (Faculty Member 5).

Their sentiment underscores the need for institutional support and systemic responses, a point echoed by another participant from the English department who notes how the responsibility cannot be taken nor the labor done without buy-in from everyone involved: "LRI cannot thrive without the support and the integration of all actors in our community of learning because systemic needs require a systemic response. Such an approach would include serious consideration of the challenges faced by students and instructors as the university expands their international student population" (Faculty Member 4). Articulating how LRI cannot succeed without the active participation and support of all stakeholders from across the university, this participant speaks to the need for a comprehensive, institution-wide approach to addressing the challenges faced by both students and instructors in an internationalized university.

These insights underscore the importance of individual instructor responsibility and effort, while also emphasizing that these efforts are most impactful when complemented by institutional support.

Theme 2: Linguistic Overwhelm

In examining the second theme, we encountered another layer of complexity in the instructors' experience with LRI—a feeling that we have termed "linguistic overwhelm," which can pose a barrier to exploring and applying a linguistically responsive lens to their pedagogical practices. This theme captures the sense of being daunted by the potential workload and energy required to fully commit to LRI, as expressed by a Biology professor: "I have a feeling that a classroom that fully commits to LRI may look very different, and I'm not sure I have the energy reserves to make drastic changes at the moment" (Faculty Member 2). This quote reveals a sense of apprehension about the magnitude of change that LRI might necessitate, and a concern about whether they have the capacity to undertake such a transformation. This feeling of "linguistic overwhelm" can pose a significant barrier to the adoption and application of a linguistically responsive lens in teaching.

In response to this perceived workload, some instructors are seeking support outside the classroom. A faculty member from Environmental Science and Geography shares how they rely on SFU's SLC, the student academic support unit, to help manage the load: "I lean heavily on the SLC for this work, which helps ease the burden on me as the instructor" (Faculty Member 10). This reliance on external support services suggests the importance of institutional resources to aid instructors in implementing LRI. It also reinforces the theme we first discussed above, the importance of a systemic approach, one that extends beyond the individual instructor and involves support and resources from the wider SFU community.

Theme 3: Shifting Instructor Identities

In the third theme, shifting instructor identities, we observed a change/shift that many instructors experienced during LRCIS. This theme embodies the gradual change in instructors' self-perceptions and their emerging roles in addressing language barriers in their classrooms.

An engineering professor, for instance, shared a revelation about their role in mitigating language barriers for EAL students, a responsibility they had not previously considered: "While I have always been aware of the fact that language is sometimes a barrier for my ESL students, it had not occurred to me to think about my role as an instructor in mitigating this barrier" (Faculty Member 1). This newfound awareness signifies a shift in mind-set, a reevaluation of their role as an instructor, which was prompted by their participation in the series.

Similarly, another faculty member reflected on their evolving perspective toward multilingual students, moving toward an asset-oriented approach and critically examining their own classroom practices: "The idea of a monolingual university as a myth is powerful! I have thought more about the student-positive perspective, including ways my practice has been consistent with that and ways it has not been" (Anonymous, Evaluation Form). This reflection suggests a growing awareness of the value of linguistic diversity and a willingness to align their teaching practices with an LRI lens.

Yet another participant described how their awareness of the language barriers EAL students face has been heightened, and how they have been inspired by the various strategies to overcome these barriers:

> My eyes were opened to a lot of different ways in which language can trip up EAL students, and I was inspired by the many ways that people can approach removing these stumbling-blocks. I don't feel like I'm ready to solve all of these problems, but I feel much more aware, and have lots of other people's clever ideas marinating in my brain now. (Anonymous, Evaluation Form)

Building upon this idea of increased awareness, when asked if the series enhanced their knowledge of linguistically responsive classrooms and pedagogy, 80 percent of participants agreed or strongly agreed with the statement (LRCIS Evaluation Form). It appears most instructors experienced a shift in their understanding and potentially their approach to teaching. This shift is a key aspect of the changing mind-sets that some participants experienced. As instructors gain more knowledge about LRI, they may begin to see their roles differently, moving from being solely content instructors to becoming language instructors as well.

The course evaluation asked participants about this notion of being a language teacher. Specifically, they were asked if they agreed with the statement: "The instructor series increased my awareness of my role as a disciplinary language teacher." Unlike previous questions on the evaluation, the responses indicate a range of opinions on this issue. While 20 percent of participants disagreed and 10 percent remained neutral, suggesting limited shift in their perception of their role as disciplinary language teachers, 50 percent of participants (20 percent agreed, 30 percent strongly agreed) indicated that the series positively impacted their self-perception and understanding of their role. These results, while highlighting the complexities and tensions inherent in the shift toward viewing oneself as a disciplinary language teacher, particularly for content faculty, are not unexpected given what we know from the literature (Airey 2012; Gallagher and Haan 2018; Murray 2016).

Taking these findings into account, it is worth noting that the journey toward identifying as a disciplinary language teacher is nuanced and may present challenges for some instructors, despite the series potentially influencing perceptions for some participants. It appears that as some instructors become more aware of the challenges EAL students face, they may start to see themselves as part of the solution, possibly transitioning from solely content instructors to also considering their roles as language instructors. This shift in mind-set suggests the potential impact of the LRCIS, hinting at how such initiatives might foster more inclusive and linguistically responsive teaching practices.

Implications, Insights, and Reflections

The instructor series demonstrates its value by moving toward enhancing the pedagogical capabilities of faculty members in fostering multilingual student success in their classrooms. In this section, we consider broader implications gleaned from the evidence in this case and reflect on potential paths for program refinement, possibilities for building on and assessing impact, and opportunities for future study.

The Linguistically Responsive Instructor Series seeks to meet the challenge of how our uniquely embedded EAL consultant team could, drawing on our shared expertise as applied linguists, practitioners, and educational developers, cocreate a faculty-facing intervention which would effectively move the needle on pedagogical approaches and attitudes toward meeting the needs of multilingual students in an internationalized university. The series found success in that the participant instructors were able to reflect on and redesign tools, measures, and activities in response to the linguistic complexity of their classrooms. Instructor data showed an evolution in thinking in some cases around their responsibilities and roles as disciplinary language teachers, while also acknowledging the complexity of addressing this challenge in a post-pandemic public university, without also adding to their own workload and sense of being overwhelmed. While questions arose around institutional responsibility, each instructor took steps toward praxis, demonstrating a measure of growth and development in their teaching practice.

Building on the strengths of the program design, in the immediate future we anticipate regularly soliciting feedback from faculty members across the university to understand their evolving concerns, limitations, and preferences in meeting the challenge of linguistic diversity in the internationalized university, and we will adjust the LRCIS program accordingly. Following the series, formally establishing a community of practice (Wenger 1998) that facilitates the sharing of experiences, including contextualized LRP teaching challenges and successes among former and future series participants, would support ongoing reflection and reinforce attitudinal growth among individuals and our institution.

The challenge remains around increasing awareness and interest among time and attention-starved faculty, especially in post-pandemic environments of fiscal austerity, where monetized incentives are no longer possible. Institutions such as ours, which recognize the need to reinforce effective teaching as a measure of student satisfaction, may need to find alternative means to incentivize faculty to address complex teaching challenges. Some examples include offering time buy-outs, additional TA support, or awards and recognition around teaching innovation which support the goals of true inclusion and diversity. For our team, continuing to explicitly align the series with university priorities and articulated goals around inclusivity in teaching (i.e., EDI initiatives) may help preserve institutional (and faculty) buy-in. Furthermore, by framing LRP as an integral component of the institution's broader EDI initiatives, we can emphasize its role in fostering an inclusive, accessible academic environment that recognizes and values the diverse backgrounds of all students.

While the immediate impact of the series is clear from the evolving attitudes expressed by participants toward their positionalities and responsibilities as disciplinary language teachers, we understand instructor identity reformation to be an ongoing and iterative process of development (Norton 2013). Conducting longitudinal studies to track situated instructor attitudes over time, as well as the long-term effects of the program on participants' teaching practices and their multilingual students' learning experiences, would best inform any measures of success. Alternatively, partnering with faculty to engage in action research through the scholarship of teaching and learning would promote a deeper understanding of their own teaching contexts and the potential impact of situated, LRI.

Broadly speaking, our goals as educational developers and program designers for this series were to support faculty struggling with linguistically diverse classes; to build a community of trust and credibility with and among faculty participants; to build our team's capacity to create responsive, innovative faculty development programs; to help legitimize our work in the eyes of the university teaching community; and ultimately, to contribute to multilingual student success. In many ways, this series has accomplished these aims through the design and execution of the series. How much impact our team ultimately has is a question for further exploration and analysis over time. Questions remain about possibilities of scale and how programming like this will be impacted by the ongoing cycle of fiscal constraint faced by the public postsecondary sector. It is our hope that with future iterations and more offerings we will be able to continue to impact the teaching practices in the internationalized university.

Good teaching responds to the needs of the students, whoever they are, in front of the instructor. This series, or these artifacts (which meet the need of one specific linguistic and pedagogical context), is not the one and final answer to this challenge. It is clear that faculty must be institutionally supported to appropriately enact their roles as disciplinary language teachers in an ongoing way, to continue to meet students where they are, with linguistic complexity or otherwise. This series forms one small part of the institutional support we provide. This support is bolstered by our faculty consultation services, the educational resources we develop, and the responsive teaching community we foster. Our comprehensive support also encompasses various initiatives such as workshops, self-directed resources, and sessions at faculty orientations and symposia. We also contribute to the training of SFU's TAs and provide international teaching assistants training, further enhancing our support structure. Moreover, we partake in broader center initiatives and bring an EAL perspective into focus, as exemplified by our involvement in the Rethinking Course Design workshop. Our commitment to linguistic diversity extends to collaboration with campus partners in organizing a weeklong celebration of multilingualism at SFU, signifying our dedication to creating a diverse and inclusive learning environment. Shifting entrenched attitudes held by institutions and faculty alike toward multilingual students requires sustained and intentional efforts, much like any change. It comes slowly and then sometimes all at once. How we might best push our practice forward toward that change and measure the impact for faculty and students is what we will continue to investigate as our situated and unique EAL educational development team evolves.

References

Airey, John. 2012. "'I Don't Teach Language.' The Linguistic Attitudes of Physics Lecturers in Sweden." *AILA Review* 25, no. 25: 64–79. https://doi.org/10.1075/aila.25.05air.

Anderson, Tim. 2015. "Seeking Internationalization: The State of Canadian Higher Education." *Canadian Journal of Higher Education* 45, no. 4: 166–187. https://files.eric.ed.gov/fulltext/EJ1086913.pdf.

Andrade, Maureen S. 2010. "Increasing Accountability: Faculty Perspectives on the English Language Competence of Nonnative English Speakers." *Journal of Studies in International Education* 14, no. 3: 221–239. https://doi.org/10.1177/1028315308331295.

Arkoudis, Sophie, Lachlan Doughney, Australia. Office for Learning and Teaching, issuing body, and The University of Melbourne, issuing body. 2014. "Good Practice

Report – English Language Proficiency." *ResearchGate*. Canberra: Department of Education, Skills and Employment. https://www.researchgate.net/publication/264544663_Good_Practice_Report_-_English_Language_Proficiency.

Bettinger, Eric P., and Bridget Terry Long. 2009. "Addressing the Needs of Underprepared Students in Higher Education: Does College Remediation Work?" *Journal of Human Resources* 44, no. 3: 736–771. https://doi.org/10.1353/jhr.2009.0033.

Bothwell, Ellie. 2017. "Overseas Student Enrolment in Canada Rises by 11 Percent." Times Higher Education. November 22, 2017. https://www.timeshighereducation.com/news/overseas-student-enrolment-canada-rises-11-cent.

Briguglio, Carmela. 2014. *Working in the Third Space: Promoting Interdisciplinary Collaboration to Embed English Language Development into the Disciplines*. Sydney: Office for Learning and Teaching.

Brinton, Donna, Marguerite Ann Snow, and Marjorie Wesche. 2003. *Content-Based Second Language Instruction*. Michigan Classics Edition. Ann Arbor, MI: University of Michigan Press.

Burke, Zoe, Jennifer Haan, and Colleen Gallagher. 2020. "Faculty Development for Teaching International Students." *Journal of International Students* 10, no. 3: 776–781. https://doi.org/10.32674/jis.v10i3.1168.

Cilliers, Francois J., and Nicoline Herman. 2010. "Impact of an Educational Development Programme on Teaching Practice of Academics at a Research-Intensive University." *International Journal for Academic Development* 15, no. 3: 253–267. https://doi.org/10.1080/1360144X.2010.497698.

Duff, Patricia, and Tim Anderson. 2016. "Case Study Research." In *The Cambridge Guide to Research in Language Teaching and Learning*, edited by James Dean Brown and Christine Coombe, 112–118. Cambridge, UK: Cambridge University Press.

Evers, Frederick, Shirley Hall, Judy Britnell, Bettina Brockerhoff-Macdonald, Lorraine Carter, Debra Dawson, Donald Kerr, Joy Mighty, Jillian Siddall, and Peter Wolf. 2009. "Faculty Engagement in Teaching Development Activities Phase 1: Literature Review." https://heqco.ca/wp-content/uploads/2020/03/Faculty-Engagement-in-Teaching-Development-Activities2.pdf.

Gallagher, Colleen E. and Jennifer E. Haan. 2018. "University Faculty Beliefs about Emergent Multilinguals and Linguistically Responsive Instruction." *TESOL Quarterly* 52, no. 2: 304–30.

Gay, Geneva. 2002. "Preparing for Culturally Responsive Teaching." *Journal of Teacher Education* 53, no. 2: 106–116. https://doi.org/10.1177/0022487102053002003.

Gee, James Paul. 2003. "What Video Games Have to Teach Us about Learning and Literacy." *Computers in Entertainment* 1, no. 1: 20. https://doi.org/10.1145/950566.950595.

Goldsmith, Rosalie, and Keith Willey. 2016. "'It's Not My Job to Teach Writing': Activity Theory Analysis of [Invisible] Writing Practices in the Engineering Curriculum Practices in the Engineering Curriculum." *Journal of Academic Language and*

Learning 10, no. 1: A118–A129. https://journal.aall.org.au/index.php/jall/article/view/383.

González-Howard, María, and Enrique Suárez. 2021. "Retiring the Term English Language Learners: Moving toward Linguistic Justice through Asset-Oriented Framing." *Journal of Research in Science Teaching* 58, no. 5: 749–752. https://doi.org/10.1002/tea.21684.

Haan, Jennifer E., and Colleen Gallagher. 2021. "Situating Linguistically Responsive Instruction in Higher Education Contexts: Foundations for Pedagogical, Curricular, and Institutional Support." *TESOL Quarterly* 56, no. 1. https://doi.org/10.1002/tesq.3087.

Haan, Jennifer E., Colleen Gallagher, and Lisa Varandani. 2017. "Working with Linguistically Diverse Classes Across the Disciplines: Faculty Beliefs." *Journal of the Scholarship of Teaching and Learning* 17, no. 1: 37–51. https://doi.org/10.14434/v17i1.20008.

Jin, Li, and Jason Schneider. 2019. "Faculty Views on International Students: A Survey Study." *Journal of International Students* 9, no. 1: 84–99. https://doi.org/10.32674/jis.v9i1.268.

Johnson, Joy. 2020. "Equity, Diversity and Inclusion Commitments." Simon Fraser University. https://www.sfu.ca/president/statements/community-messages/2020/equity-diversity-and-inclusion-commitments.html.

Knight, Jane. 2013. "The Changing Landscape of Higher Education Internationalisation – For Better or Worse?" *Perspectives: Policy and Practice in Higher Education* 17, no. 3: 84–90. https://doi.org/10.1080/13603108.2012.753957.

Ladson-Billings, Gloria. 1995. "Toward a Theory of Culturally Relevant Pedagogy." *American Educational Research Journal* 32, no. 3: 465–491. https://doi.org/10.3102/00028312032003465.

Lin, Angel M. Y. 2016. *Language Across the Curriculum & CLIL in English as an Additional Language (EAL) Contexts*. Singapore: Springer Singapore. https://doi.org/10.1007/978-981-10-1802-2.

Marshall, Steve. 2009. "Re-Becoming ESL: Multilingual University Students and a Deficit Identity." *Language and Education* 24, no. 1: 41–56. https://doi.org/10.1080/09500780903194044.

Meyer, Oliver, Do Coyle, Ana Halbach, Kevin Schuck, and Teresa Ting. 2015. "A Pluriliteracies Approach to Content and Language Integrated Learning – Mapping Learner Progressions in Knowledge Construction and Meaning-Making." *Language, Culture and Curriculum* 28, no. 1: 41–57. https://doi.org/10.1080/07908318.2014.1000924.

Murray, Neil. 2016. *Standards of English in Higher Education: Issues, Challenges and Strategies*. Cambridge: Cambridge University Press.

Murray, Neil. 2022. "A Model to Support the Equitable Development of Academic Literacy in Institutions of Higher Education." *Journal of Further and Higher Education* 46, no. 8: 1–12. https://doi.org/10.1080/0309877x.2022.2044019.

Norton, Bonny. 2013. *Identity and Language Learning: Extending the Conversation*. Bristol: Multilingual Matters. https://doi.org/10.21832/9781783090563.

Paris, Django, and H. Samy Alim. 2017. *Culturally Sustaining Pedagogies: Teaching and Learning for Justice in a Changing World*. New York: Teachers College Press.

Ryan, Janette. 2005. "Improving Teaching and Learning Practices for International Students: Implications for Curriculum, Policy, and Assessment." In *Teaching International Students: Improving Learning for All*, edited by Janette Ryan and Jude Carroll, 92–100. London: Routledge.

Ryan, Janette, and Rosemary Viete. 2009. "Respectful Interactions: Learning with International Students in the English-Speaking Academy." *Teaching in Higher Education* 14, no. 3: 303–314. https://doi.org/10.1080/13562510902898866.

Simon Fraser University (SFU). 2021. *An Update on the Supports and Services Facing SFU Students for Whom English is an Additional Language*. Burnaby: Simon Fraser University

Stohl, Michael. 2007. "We Have Met the Enemy and He Is Us: The Role of the Faculty in the Internationalization of Higher Education in the Coming Decade." *Journal of Studies in International Education* 11, no. 3–4: 359–372. https://doi.org/10.1177/1028315307303923.

Tavares, Vander. 2021. *International Students in Higher Education: Language, Identity, and Experience from a Holistic Perspective*. Lanham: Lexington Books.

Wallace, Amanda, Valia Spiliotopoulos, and Roumiana Ilieva. 2020. "CLIL Collaborations in Higher Education: A Critical Perspective." *English Teaching & Learning* 44: 127–148. https://doi.org/10.1007/s42321-020-00052-4.

Wenger, Etienne. 1998. *Communities of Practice*. Cambridge: Cambridge University Press.

WIDA—University of Wisconsin-Madison. n.d. "Understanding Multilingual Learners." wida.wisc.edu. https://wida.wisc.edu/teach/learners.

Wingate, Ursula. 2015. *Academic Literacy and Student Diversity: The Case for Inclusive Practice*. Bristol: Multilingual Matters.

Zappa-Hollman, Sandra, and Joanne A. Fox. 2021. "Engaging in Linguistically Responsive Instruction: Insights from a First-Year University Program for Emergent Multilingual Learners." *TESOL Quarterly* 44, no. 4: 1081–1091. https://doi.org/10.1002/tesq.3075.

12

Closing Reflections

Kumari Beck and Roumiana Ilieva

Working closely with our colleagues in producing this book has been a moving experience. Prior to this book, we had been working with each of them in varying capacities, co-teaching, researching, developing programs, serving on university committees, in supervisory relationships, and felt we already knew each of them through that work. The experience of producing material for a book, however, was a very different one; it has taken our collegiality and working relationship to a different level, for which we are grateful. We need these connections and a sense of a collective to stay true to our academic commitments in these times of internationalization "gone mad," an academy under neoliberal pressures, escalating social issues, and a planet under stress.

In reflecting on the book itself, one way to make sense of the experiences and practices shared in the chapters of this book is to connect them to the ROAD-MAPPING framework (Dafouz and Smit 2020) we discussed in our introductory chapter, which highlights the multidimensionality of the internationalization process we have just written about. Drawing on this framework, we can say that all of the chapters in the book shed light on practices and processes of learning and teaching or supporting others in these processes in the institution. All chapters also illuminate the varied beliefs and activities of diverse agents as they engage in these practices. Global, but also institutional (i.e., local) forces that drive internationalization, especially with regard to economic rationales for internationalization, are also commonly mentioned across the board (see in particular Chapter 1). References to (mostly) implicit, but also occasionally explicit, policies around language (i.e., (language) Management) and the role of English in the institution are also present (see in particular Chapters 2, 3, and 8). The reference to academic disciplines is very evident in the chapters that reflect collaborations between applied linguists and disciplinary faculty to support multilingual students in the university (see Chapters 9–11). The cultural facets of practices and processes of internationalization are highlighted specifically in chapters that engage in-depth with cultural difference (see Chapters 1, 4–8). The power relations embedded in engaging with internationalization in an Anglo-dominant context, while not referred to directly in some of the chapters, seem to permeate all accounts shared in the book and are very clearly evident in Chapter 3. Discourses, or how university stakeholders talk about and interpret their experiences, while varied, point to the paramount importance of considering the multifaceted nature of internationalization in today's world embedded within a language/culture nexus. It is our contention that paying particular attention to shifting the discourses that currently frame internationalization is one way to move forward in imagining this complex phenomenon differently.

We have also reflected on the elements that we think are missing in this book. We did state that our intention was to gather whatever our colleagues were working on at the time, rather than try to get representation of the range of issues facing us. It is important, however, to recognize and mark the missing voices and perspectives. To gain a fuller picture of the university environment, we need to hear from a wider range of students. We need the perspectives of administrators to understand the tensions and dilemmas that they possibly face. The voices of the custodial staff, the invisible, low paid workers who maintain the services and buildings, are mostly absent from any account of university life.

Most importantly, we mark the absence of Indigenous voices from this collection, reflecting how we still work in silos. Our colleague Michelle Pidgeon and Kumari have written about the deep divides between Indigenization and internationalization in higher education (Beck and Pidgeon 2020), noting the common influences of imperialism that have affected both our fields and advocated for dialogues among us. Pidgeon and Beck argued that "a wholistic, decolonial framework drawn from Indigenous values and principles could advance a principled internationalization of higher education" (2020, 385). As authors of the present book, we believe that this is an important commitment to engage in decolonizing our universities, and that we have much to learn from Indigenous knowledges, peoples, and ways of being. This is something to work toward.

In closing, we return to the question of moving forward in our work. We had hoped that the pandemic was an opportune time to hit pause on internationalization work, and that this desire to do so was widespread. Three years later, however, we are disappointed to see that our institutions are seeking to do more rather than better. In this moment, we reflect as academics on what our collective responsibilities are toward not just our work in internationalization, but to society at large. We acknowledge here the influences of Vanessa Andreotti, Sharon Stein, and the Gesturing Towards Decolonial Futures Collective on our thinking. The notion of "imagining and acting otherwise" (Andreotti et al. 2016, 13) has been guiding our work at our Centre for Research on International Education. Although we recognize that such imaginings and actions may be imperfect and even impossible at times, it is a commitment that keeps us turned toward just futures.

References

Andreotti, Vanessa, Sharon Stein, Karen Pashby, and Michelle Nicolson. 2016. "Social Cartographies as Performative Devices in Research on Higher Education." *Higher Education Research & Development* 35, no. 1: 84–99.

Beck, Kumari, and Michelle Pidgeon. 2020. "Across the Divide: Conversations on Decolonization, Indigenization and Internationalization of Higher Education." In *International Education as Public Policy in Canada*, edited by Merli Tamtik, Roopa Desai Trilokekar, and Glen A. Jones, 384–406. Montreal: McGill- Queens University Press.

Dafouz, Emma, and Ute Smit. 2020. *ROAD-MAPPING: English Medium Education in the Internationalised University*. Cham: Springer International Publishing.

Contributors

Brent Amburgey is Lecturer in the American Studies Program at Willamette University, Salem, USA. He is also a Ph.D candidate in the Languages, Cultures and Literacies program at Simon Fraser University. His forthcoming doctoral thesis is on the topic of plurilingualism, specifically the plurilingual practices of students studying at an English-medium university in Canada. Brent has taught English and various topics in communication in university contexts, including Japan, Canada, and the United States.

Kumari Beck is Associate Professor, Co-director for the Centre for Research on International Education, and Co-Academic Coordinator of the Equity Studies in Education Master's program in the Faculty of Education at Simon Fraser University, Burnaby, Canada. Her research interests span internationalization of higher education, international education, internationalization of curriculum, and equity issues in education. Her work history in immigrant settlement programs and community development has informed much of her academic work. Recent publications include chapters in *Research with International Students, International Students from Asia in Canadian Universities, Curriculum Studies in Canada*, and in the *Journal of International Students*.

Jas K. Uppal-Hershorn is Assistant Professor at the University of the Fraser Valley, Abbotsford, Canada, in the Teacher Education Department. Jas's extensive experience in teacher education includes pre-service and in-service teacher education in BC and internationally; teacher mentorship; and program development in K-12 schools, school districts, and in graduate studies. Her scholarship interests include decolonizing curriculum, (inter)cultural learning, teacher inquiry and change, and praxis for equity in teaching and mentoring. She is strongly committed to exploring the praxis of teaching, with a focus on self-reflexivity.

Roumiana Ilieva is Associate Professor in the fields of applied linguistics and second/additional language education and Co-Director for the Centre for Research on International Education at the Faculty of Education at Simon Fraser University, Burnaby, Canada. Her research interests include internationalization of higher education, language teacher identities and agency, academic identity construction, interdisciplinary collaborations for multilingual student success, language and culture, migration and integration. Her most recent publications focus on disciplinary and language faculty collaborations, and on pre-service teacher identity and agency with articles appearing in the journals *Higher Education Research & Development* and *Canadian Modern Language Review.*

Chelsey Laird is Director of the University Mobility for Asia and the Pacific International Secretariat, located in Vancouver Community College, Vancouver, Canada. She is a scholar-practitioner with over a decade of professional experience in internationalization of higher education in Canadian higher education institutions and government agencies. In her roles at various postsecondary institutions, she has been involved with program development, international student advising and support, student services, staff support, program leadership, and administration services related to teaching and learning in the international education sector. She is a doctoral student in the Faculty of Education at Simon Fraser University, Burnaby, Canada.

Steve Marshall is Professor in the Faculty of Education at Simon Fraser University, Burnaby, Canada. His research focuses on academic literacy and plurilingualism in Canadian higher education, as well as international teacher education. He recently published, coauthored with Arlene Kent Spracklin, a study of university educators from four Southeast Asian countries and the impacts of graduate studies in Canada: "'We are in country; Why do we have to resort to Western ways of doing things?': An analytic framework for knowledge application in language teachers studying abroad" (2022).

Camila Miranda is Academic Advisor at Northeastern University in Vancouver, Canada. She holds a Bachelor's degree in Anthropology from Pontifícia Universidade Católica de Campinas, Brazil, and a Master of Arts in Education degree from Simon Fraser University, Burnaby, Canada. Her graduate research focused on the experiences of students, faculty, and staff with linguistic diversity in an internationalizing university in Canada. With over a decade of experience in the field of education and a passion for guiding students, Camila's educational background and research experience allow her to provide valuable insights and support to students navigating the complexities of higher education.

Aisha Ravindran was Associate Professor of teaching in the Faculty of Creative and Critical Studies at the University of British Columbia, Okanagan, Kelowna, Canada. She received a posthumous Ph.D degree in Languages, Cultures, and Literacies at Simon Fraser University, Burnaby, Canada, and held a Ph.D degree in English Literature from Mahatma Gandhi University, Kottayam, India. Her research interests were in internationalization of higher education; academic writing in multilingual, multicultural, and globalized environments; the intersections of language, culture, and literacies; student and teacher agency and identities. Her most recent publication, "The Interview-Event-*Agencement* as Creative Movement and Methodological Disruption" (2022) appeared in *Reconceptualizing Educational Research Methodology*.

Fiona Shaw is Associate Director of Inclusive Teaching at Simon Fraser University, Burnaby, Canada, and leads a team of Educational Developers and English as an Additional Language (EAL) Consultants in portfolios, including Equity, Diversity, and Inclusion, antiracism, accessibility, decolonial teaching practices, and multilingual learner success. She has successfully designed, developed, and facilitated both faculty and graduate facing teaching programs, online and in-person, in collaboration with diverse university and community partners. Fiona is dedicated to fostering responsive, innovative pedagogical and curricular design practices and is interested in the ways in which instructors enact compassion and intentionality in their teaching practices.

Eilidh Singh is an EAL Consultant in the Centre for Educational Excellence at Simon Fraser University, Burnaby, Canada. Her work focuses on using a flexible, evidence-based approach to facilitate EAL support for all faculty and TAs. This includes creating and delivering workshops, collaborating on an instructor series exploring linguistically responsive pedagogy, offering consultations, developing materials, contributing to the work of the center, and working with campus partners on various projects highlighting linguistic diversity on campus. Her continued interest is in how multilingual learners in higher education can best be supported collectively to thrive in L1 content environments.

Michael Sjoerdsma is University Lecturer in the School of Engineering Science at Simon Fraser University, Burnaby, Canada, and Coordinator of the school's technical communication program. He teaches courses encompassing various aspects of technical communication and engineering and society: Form, Style, and Professional Genres; Engineering, Science, and Society; Graphical Communication for Engineering; Spatial Thinking and Communicating; Project Documentation and Team Dynamics; Social Responsibility and Professional Practice; and Human Factors and Usability. His current research interests focus on students' concepts of success as they transition to first-year engineering and the persistence of engineering students as they complete their degrees.

Valia Spiliotopoulos is Assistant Professor at the University of Ottawa, Ottawa, Canada, and teaches in the Immersion, Teacher Education, and Master's program in Bilingual Studies in English and French. Her research interests focus on content and language integrated learning, academic writing, technology-based language learning, and assessment. She has held leadership roles in teacher education and faculty development centers in order to advance equity and inclusion programs and initiatives in linguistically and culturally diverse educational contexts.

Amanda Wallace serves as an EAL Consultant in the Centre for Educational Excellence at Simon Fraser University, Burnaby, Canada. In this role, she collaborates with faculty to create linguistically responsive curricula and innovative teaching methodologies. Prior to her work at SFU, Amanda taught English for Academic Purposes at Seoul National University, Seoul, South Korea, gaining valuable insights into the needs of multilingual students. She is currently a Ph.D candidate, with a significant aspect of her research focused on interdisciplinary collaboration between applied linguists and faculty to better support multilingual students. Her latest publication is "CLIL Collaborations in Higher Education: A Critical Perspective" (2020).

Zhihua (Olivia) Zhang is Director of Education at Trinity Language Centre of Trinity Western University, Richmond, Canada. She leads an exceptional team of faculty and staff and oversees curriculum and program design and development, teacher training and evaluation, and quality assurance. Olivia's research interests include teaching and learning English as an additional language, inclusive curriculum and pedagogy, international student experiences, and narrative inquiry as a methodology. Olivia is passionate about intercultural communication and collaboration in teaching and research. She earned her Ph.D in Languages, Cultures, and Literacies in the Faculty of Education at Simon Fraser University, Burnaby, Canada.

Index

academic language and literacy skills   198, 203, 213, 219
academic language development   196
academic standards   50, 53, 60, 61, 65
academic studies   71, 74, 80, 82, 87
academic success   194, 196
accessibility   235, 240
accommodation(s)   50, 53, 61, 65
accountability   211–13, 224
accreditation   192–6, 213, 217, 222, 225
admission (university)   71, 72, 74, 83, 86
agency   72–6, 85
ambivalence   136–8
Anglo-dominant   1, 12, 14–16
application of knowledge   129, 130, 133, 137, 142, 143
applied linguistics (AL)   11, 12, 16, 49–52, 63, 66, 236–8
 critical AL   54–6, 64–5
applied linguists   193, 197, 201–3, 205
asset-oriented   244–6

BANA (Britain, Australia, and North America)   91, 93, 96, 103, 104
barrier/barriers   244, 245, 247
boundary   112, 113
 edge of a boundary   117, 119–23
business discourse   220, 221, 224, 225
buy-in   234, 236, 245, 249

Canada   71–80, 82, 84, 86
 Canadian Engineering Accreditation Board (CEAB)   192–4
capital   75–7, 82–6
Centre for English Language Learning, Teaching and Research (CELLTR)   194, 195, 200, 202, 205
China   71–4, 76, 78–80, 84
collaborations   195, 197, 201
collaborative model/partnerships   202, 203, 205
colonial/coloniality/colonialism   5, 6, 10, 13, 28, 34, 55, 63, 94, 111, 181, 182

comfort zone   114–22
communication skills   192, 193, 196
content area/content/disciplinary faculty   49, 54, 58, 60–2, 64, 65, 197, 201, 203, 205, 237, 238, 247
content-based, content, and language integrated   214, 219, 220, 222, 224
cultural difference, *see* difference
cultural diversity   9–11, 16, 18, 26, 28, 29, 33–7, 40, 43, 163, 171–3, 178, 180, 185, 191, 217, 221
cultural transformer(s)   91, 97, 103, 104
culture   10–11
 intercultural communication   10, 94, 221
 intercultural learning   3, 10, 17
 language and culture   10–11
curriculum/curriculum studies   26–8
 curriculum as lived   29, 113, 122
 curriculum as plan   29, 34, 42–4
 curriculum in third space/third-space curriculum   30–2, 38, 43, 44

deficit discourse/perspectives   198, 217, 219, 236, 237, 243
designer/ideal immigrants   92, 93, 95
diagnostic reading assessment   202
difference   5, 11, 16, 17
 cultural difference   110, 112–14, 116, 118–20
 encounter with difference   6, 16, 111
 relational sites of difference   122
disciplinary   234, 237, 238, 240, 243, 247–50
 disciplinary courses   234, 237
 disciplinary discourse(s)   196, 203, 243
 disciplinary faculty   240, 247–50
 disciplinary language and literacy skills   238
 disciplinary/professional identity   51, 60, 66
discipline-specific   196

discipline-specific academic
  language   195
discipline-specific language and
  literacy skills   205, 238
discipline-specific PELA   197
discomfort   111, 113, 115, 116, 120, 122
  (dis)comfort   113, 116, 119–23
discrimination   173, 183

EAL students   191, 194, 196
educational developer(s)   233, 237, 248,
  249
educational development   236, 237, 250
embedded language support   199
  embedded model   195, 202
  embedded support   205
engineering   191–3, 197
  engineering-specific PELAS   197
English as a lingua franca   129, 130, 135
English as an additional language
  (EAL)   191, 194, 195, 200, 202,
  233, 235, 250
  EAL support   234–6
English language proficiency   196, 203
English language teachers   129–31, 135,
  142
English learning   71, 72, 74, 76–8, 84, 85
English test(s)   71, 73, 74, 76, 80, 85, 86
  English language proficiency
    exams   196
  English test score(s)   71, 76, 80, 86
  standardized English test(s)   71, 73, 74
  standardized language tests   82
Equity, Diversity, and Inclusion
  (EDI)   235, 236, 242, 249
experiences (of language learners)   71–5,
  77, 78, 80, 83, 85

faculty/faculty members   5, 7, 8, 10, 15,
  16, 18, 25–70, 96, 147, 149, 152,
  154, 160, 163, 170, 173, 181–4,
  193–5, 234, 236, 237, 245, 247–50,
  see also "instructors"
Faculty of Applied Sciences (FAS)   191,
  195
future   73–5, 77, 80, 84, 85

graduate attributes   192–4, 198

hybridity   95, 98, 99, 101

identity/identities   72–8, 82–5, 95,
  99–103
ideology/ideologies   75, 76, 81, 83, 94,
  97, 101, 104, 171–3, 176–8, 183, 184
IELTS   71–4, 77–85, 196
immigration   92, 93, 103, 104
impact assessment   213, 216, 222, 224
inclusive, inclusion, inclusivity   239, 248,
  249
  inclusive teaching approaches   234,
    235, 239
inquiry-based learning   135, 138, 139,
  141
in-service (teachers)   129, 130, 132–4,
  142
institutional ethnography (IE)   2, 175,
  185
institutional policy and structures   200–2
institutional responsibility   202, 205, 244,
  245, 248
institutional support   200, 205, 245, 246,
  250
instructor/instructors   243, 245–8, 250,
  see also faculty
  content instructors   248
  instructor identity/ identities   244,
    246, 249
  instructor workload   244, 246, 248
  language instructors   248
intercultural   110, 111, 113, 115, 116,
  119–23
  intercultural capital   91, 94, 95,
    97–102, 104
  intercultural competence   10, 27, 94
  intercultural encounter   111–13, 123
  intercultural learning   109–11, 180,
    185
  intercultural relations   110
international education   72, 76, 79, 80,
  see also internationalization
internationalization (of higher
  education)   1–7, 18, 25, 49–51,
  53–5, 57–62, 65–6, 72, 78, 86, 129,
  130, 134, 135, 152, 154, 159, 161,
  171, 177, 169–80, 183–6, 191, 192,
  204, 233, 237–9
  definitions   3, 4
  ethical   10, 11, 49, 66, 171, 185
  historical context (Canada)   5–6
  policies   6–7

internationalizing (the) curriculum (IOC)   26-8
international student(s)   5-11, 16, 17, 26, 27, 32, 33, 35-8, 40, 43, 50, 51, 57, 59, 62, 65, 66, 72-5, 77, 78, 80, 82-6, 91-3, 95-7, 103, 104, 152-61, 170, 171, 173, 176, 178-81, 183, 184, 185, 186, 191, 202-4, 212, 213, 216, 219, 220, 226
   Chinese international students   71-5, 77, 83
investment   72-7, 81-5

Japanese English teachers   131, 134

language   245-9
   barriers   245-7
   development   195, 196, 203
   ideology/ideologies   55, 56, 65, 171, 172, 177
   literacy skills   198, 203, 205, 235-7
   literacy support   198, 200
   matters/issues   49-51, 54-8, 61, 62, 64, 65, 170, 172, 175, 179, 193, 203, 204
   proficiency   51, 53, 64, 65
languaging   13, 14, 16, 65, 66
linguistic(s)   193, 234, 244, 245, 247, 248, 250
   linguistic complexity   234, 48, 250
   linguistic diversity/linguistically diverse   52, 53, 62, 169, 175, 183-5, 191, 194, 204, 244, 247, 248, 250
linguistically accessible   240, 244
linguistically responsive   234, 238-41, 244-9
   linguistically and culturally responsive   226, 227, 234
   linguistically responsive classrooms   236, 239, 240, 247
   Linguistically Responsive Classrooms: Instructor Series (LRCIS)   234, 239-41, 244-8
   linguistically responsive instruction (LRI)   50, 53, 55, 238, 244-7, 249
   linguistically responsive lens   245, 246
   linguistically responsive pedagogy (LRP)   234, 238, 239, 241, 248, 249
linguistic repertoires   54, 56, 66

mobility   3, 5, 7, 10, 33, 92, 94, 109, 152, 154, 155, 159, 169, 170, 185
motivation(s)   73-5, 85
multiculturalism/multicultural   10, 11, 29, 98, 170, 184
multidimensional/multidimensionality   1, 2, 14, 15
multilingual/multilingualism   49, 51, 52, 54, 60, 61, 211
   students   52, 53, 56, 57, 59, 60, 64, 66, 233, 235, 237, 241, 248-9
multiplicity   17, 29, 31, 37, 112, 113

narrative(s)   71, 72, 75, 77, 83
narrative inquiry   77
narrative writing   130, 132-4, 136, 138-42
native speaker   52, 58-60
neoliberal/neoliberal discourse   17, 18, 62, 92, 96, 150, 157, 204, 212, 213, 255, 256
nonnative English speakers   172, 173, 179, 183

pedagogy/ pedagogical   111-13, 121, 122, 233, 235, 237, 239, 244, 245, 248, 250
   pedagogical challenges   192, 196, 197, 201, 202, 204, 244, 245, 247, 249
   pedagogical dynamics   111-13, 121, 122
plurilingual   52, 53, 55, 193, 204
Post Entry Language Assessments (PELA)   192, 195-200, 205, 213, 215
power/power relations   10, 11, 13, 15, 16, 75-7, 81-4, 110-12, 120, 201
professional development   129-31, 133, 134, 136, 138, 139, 142, 156, 164, 202, 233, 242

qualitative methodology/methods   32, 57, 95, 113, 151, 152, 169, 175, 240
quality assurance   213, 217

race, racialization   11, 111, 112, 164, 177
reading   192-4, 196-9
ROAD-MAPPING   15, 18, 255

staff   1, 4, 7–9, 12, 15–18, 74, 147–68, 180–90, 202, 204, 256
   changes to workload   156
   in higher education   148–9
   improvisation   160, 161
   intercultural skills, fluency, literacy   155, 164
   international experience[s]   154–6, 163
   professional development   156, 164
   Third Space Professional (TSP)   150, 151
standard language   173, 176, 178, 184
study abroad   109–13, 115, 118–20, 122, 123, 130, 132, 133, 137
   international practicum   109–12
superdiverse/superdiversity   49, 51, 52, 55, 56
sustainability   4, 6, 9, 129, 134, 136, 143

teaching   3, 9, 12, 15–17, 25–55, 59, 60, 62–4, 71, 96, 99–102, 109, 110, 113, 119, 120, 129–31, 134, 135, 137, 138, 141, 144, 173, 192, 194, 197, 201, 205, 220–2, 224, 225, 227, 233–8, 246–50, 255
   Canadian way (of teaching)   139, 140, 143
   inclusive teaching strategies   234, 235, 239
   teaching assistants   234, 249, 250
   Western (teaching approaches)   129, 131, 135, 136, 143, 144
Teaching English to Speakers of Other Languages (TESOL)   94–8, 100, 102–4, 194
tensioned space   113, 120–3
tensions   9, 16, 25, 29, 30, 32, 52, 58, 59, 61, 65, 102, 113, 157–9, 164, 202, 247, 256
Test of English as a Foreign Language (TOEFL)   71, 73, 194, 196
textbooks   131, 134, 139, 141, 142, 144
Third Space/third space   17, 31, 32, 95, 100, 104, 147, *see also* "third space curriculum"
Third Space Professional (TSP)   150, 151
transcultural university   169, 170, 174

uncertainty   7, 31, 53, 117, 119–21, 237
unfamiliar/unfamiliarity   113, 115–19, 121
Universal Design for Learning (UDL)   235, 236

vulnerability   119–23

whiteness   6, 10, 11
writing-intensive   215, 216, 220–2, 225

Zone of Between   29, 31, 40, 43, 44

www.ingramcontent.com/pod-product-compliance
Lightning Source LLC
Chambersburg PA
CBHW071811300426
44116CB00009B/1273